Gimme Five

Mike Jonker

acknowledgements

I would first like to thank my beautiful wife Heidi, my best friend and biggest fan. You are the best thing that ever happened to me. Your support on this project has been invaluable. I love you x 3!!!

I would also like to thank my boys, Noah (Butter) and Jack (Bang) for allowing me to *use* you both to illustrate biblical principles. I am a very proud daddy. I love you guys! Go MAVS!!!

I am also thankful for my loving parents. Dad, you are the man I want to be and the type of man every son should have for a father. Mom, you are a peacemaker, and you have taught me so much about valuing and appreciating people. I love you both.

I also want to thank my mom-in-law. Mama, I am so blessed to have you in my life. I love you and appreciate the constant support you show me and my family.

There are many other family and friends that I could mention here, who have encouraged me through this process. Unfortunately, one page fills up really quick, and I don't have enough room to adequately thank you all. Hopefully, you know who you are. Thank you so much. I love all of you.

Lastly, and most importantly, I would like to thank my Lord and Savior Jesus Christ for entrusting me with this message and for giving me the grace to write it. It's a good thing the Holy Spirit is a genius. I love You, Lord.

foreword

Michael has been writing these daily challenges for almost three years. Every week or two he would send me a set of five as he finished them. It didn't take long for me to realize that they were something special. I printed each set, placed it in a ring binder, and began to use them as part of my own daily devotion. I found myself looking forward to each installment and missing them when there were gaps in his writing.

I forwarded a few of them to friends and relatives who immediately requested that I keep them coming. They have been used as source material in home group Bible studies, and they have been passed on as material for mentoring others with needs in a specific area.

The best way to describe each entry is that it is based on Scripture; it is brief, and is simple to relate to. Most important, it contains something you can do each day to enrich your Christian walk and/or provides practical instruction on how to treat others as Christ would treat them.

For those of you who have not yet begun the habit of a daily devotion and would like a simple structure to get started, I would suggest you read the first challenge entitled "gimme five" and try it. It is a terrific guide for spending the first five minutes of each day communicating with God. Then add a minute to read one of these daily challenges, and you will be well on your way to forming a life changing daily habit.

Enjoy!

Dan Jonker Jr.
(Author's proud father)

gimme five

> **Mark 1:35** – *Very early in the morning, while it was still dark, Jesus got up, left the house and went off to a solitary place, where he prayed* (NIV).

If your days are anything like mine, then you spend the majority of them surrounded by other people. If you're married, your spouse is usually around. If you have children still living at home, then your time is certainly in demand. If you work, your workplace probably has multiple people that you just can't seem to avoid. Sometimes it seems like people are everywhere! And if they're not physically present, they can reach you by phone, text or some other means of communication.

It's because of this fact that it is vitally important for us to spend quality time with God on a daily basis—alone. Jesus even realized how important this truth is. The Bible says that He woke up very early, before dark, left the place where He was staying and found a solitary place to pray.

My challenge to you today is to do the same thing every day. Start your day by finding a solitary place where you and God can communicate. It's so much easier to hear God's voice when others are not fighting for your attention.

I want to introduce to you the "Gimme Five Principle." Simply give God the first five minutes of each day. For some of you that may not seem like a lot, but for others of you five minutes is more than the zero you typically give God in the morning. If you're at a loss as to how to spend those five minutes, allow me to further explain "Gimme Five."

For the first minute, give God praise (**Psalm 9:1-2**). It's amazing how quickly the atmosphere changes when you begin by lifting Him up. In the second minute, repent (**1 John 1:9**). Lay down your sins and purpose to live differently. Make your requests known to God in the third minute (**1 John 5:15**). Ask Him for whatever you need. Yield or surrender your will to His in the fourth minute (**Romans 12:2**). God has a purpose for every day, not just Sundays. Lastly, take a minute to read His word.

God's masterpiece

Every week in children's church, the kids are given a power verse (or memory verse). My wife Heidi writes the verse on a dry erase board in big, bright letters, and prizes are given to the kids who memorize it before service ends. We have a lot of fun with it, and you'd be amazed at how much Scripture the kids can quote because of the power verse games we play.

One Thursday morning I was setting up chairs in the children's building, and I noticed that Heidi had already written the next Sunday's verse on the board. The verse for the week was **Ephesians 2:10**. I was greatly encouraged as I read how we are God's masterpiece and that He created us.

I'll be honest with you. There are many days that I don't feel like a masterpiece. In fact, I often feel more like a four-year old's finger painting. Many people look at their lives and see a mess. Their flaws and failures overwhelm them, and they are confused as to why they even exist. They question everything from their hair color to body shape to their accent.

Perhaps you are unhappy with yourself on some level today. Maybe you are not pleased with your physical appearance, or you may not like the direction your career is going. There could be multiple areas of your life that you're not satisfied with. If so, I have a word for you today. *You are God's masterpiece.* Don't ever forget it!

He created you anew in Christ. If you can grasp this revelation, it will completely alter the course of your life. When you realize that you are God's masterpiece in Him, you can then begin to do the good things that God planned in advance for you to do. Hallelujah! Now *that* will make you shout.

spell check

1 Thessalonians 5:23 – *May God himself, the God of peace, sanctify you through and through. May your whole spirit, soul and body be kept blameless at the coming of our Lord Jesus Christ* (NIV).

If you've ever typed any kind of a document on a computer, then you are probably familiar with the spell check option. It's most commonly used after typing to check for spelling errors. When selected, the spell check option will underline all the words that may be spelled wrong in red (some programs even underline misspelled words as you type). Some of you know exactly what I'm talking about because your whole page turns red when you press the button!

Spell check is great for many reasons. It turns average spellers into great spellers, and it prevents many college students from spelling like second graders. The best feature of spell check is that it not only indicates when a word may be spelled wrong, it gives different options as to how to correct the spelling.

I remember typing papers in college. I would get into the groove and start feeling pretty good about myself. The thoughts would flow through my fingers onto the screen, and I would race to the conclusion. Once finished, there were many times I would print papers without doing a spell check. I was convinced I didn't need to because I was a solid speller, but some of my papers would come back with errors. Why? I didn't use spell check.

The Holy Spirit works a lot like spell check. When He is allowed to, the Spirit of God will shine a light on the dark places of our lives. He will show us the things that are unpleasing to Him. And just like spell check, He doesn't just point out our flaws. He gives us practical solutions through the Word and prayer.

I want to encourage you today to allow the Holy Spirit to evaluate your life. Even if you are a godly person, He will reveal to you the hidden areas of your character that need work. You certainly want to do this at least once a day (possibly at the end), but you may need to "check for errors" all throughout the day.

positioned in Christ

> **Ephesians 1:19-21** – 19 *That power is like the working of his mighty strength,* 20 *which he exerted in Christ when he raised him from the dead and seated him at his right hand in the heavenly realms,* 21 *far above all rule and authority, power and dominion, and every title that can be given, not only in the present age but also in the one to come* (NIV).

Perhaps you are familiar with the three most important words in real estate: location, location, location. I recently heard Dr. David Remedios preach a message on that very subject. It is vitally important for us to understand where the Father is located, where Jesus is located and where we are located.

God the Father is seated on the throne (**Psalm 47:8**), and Jesus sits at the right hand of God in the heavenly realms (**Mark 16:19**). Scripture indicates that Jesus sits *far* above all rule and authority, power and dominion, and every title that can be given. He has incomparably great power (**Ephesians 1:19**). In fact, God has placed *everything* under His feet (**Ephesians 1:22**). Glory!

But that's not even the best part. Look at **Ephesians 2:6** – *And God raised us up with Christ and seated us with him in the heavenly realms in Christ Jesus* (NIV). Those who are in Christ have been seated with Him in heaven. Wow! I can hardly hold back my excitement as I write this.

God has already prepositioned you for victory. He has placed everything under your feet in Christ. The only way you and I can be defeated is if you *choose* to step down from your place of authority and engage the enemy. Satan has already been defeated, and he knows it. So he makes it his mission to get you out of your position in Christ. That's the only way he has a chance. If you remain in your place of authority, the devil has to get through the Father and Jesus in order to get to you. And that's not happening.

> **1 Peter 3:22** – *Now Christ has gone to heaven. He is seated in the place of honor next to God, and all the angels and authorities and powers accept his authority* (NLT).

Satan meets needs too

Matthew 4:2-3 – 2 *After fasting forty days and forty nights, he was hungry.* 3 *The tempter came to him and said, "If you are the Son of God, tell these stones to become bread"* (NIV).

To say Jesus was in a vulnerable state in the above passage would be an understatement. He had just finished a forty day fast. If you have ever fasted food and drink for any length of time, then you know how difficult of a sacrifice this was. Going *one* day without food and drink is hard enough!

As a teenager I once ate and drank only bread and water for ten days. At the end of those ten days, I was in great need of nourishment. I am a thin person to begin with, so I was almost sickly looking after the fast. Don't get me wrong. God sustained my health for the duration of the fast, but I still lost quite a bit of weight. When it was over, I was hungry. I can't even begin to imagine how hungry Jesus must have been after forty days!

When the devil approached Jesus in Matthew 4, Jesus was in great need. Satan knew Jesus had been fasting, so he offered Him some reasonable advice. "If you're really the Son of God," he said, "turn these rocks into bread." Jesus needed food, so Satan offered Him a way to get some.

Satan recognizes the needs people have just like God does, and he is more than willing to meet those needs if we allow him to. He is a deceiver and manipulator. His solutions sound legitimate, and they may even meet our needs temporarily, but his methods have no lasting benefit. They will only leave us in greater need in the end.

Perhaps you find yourself in need today. God desires to meet your need, but so does the devil. It's important for you to have discernment because Satan's counterfeits can closely resemble God's authenticity. Stay close to God and listen to His voice. He is more than able to meet every one of your needs!

2 Corinthians 11:14 – *And no wonder, for Satan himself masquerades as an angel of light* (NIV).

spit for spit

Matthew 5:38-39 – 38 *"You have heard that it was said, 'Eye for an eye, and tooth for tooth.' 39 But I tell you, do not resist an evil person. If someone strikes you on the right cheek, turn to him the other also"* (NIV).

The other day our family was driving home from one of Jack's soccer games, and our boys had a friend in the backseat with them. They were getting along really well. Then all of a sudden Jack blurted out, "Hey, Noah spit on me!" Not two seconds later, Noah countered with, "He spit on me first!"

Heidi told both of them to quit spitting, and I decided it was time for a teaching moment. I said to Noah, "When Jack does something he's not supposed to, he is the one who's going to get into trouble, not you. But if you do the same thing back to him, you're both going to get into trouble. Do you like getting in trouble?" "No," he replied. I finished, "Then don't do something wrong just because someone else does."

That little altercation between our boys got me to thinking about the lesson Jesus taught in Matthew 5. In **Exodus 21:23-25**, Israel was taught to take life for life, eye for eye, tooth for tooth, hand for hand, foot for foot, burn for burn, wound for wound and bruise for bruise. Jesus introduced a new methodology.

He taught not to resist an evil person, but instead to absorb his blows without retaliation. He also demonstrated this principle while on the cross. **1 Peter 2:23** – *When they hurled their insults at him, he did not retaliate; when he suffered, he made no threats* (NIV). We should learn from His example.

Revenge is instinctual for most people, but it is not the way of love. Taking an eye for an eye leaves you and the other person blind in one eye. Taking a tooth for a tooth leaves both you and your offender looking like hockey players. Noah and Jack were both left covered in spit. Exchanging wrongs leaves both parties hurt. So how should you respond when someone wrongs you? Look at what Jesus did in the second part of **1 Peter 2:23**. He entrusted Himself to Him who judges justly, and you should too.

the winds of change

> **Deuteronomy 28:2, 6** – 2 *And all these blessings shall come upon you and overtake you, because you obey the voice of the Lord your God:* 6 *Blessed shall you be when you come in, and blessed shall you be when you go out* (NKJV).

When Heidi and I were first married, we moved to a small town in northeast Arkansas where we served as the youth pastors at a church there. There was a couple in our church that had a five-year-old son that Heidi and I would babysit for on occasion. He was a sharp little boy, and he was quite the character. We never really knew what was going to come out of his mouth.

One night we were watching after him, while his parents were out together, and we decided to go to Wal-Mart. I don't exactly remember what it was we were shopping for, but I'll never forget something he said. He looked at Heidi, "The winds of change are blowing for me."

It was actually quite funny to hear a five year old say something like that, but he was right. His mom was pregnant, and I guess his parents were trying to prepare him for the major change that was coming. I'm sure they had said something to him about the winds of change blowing, and he just repeated what he heard. He didn't understand everything that was going on, but Heidi and I could tell he was well aware that he was in transition. He still felt a little vulnerable and unsure, but his parents did their best to comfort him and prepare him for what was coming.

Perhaps you find yourself in transition today, and you are uncertain about the next step in your life. Like that little boy, you just need some reassuring from your heavenly Father. My wife once said this to me as we were transitioning, and I believe the Lord is saying the same to you: "You are blessed going in, and you are blessed going out."

You may not understand all that is going on right now, but you will be blessed as you come out of where you are and into where you are going. The Bible says that God's blessings will overtake you, as you are obedient to His voice. Hallelujah!

too much of a good thing

2 Kings 4:6 – *When all the jars were full, she said to her son, "Bring me another one." But he replied, "There is not a jar left." Then the oil stopped flowing* (NIV).

Not long ago, Heidi's family invited us over for dinner. Her dad was in charge of cooking. We were very excited, and he didn't disappoint. There was enough food to satisfy the whole neighborhood! He grilled hotdogs and ribs. There was homemade potato salad and baked beans, not to mention the 14-pound piece of beef he threw on the pit. There was also garlic bread, sweet tea and the bread pudding my wife made.

Usually when we eat over at someone's house, no matter who's cooking dinner, I can find at least one or two things I'm not going to eat. That was not the case on this day. As I looked the spread over, I knew I was going to hurt myself. And after they asked me to bless the food, I did just that.

Everything was wonderful, and even after everyone had stuffed themselves, there was enough food leftover to feed an army. I sat at the table for about thirty minutes before I could move. I normally don't eat like that, but on that day I ignored my better judgment. My stomach had no vacancy. Even though there was plenty of delicious food left, I couldn't have eaten anymore if I tried. Eventually I was able to go play in the yard with the kids.

Likewise, many believers gorge themselves on the knowledge of God, but they don't apply it to their lives. Others get prayed for and hands laid on them service after service, but they remain unchanged. Many of them are good people, but they can't do anything but sit at the table because they are too full to move. Nothing else can come in, and nothing is going out.

God blesses us to be a blessing. What are you doing with what you have received from Him? Perhaps you have become stagnant in your walk with God. You may still be faithful to church, but you are too inwardly focused. I challenge you to be an encouragement to others. Heaven never runs out of supplies; we simply run out of emptiness. Pour yourself out today.

the allure of Christ

Zacchaeus was not a good man. Luke records that he was rich, and it's widely known that he made his fortune by overtaxing the people of Jericho. He also likely suffered from "short man's syndrome," as the Bible says he was short in stature (**Luke 19:3**). In fact, a popular kids song depicts Zacchaeus as a "wee little man." It's okay to laugh a little.

Even though he was an ungodly person, Zacchaeus was desperate to see Jesus. As Jesus passed through his town, he ran ahead of the crowd and climbed up a sycamore tree so he could see Him. I admire Zacchaeus' enthusiasm and perseverance. He put forth more effort to meet Jesus than a lot of *Christians* do today, and it paid off. Jesus invited Himself over to Zacchaeus' house where they sat down together face to face. How awesome!

The fact that Zacchaeus stopped at nothing to see Jesus is quite impressive, but that's not what I want to focus on today. Allow me to draw your attention away from *what* Zacchaeus did to *why* he did it. There was something so unique and attractive about Jesus that this crooked tax collector was drawn to Him. The allure of Christ was too much for a known embezzler to ignore.

Zacchaeus was so taken by Jesus that he forgot about his reputation and was overcome with a desire to know Him. The love of God on the inside of Jesus is what reeled Zacchaeus in, and it's the love of God on the inside of us that will attract the lost today.

Are people drawn to Christ by the way you live your life? When others are around you, do they sense the love and purity of God? Our lives should reflect Jesus to the lost. My prayer is that your life will create desperation in others to know Him.

when wrong seems right

Luke 19:9-10 – 9 *And Jesus said to him, "Today salvation has come to this house, because he also is a son of Abraham:* 10 *for the Son of Man has come to seek and to save that which was lost"* (NKJV).

My wife and I moved back to her hometown of Forest Hill a little over five years ago. Heidi was hired to be the full-time children's pastor at her home church, and I was later hired on as the youth pastor. Our church is unique in that there are multiple families that drive long distances to attend services. One of the cities they come from is Leesville (about an hour drive one way).

There are basically two routes from the church to Leesville. One of them takes state highways, but the mileage is more. The other takes two lane roads through the backwoods of central Louisiana, but the mileage is less. They both take about the same amount of time (give or take a few minutes). I still remember the first time Heidi and I were asked to go make visits in Leesville.

We opted to go through "the sticks." The trip there was seamless, but I can't say the same for the trip back home. Everything was going well until we rolled into a small town called Hineston. It was there that we were supposed to take a right onto Highway 112. I was not aware that there are two possible right turns onto Highway 112. One goes to Forest Hill (the one we wanted), and the other takes you to Union Hill (the one I took). It took me twenty minutes to realize we were going the wrong way.

I was confused because it is the same highway and a right turn is needed to access them both, but they go in different directions. I turned around and went back. Following God's will can be a lot like this. Many times we are going along God's path for our lives, and we get slightly off. It's easy to do because sometimes the wrong way looks quite similar to the right way.

Maybe today you have veered from God's plan. If so, here's a truth you need to hear: The road you need to take is right where you left it. Go back to where you got off track and begin to obey Him again. Ask Him for discernment. God is faithful!

like a child

Luke 18:16-17 – 16 *But Jesus called the children to him and said, "Let the little children come to me, and do not hinder them, for the kingdom of God belongs to such as these.* 17 *I tell you the truth, anyone who will not receive the kingdom of God like a little child will never enter it"* (NIV).

Working with children for the last five plus years has been one of the greatest privileges of my life. There is nothing more rewarding than to witness a four-year old get a revelation of who Jesus is and how much He loves her. It's absolutely beautiful.

I was brought to tears, just the other day, as I watched a little girl worship God as if no one else was around. I wept, as I thought about the adversity she has faced in her short life, and I marveled at her ability to close off everything and crawl up in Jesus' lap. She was no doubt singing to Him face to face.

Children have such great faith. If you tell a child that Jesus heals, she believes He can heal. If you say to her that Jesus is always with her, she will know that she is never alone. Tell a child that God loves her unconditionally, and she will not think otherwise, no matter how bad she messes up. But all children grow up, and many of them grow out of faith.

There is a natural maturing process that takes place as a person moves from childhood to adulthood. God intended it to be that way. The move from dependence to independence is a sign of health in a person's life, but there is one area that God desires for us to remain totally dependent. That is the area of faith.

In order for you to mature spiritually, you have to maintain a childlike faith. An "adult-like" faith often explores other options before turning to God. Children don't even realize there are other options. I want to encourage you today. Don't put your trust in God as a last resort. No matter what you may be facing, God is the answer. Choose to have faith in Him like a child.

Matthew 18:4 – *"So anyone who becomes as humble as this little child is the greatest in the Kingdom of Heaven"* (NLT).

six-foot goal superstars

1 Peter 5:3 – *Don't lord it over the people assigned to your care, but lead them by your own good example* (NLT).

Our oldest son Noah just recently celebrated his eighth birthday. He is a basketball fanatic, so Heidi's mom (Granny) gave him an adjustable hoop that goes up to six feet high. He loves it, and so do I! Noah, Jack and I have played some epic games of two-on-one in our playroom, and Heidi even gets in on the action from time to time.

I have to admit that sometimes I feel like a superstar playing on the six-foot goal. Even though the boys play against me two-on-one, I can still crush them every time if I want. Blocking their shots is effortless for me, and I can score on them at will. It's very easy to frustrate them, though, if I block too many of their shots. But my goal is not to upset them, so most of the time I let them win. Occasionally, I'll win a couple to save face.

Not long ago, after one such game, I got to thinking about how many people in leadership stunt the development of those they are leading (You may find this random, but it's how my mind works and how God often speaks to me). I thought how if I were to block every single shot my boys take, and win every game fifty to zero, it would not take long for them to become discouraged and quit. Not to mention, they would have little respect for me. Sure, I'd be a six-foot goal superstar, but at what cost?

Many people, in various positions of authority, have become six-foot goal superstars. They prevent those who they are leading from reaching their potential, and they stifle the dreams of others for whatever reason. They constantly "block the shots" of the people they lead. They may recognize the gifts in others, but they do not celebrate them.

Think on this: Who are you leading? Parents, are you setting your children up for failure? If you are an employer, does a more talented employee threaten you? Church leaders, are you afraid to utilize people's gifts because they might show you up? Purpose to make your ceiling somebody else's floor today.

blocked shots

Psalm 119:86 – *All your commands are trustworthy; help me, for men persecute me without cause* (NIV).

Unfortunately, many leaders are stifling the success of the people they are leading. There are a variety of reasons why leaders act this way, but the majority of them do so because they are insecure. An insecure leader does not want to feel inferior to his subordinates, nor does he want to be perceived that way. So he constantly "blocks the shots" of those he leads and does not allow them to succeed.

I addressed this type of leader yesterday, and today I want to encourage those of you who are under such leadership. There are many talented individuals who are unable to thrive because their leaders are insecure. Perhaps you feel oppressed today by the very person that should be your biggest fan and ally. I have been there before, and it is an unenviable position.

One of the myths that keep people in prolonged bondage is that leaders are untouchable. Honoring authority is a godly principle, but doing so does not mean that you have to accept being mistreated. You can honor your leader and not agree with him. If a leader in your life is taking advantage of you, or you feel he is purposefully stunting your development, you have every right to approach him about it. But do so in love and with a good attitude. Do not act hastily. Seek the counsel of the Holy Spirit, and consult the word of God. Allow Him to lead you.

If you are frustrated today, remain faithful and under authority. Doing so may lead you into more trying times, but remember that God is faithful and true to His word. Do not lose heart or get down on yourself. God is aware of your gifts, and you will have the freedom to flourish in due season. Sometimes it takes a bad leader to prepare us for what God has next.

Psalm 75:6-7 – 6 *For promotion cometh neither from the east, nor from the west, nor from the south.* 7 *But God is the judge: he putteth down one, and setteth up another* (KJV).

grace, the enabler

> **Romans 5:20-21** – 20 *Moreover the law entered that the offense might abound. But where sin abounded, grace abounded much more,* 21 *so that as sin reigned in death, even so grace might reign through righteousness to eternal life through Jesus Christ our Lord* (NKJV).

In order to fully understand what Paul was teaching here, we need to continue reading in **Romans 6:1-2** – 1 *What shall we say then? Shall we continue in sin that grace may abound?* 2 *Certainly not! How shall we who died to sin live any longer in it?* (NKJV). Grace does not give us a license to sin, but many people live their lives as if it does. They probably wouldn't admit it, but the fruit of their lives reveals their true heart condition.

Many people refuse to do right because they are enabled to do wrong. There are adult children who never grow up because their parents cover up their immaturity with excuses. Others who have a poor work ethic and a bad attitude on the job remain unproductive because their bosses avoid confrontation.

When a person in authority condones the wrongdoing of someone, it is to the detriment of all the others under his or her authority. Someone reliable ends up pulling the dead weight of the person being enabled, and he usually does so reluctantly. Maybe you understand where I'm coming from today.

Unfortunately, this is exactly how many Christians view grace. They take advantage of the sacrifice Jesus made on the cross, and they maintain their sinful nature using grace as a cover-up. This perverted grace breaks the heart of God. He desires for us to move on to maturity (**Hebrews 6:1**).

Grace *is* an enabler, but it does not give us a free pass to sin. On the contrary, grace enables us to do what we cannot do in our own strength. It enables us to be forgiven and made righteous in God's sight and to persevere through severe trials. Grace enables us to live holy lives and to love our enemies as ourselves. Paul wrote that grace reigns *through* righteousness. Conduct yourself today in a manner worthy of receiving God's grace.

perverted vs. pure

2 Corinthians 6:1 – *As God's fellow workers we urge you not to receive God's grace in vain* (NIV).

We took a glance at grace yesterday, but I felt it necessary to take a deeper look today. I believe there is a perverted grace, and there is a pure grace. Perverted grace enables wrong behavior; pure grace enables right behavior.

Many people are enabled to do wrong because they are not held accountable for their actions. Instead, others make excuses for their poor behavior (I gave a couple of examples yesterday). This form of "grace" is highly prevalent both in and out of the church. There are two questions we need to ask ourselves. First of all, is someone else enabling me by perverting grace? And secondly, am I enabling someone else by perverting grace?

Grace is not meant to cover up our weaknesses or excuse our wrongdoing, but rather to strengthen us when we are weak. **2 Corinthians 12:9** – *But he said to me, "My grace is sufficient for you, for my power is made perfect in weakness"* (NIV).

There are plenty of things that God requires of us that we cannot do in our own strength. I briefly mentioned a few yesterday, but I want to give you a couple more. God expects us to forgive others as He forgave us (**Colossians 3:13**). Grace enables us to do so because there are certain people we would never forgive on our own.

Other times God's grace enables us to give when we don't feel like we have anything left to give. **2 Corinthians 8:3** – *For I testify that they gave as much as they were able, and even beyond their ability* (NIV).

I believe God's grace actually gives us supernatural ability and enhances our inabilities. Perhaps your view of grace has been a warped one. My prayer is that the eyes of your understanding will continue to be enlightened as we go deeper.

John 1:16 – *From the fullness of his grace we have all received one blessing after another* (NIV).

grace enabled

Jude 4 – *For certain men whose condemnation was written about long ago have secretly slipped in among you. They are godless men, who change the grace of our God into a license for immorality and deny Jesus Christ our only Sovereign and Lord* (NIV).

Many people have turned God's grace into a license for immorality. It's unfortunate but true. What some fail to realize, though, is that more sin does not necessarily equate more grace in a person's life. A lot of people have fallen into error because they have manipulated Paul's teaching in **Romans 5:20** when he said, "But where sin abounded, grace abounded much more." Paul did not mean that abundant sin equals abundant grace. In fact, habitual sin guarantees separation from God.

Before I go any further, allow me to clarify the difference between grace and mercy. God's mercy is what keeps us from getting what we deserve. He extends mercy to believers and unbelievers alike. Grace is what enables us to receive forgiveness of sins and be saved. Grace is God's unmerited favor in the life of a believer. It is the influence of the Spirit of God operating in us to regenerate and strengthen us when we are weak.

Grace has to be enabled to function in our lives. So what's the key to abundant grace in the life of a believer? I'm glad you asked. Grace can either be accepted or rejected. We accept grace, and enable it to function, when we crucify our sinful nature. Paul said that grace reigns through righteousness (**Romans 5:21**).

Christ made us righteous through His death, burial and resurrection. Our good works do not make us righteous. We accept the work He did on the cross by crucifying our sinful nature. Crucifying the sinful nature does not mean we will never sin again. What is does mean is that when we do sin, grace will be enabled to cover us. Hallelujah!

Romans 8:12 – *Therefore, brothers, we have an obligation—but it is not to the sinful nature, to live according to it* (NIV).

20

the evidence of grace

> **Acts 11:21-23** – 21 *The Lord's hand was with them, and a great number of people believed and turned to the Lord.* 22 *News of this reached the church at Jerusalem, and they sent Barnabas to Antioch.* 23 *When he arrived and saw the evidence of the grace of God, he was glad and encouraged them all to remain true to the Lord with all their hearts* (NIV).

My wife and I traveled and ministered in various churches in the South for a season. It was a great time! A few of the churches we went into were vibrant and full of the Spirit of God. Many of them were small congregations, but we could tell that our *big* God was present there on a regular basis. The people expected great things.

Unfortunately, the majority of the churches we were invited to were on life support. Going to church had become more about ritual than relationship. There was no expectation in those places. Well, actually there *was* expectation, but what they expected was dry and dull. As soon as we stepped foot into those type of churches, we knew it was going to be tough.

Scripture records that a great number of people were receiving salvation at the church in Antioch. News spread to the church in Jerusalem, so they sent Barnabas to go check it out. Who knows what his thoughts were as he traveled to Antioch. Perhaps he thought, "I wonder what's *really* going on over there?" or maybe he was just full of excitement.

We don't know what he thought, but I love what he saw. When he arrived at Antioch, he *saw* the evidence of the grace of God and he was glad. He encouraged them to remain true to the Lord with all of their hearts. That's what the evidence of grace is—remaining true to the Lord with all of our heart.

What kind of a first impression do you make? Do people see the evidence of grace in your life, or does your life appear to be a drag? Where there is grace, there is life. Others should be able to notice that God's unmerited favor rests on you, and the grace on your life should compel others to Christ.

no dispute

Not long ago I was checking the account balance of our credit card online when I noticed that a certain vendor had overcharged us. As a matter of fact, we had been charged twice for a transaction that was in excess of three hundred dollars. Needless to say, I was not amused, but I understood that these kinds of accidents happen quite often.

I quickly got the credit card company on the phone and disputed the charge. Over the next several weeks, I had to endure the charge disputing process. It started with the phone call. I told my side of the story and why the charge should be removed from my account. Moments later my online account noted the dispute, and then a few days later I received a letter from the credit card company stating that the vendor had been notified of the charge in question. It was very frustrating, especially since I was innocent.

I checked our online account everyday to see if the charge had been dropped, and everyday it was still there. It notified me that the charge was being disputed, but my credit limit was still being affected. Though it was in dispute, the charge was held against me. Finally, after weeks of waiting, the charge was canceled and my account balanced out. I finally had peace.

I am so thankful there is not a charge disputing process when it comes to canceling our record of sin. There actually is *no* dispute. We do not have to plead our case before God and tell Him why certain charges should be dropped. He canceled the record against us by nailing it to the cross. Hallelujah! If that doesn't make you shout, I don't know what will.

Do not forfeit your peace fretting over charges that Jesus has already dropped. There is no waiting period. Thank Him for vindicating you today. You've been found innocent of all charges!

as the wicked prosper

Psalm 73:3 – *For I was envious of the arrogant as I saw the prosperity of the wicked* (NASB).

Most believers, at one time or another, have felt like the psalmist in the above verse. It's very difficult to watch the wicked prosper while you suffer, especially if you are being faithful to God's purpose. When the unrighteous seem to have it made, righteousness often becomes burdensome. When righteousness becomes burdensome, unrighteousness becomes more appealing.

This was definitely a point of contention for the psalmist because he voiced his displeasure again in verse 12, "Behold, these are the wicked; and always at ease, they have increased in wealth." I can definitely relate to his frustration.

When Heidi and I were first married, we served at a particular church as the full-time youth pastors. Heidi helped me, and she also substituted at the local schools when needed. Money wasn't growing on trees, but we were doing fine for a newlywed couple in the ministry. It also helped that we didn't have kids yet.

After we had been on staff for about five or six months, the church fell on hard times. And to make a long story short, our pay was cut twenty-five percent. Needless to say, I did not take it very well. I kept my composure in public (because I had to), but inside I was boiling. I could not understand why God would allow something like that to happen to one of His own.

It didn't make sense. I remember yelling at Him, "Why God?! How could you let this happen to us? Didn't *You* call us to this place? Now You're going to make us poor! How is it that *this* person lives like the devil and doesn't have to worry about anything?" Maybe you can understand where I was coming from.

After I was done pitching a fit, God gently reminded me that He *had* called us to that place. Then He proceeded to open up doors. Heidi was able to substitute full-time for twelve straight weeks while two different teachers were on maternity leave. She was given a full-time salary, and we were actually better off than before my pay cut! Be encouraged today. Don't envy; trust God.

no need to understand

Psalm 73:4 – *For there are no pains in their death, and their body is fat* (NASB).

Another version of this verse states that *they have no struggles; their bodies are healthy and strong* (NIV). The psalmist was frustrated that the wicked were healthy while he suffered. One thing I doubt I will ever understand is why godly people get terminally ill. And I surely don't get why innocent children die young from incurable diseases. They just don't deserve it. Even so, we have to be careful not to allow our inability to understand to cause us to resent God or anyone else.

Two and a half years ago, my dad was diagnosed with esophageal cancer. He has never smoked and never drank. He is a godly man, a fair man and a hard worker. He has always put the needs of others above his own, especially our family's. He is the type of man that every child should have for a father.

When I received the news of his prognosis, I wept bitterly. But it wasn't the kind of cry that results from entertaining worst-case scenarios (those cries came later). My initial reaction was rage. I recall the conversation I had with God. It went something like this: "Seriously?! Why *my* dad? There are plenty of people in the world who deserve this, and my dad isn't one of them!" I even suggested some possible replacements. I was offended.

This is the same pit that so many people have fallen into. While I was pointing out all the unrighteous people who I thought were more deserving of cancer, I was really pointing the finger at God. I was angry with Him for something He didn't do. God is not the author of sickness and disease.

Don't let yourself become bitter because you can't figure out why God allows bad things to happen to good people. God's thoughts and ways are higher than ours. I found peace again when I relinquished the need to understand. So can you.

Psalm 73:16 – *So I tried to understand why the wicked prosper. But what a difficult task it is!* (NLT)

rut in His will

Joshua 6:3-4 – 3 *March around the city once with all the armed men. Do this for six days.* 4 *On the seventh day, march around the city seven times, with the priests blowing the trumpets* (NIV).

Have you ever felt like you were stuck in a rut, but at the same time you knew you were in the center of God's will? You may be in that place right now! Feeling this way does not make you a bad person; it means you're a normal person. Most believers, whether they want to admit it or not, have been "stuck" in God's will at one time or another.

I believe there are three words that you need to remember when it comes to following God's perfect will for your life. They all start with the letter *p*—Promise, Plan and Performance. God promised Israel that He was going to deliver Jericho into their hands (**Joshua 6:2**). Then He gave them the plan they were to follow in order to ensure victory (**Joshua 6:3-5**). After receiving the promise and the plan, Israel then had to perform, or execute, God's plan in order to receive the promise (**Joshua 6:6-20**).

God has made similar promises to every believer, and He has given us the plan to receive them in His word. But most people miss out on His promises because they give a less than stellar performance when executing the plan.

As Israel paced around Jericho time after time, their steps created a rut. With each passing day, the rut grew deeper and deeper and deeper. They knew they were doing what God had said, but I imagine some thought He was crazy. Others probably got bored or wanted to quit. By day five or six, some of them likely begged for a change of scenery or a break in their routine.

I want to encourage you today. Remain faithful and keep a good attitude as you follow God's plan for your life. It's easy to lose interest or give up when His will seems routine. You may feel like you're in a rut now, but the promise is about to be fulfilled!

Hebrews 10:23 – *Let us hold unswervingly to the hope we profess, for he who promised is faithful* (NIV).

borrring...

> **2 Thessalonians 3:11** – *We hear that some among you are idle. They are not busy; they are busybodies* (NIV).

When you feel like you're stuck in a rut, it's very easy to become bored. I have experienced this personally, and I believe there are countless others who have as well. Perhaps you are in a state of boredom today as you follow God's plan for your life. I want to look at two things people are more inclined to do when they are bored. I'll discuss one of them today and the other tomorrow, but I don't recommend either of them.

People who are bored often become idle, or they start doing things they shouldn't do. The Bible says that idlers can become busybodies. They stop doing what it is that God has called them to do, and they start doing things God never intended for them to do. Such people are unproductive, and they are more likely to get themselves into trouble.

Homework time with our boys is a perfect example of this. When Noah and Jack get home from school, Heidi or I give them a snack, and they sit down at the table and begin their work. There are days when they are fully engaged and get everything done in a timely manner, but then there are days when they struggle to stay on task. They often do so because they are bored.

It's not uncommon to walk in and hear Noah rambling on about sports facts, while Jack does tricky maneuvers on the dining room chair. They know they're supposed to do their homework, and that they'll get in trouble if they don't, but boredom causes them to lose focus.

I truly believe that most Christians understand the importance of following God's will for their lives, but boredom can have a powerful effect on a person. Maybe God's plan for you seems too routine today. Do not get off course because you are bored. Reengage and focus on His promises.

> **Proverbs 15:21** – *Folly delights a man who lacks judgment, but a man of understanding keeps a straight course* (NIV).

overqualified

> **Joshua 6:7** – *And he ordered the people, "Advance! March around the city, with the armed guard going ahead of the ark of the LORD"* (NIV).

People who become bored with what they're doing often have a tendency to feel overqualified for the position they're in. Let me remind you that God instructed the armed men of Israel to march around Jericho, listen to the priests play music and then shout. It wasn't a very motivating plan.

I imagine that it was very difficult for the trained, highly skilled warriors to simply walk around the city. They had experienced numerous victories in battle before, and they were likely ready for combat. Scripture does not indicate how they felt or what went through their minds, but I can speak for how I would have felt.

I would have thought, "What are we doing? We have these weapons, and we know how to use them. We have crushed many enemies in combat, and we're just supposed to march around this city, playing music and then holler at the end?! This is crazy, and it will never work! Let us do what we know how to do."

Have you ever felt overqualified for the position God has you in? It's easy to feel this way when you are in a rut. Maybe you feel as if you have "outgrown" your current position and are ready to move on. The truth is no one is overqualified for what God has called him to do. His grace qualifies us.

If God has you serving somewhere that seems beneath you, He has you there for a reason. You are not being punished; you are being prepared. Remain faithful. Just because you may hold a lowly position does not mean God thinks you are a lowly person. God knows what your talents are because He gave them to you, and He will utilize them in due time. If your ego gets too big, though, you'll probably stay stuck longer than God intended.

> **Acts 20:19** – *I served the Lord with great humility and with tears, although I was severely tested by the plots of the Jews* (NIV).

skipping steps

Many people try to get ahead of God when they feel like they're stuck in a rut. Think about what would have happened if Israel had decided to only walk around Jericho once a day for five days, or if they would have walked around seven times on the third day. I doubt the outcome would have been favorable.

My wife recently reminded me that God orders our *steps*. God's will is not a series of leaps and bounds, and He often doesn't lead us down the quickest path to the promise. Most Christians would probably admit that they have a tendency to try and skip steps when they feel bored or anxious. He has ordered our steps. That means we need to follow the steps in the order He has given them. Don't try to jump ahead of Him.

When I feel stuck, I have often tried to "figure God out." It's in those times that I have rerouted myself and gotten off track. When we try to skip steps in God's plan, we reason that we know better than Him. We can be so foolish at times! His ways and His thoughts are so much higher than ours (**Isaiah 55:9**). God does not need us to revise His will for our lives.

Let me remind you that **Hebrews 12:1** instructs us to run with perseverance the race marked out for us. God has already charted a course for you to follow, but He has also give you a free will. You and I make a conscious decision daily as to whether we are going to stay the course or not.

God's plan will seem tedious at times, and other times taking a different route may seem quicker. But even if your way seems more logical, venturing from God's plan will undoubtedly delay His promises. I want to encourage you today. Take it one step at a time. As my Pastor once said, "Delay does not mean denial." Enjoy the ride. You'll eventually get there.

Proverbs 16:9 – *A man's heart plans his way, but the LORD directs his steps* (NKJV).

are you overly tired?

> **Galatians 6:9** – *Let us not become weary in doing good, for at the proper time we will reap a harvest if we do not give up* (NIV).

As the Israelite army paced around Jericho time after time, I imagine they became collectively tired. Not only were they physically tired, but they were also strained spiritually, emotionally and mentally. By day four or five, or even midway through day seven, I'm sure some were ready to call it quits.

Many believers get burned out in the rut. As I mentioned a couple of days ago, some people start doing things that God never intended for them to do. They stretch themselves too thin and become overly tired.

Let me stop right here and explain something to you. There is a difference between being tired and being *overly* tired. Everyone gets tired; no one is exempt. At the end of a productive day, your body is ready for rest. One of the keys to maintaining your physical, spiritual, emotional and mental well-being is to get an appropriate amount of sleep each night. It is natural to do so.

On the other hand, it is unhealthy for you to fall asleep when you are being counted on or when you should be taking care of responsibilities. When priorities get jumbled up, that's when people start falling asleep in class, showing up late for work and nodding off in church. A person is overly tired when he cannot function well enough to do what God has called him to do. People who burn out often stop doing God's will altogether.

If you are burned out or are on your way there, listen up. Here are three things you need to do to keep from becoming overly tired. First of all, you need to rest. Jesus said to go to Him when you are weary, and He will give you rest (**Matthew 11:28**). I don't believe it is possible to be fully rested outside of Him.

Secondly, keep a good attitude. **Ephesians 4:23** says to be made new in the attitude of your mind. This is something that needs to be done daily. Lastly, stay the course. **Proverbs 15:21** – *Folly delights a man who lacks judgment, but a man of understanding keeps a straight course* (NIV).

29

discerning relationships

John 2:24-25 – 24 *But Jesus [for His part] did not trust Himself to them, because He knew all [men]; 25 And He did not need anyone to bear witness concerning man [needed no evidence from anyone about men], for He Himself knew what was in human nature [He could read men's hearts].* (AMP)

There must be balance in our relationships with others. In the above passage, Jesus taught us a very valuable lesson concerning this matter. I pray today that complete health would be restored to all of your relationships. Hallelujah!

While in Jerusalem, Jesus performed many signs, wonders and miracles. And because of the great works He did, many people believed in Him and identified themselves with His party (**John 2:23**). But Jesus did not trust Himself to them. Why?

I don't believe Jesus was suspicious of them, but He understood human nature. He knew well enough not to trust Himself to them in an unbalanced way. He could read their hearts, and He simply refused to give more of Himself to them than they were capable of handling.

Listen to what I'm saying today. I'm not telling you to be suspicious of everyone and to never trust in relationships. What you need to understand, though, is that you must not rely on others more than you rely on God. Do not act hastily when it comes to trusting others with yourself. All humans are fallible. We cannot expect them to properly handle what is meant for God alone.

The level of trust you give to people should vary. It's not suspicion to be cautious before sharing your time, resources and the intimate details of your life with another person. It's called using discernment. I encourage you to evaluate your relationships. Are you relying on someone else to fill a role that should be reserved for God? Put your total trust in the Lord today. Doing so is safe, reliable and rewarding.

Psalm 146:3 – *Put not your trust in princes, in a son of man, in whom there is no help* (AMP).

---

people are the way they are

Isaiah 11:3 – *His delight is in the fear of the LORD, and He shall not judge by the sight of His eyes, nor decide by the hearing of His ears* (NKJV).

I used to be very judgmental and critical. I would make snap judgments about a person's character based on things I saw them do or say. Without knowing who they were or where they came from, I would characterize them by the limited knowledge I had about them. I was the assumption making pro.

If someone made a stupid decision, I labeled him as stupid. If I heard someone say something that did not make sense to me, I presumed he had no sense at all. If a person constantly struggled with a certain sin, I figured he must be a weak-willed individual. I did not even realize how critical I had become. After all, being judgmental comes naturally.

Then one day the Holy Spirit spoke up on the inside of me. I had just cast judgment on someone when I heard His voice say, "People are the way they are for a reason." That was it; that was all He said. I thought about it for a while, and then the revelation started to come.

People are the way they are for a reason, and just because I don't understand or necessarily agree with their reasoning, does not give me the right to judge them. I immediately felt convicted. How many times in my life have I assumed things about people that just are not true? Just because I think someone makes a dumb choice does not mean he is dumb. In fact, if I were to ask the person if *he* thought *he* was dumb, I doubt he'd say yes. He'd probably say *I* was dumb.

The fact of the matter is people in your life will make ill-advised decisions from time to time. Instead of casting immediate judgment, ask the Holy Spirit to help you understand where the person is coming from. Then you might be able to help.

John 7:24 – *"Stop judging by mere appearances, and make a right judgment"* (NIV).

the coast is clear

Jeremiah 7:9-10 – 9 *"Will you steal and murder, commit adultery and perjury, burn incense to Baal and follow other gods you have not known,* 10 *and then come and stand before me in this house, which bears my Name, and say, 'We are safe'—safe to do all these detestable things?"* (NIV)

It's quite amusing to me what children will do when they don't think anyone is watching. Our boys each have their own iPod, but they are not allowed to use it without permission. They are aware of this rule, but sometimes boys cannot help themselves.

Heidi and I used to keep their iPods in the top drawer of one of our bedside tables. It was a great hiding place until they found out we were stashing them there. So our oldest son Noah started sending Jack on covert missions to fetch the iPods. He didn't care if his younger sibling took the fall.

It didn't take long for Heidi and me to catch on to what they were doing, so we started storing the iPods on the top shelf of one of our bookcases. One day I walked by the shelf and noticed the iPods were missing. I first thought Heidi might have moved them, but then I heard gaming sounds coming from the back room. They were busted, but I was curious as to how they got them down. So I put them back on the same shelf.

Later that day, I secretly watched as Jack went into his bedroom, got a stool, carried it to the bookshelf and stood on it to reach the iPods. He would never have done it if he'd known I was watching. I'm sure he thought, "The coast is clear. I'm safe."

Everything we do in secret is seen by God. Do you have some shameful habits that you practice in private? Many believers are faithful to attend church, but they cheat on God at home. Be a person of integrity. If you are doing things that you know God does not approve of, stop! Repent, and begin to do what is right.

Jeremiah 7:11 – *"Has this house, which bears my Name, become a den of robbers to you? But I have been watching!"* declares the Lord. (NIV).

start to finish

Romans 5:3 – *And not only this, but we also exult in our tribulations, knowing that tribulation brings about perseverance* (NASB).

The world is full of starters, but there are far fewer finishers. Many people are gung-ho at the outset of certain tasks, but once there is the slightest opposition, they lose heart and give up. Perhaps you're one of them. God's desire is for us to develop perseverance in every area of our lives. He wants us to be finishers and to remain motivated when we face difficulty.

A lot of people flee from adversity because they are scared of conflict. They avoid hardship, but many times God leads us into trials. He allows us to walk through tough times in order to develop perseverance in us. Most people lack the ability to finish because they either run or quit when they encounter adverse circumstances. Perseverance only develops when our faith is tested (**James 1:3**).

Not finishing what we start is a sign of immaturity. **James 1:4** – *Perseverance must finish its work so that you may be mature and complete, not lacking anything* (NIV). If you don't discipline yourself to finish what you start, you will never be a complete person. You will lack confidence, and your faith will stumble.

Being a finisher requires great strength and self-control. The devil does not want you to finish things, so he fights you every step of the way. He attacks your mind, body and spirit. But you must remember that you are fighting the *good* fight of faith (**1 Timothy 6:12**). My wife says it is a good fight because we are fighting *from* victory, not *for* victory. Hallelujah!

Be encouraged: Do not quit! Finish what you have started. God has given you the grace and strength you need to complete the task at hand. I pray for your level of endurance to increase today.

James 1:12 – *Blessed is the man who perseveres under trial, because when he has stood the test, he will receive the crown of life that God has promised to those who love him* (NIV).

cheers and refreshments

Philemon 7 – *For I have derived great joy and comfort and encouragement from your love, because the hearts of the saints [who are your fellow Christians] have been cheered and refreshed through you, [my] brother* (AMP).

Paul is wrote this letter to Philemon while imprisoned in Rome. Obviously, Paul had seen better days, but he wrote of the great joy, comfort and encouragement he had received as a result of Philemon's love for the body of Christ. I can only hope that one day someone would write these same things about my character and devotion to the Lord.

Philemon was a man of great faith, and he was a hard worker. He was a strong leader, and he made a positive impact on the church of his day. Philemon cheered on and helped refresh fellow believers. He was a great source of encouragement.

Have you ever exerted great physical or mental energy over an extended period of time? Perhaps you have played sports or you enjoy exercising. Maybe you've participated in a series of meetings for work or attended a daylong seminar of some kind.

I've been involved in both, and they are equally draining. I've experienced physical exhaustion and mental fatigue (often at the same time). It's during those moments that I need two things in order to keep going: cheers and refreshments. Sporting events have cheerleaders and water boys, and seminars usually provide a break so you can relax and refocus.

You are surrounded by people who are tired. The last thing they need is someone nagging them or pushing them lower. When I'm worn out, I don't want to hear "boos", nor do I want someone to hand me lukewarm Gatorade. I encourage you to be an encouragement. If you need to be cheered up, serve refreshments to someone else. Be known for how you bless others.

Hebrews 3:13 – *But encourage one another daily, as long as it is called Today, so that none of you may be hardened by sin's deceitfulness* (NIV).

contentment

> **Philippians 4:11-12** – 11 *I am not saying this because I am in need, for I have learned to be content whatever the circumstances.* 12 *I know what it is to be in need, and I know what it is to have plenty. I have learned the secret of being content in any and every situation, whether well fed or hungry, whether living in plenty or in want* (NIV).

If you are reading this, odds are you can relate to Paul's condition as he wrote the above passage to the Philippians. You probably know what it is to be in need and what it is to have plenty. You've likely experienced times when you've eaten until you were satisfied, and I'm sure you have gone hungry before as well. No matter what the current circumstances surrounding your life look like, you can relate to Paul on some level. Unfortunately, this is where the similarities between Paul and most people stop.

Though Paul was writing this letter from prison, he was content. He had come to a place in his life where he was satisfied no matter what he faced. This cannot be said for many people today. In our high-paced society, there are those who have plenty, yet they never seem to have enough. Then there are those who have great need, and they tend to feel cheated.

Contentment means to be joyful and at peace with who you are and what you have. One of the greatest hindrances to being content is our tendency to compare ourselves to others. We compare everything from our circumstances to our cars to our appearances. If you consistently compare yourself to others, you likely suffer from chronic disappointment.

Paul said that he learned to be content in every situation. The key word here is *learned*. Being content is not natural; it is learned behavior. So what lesson did Paul learn? How was he able to be content writing in a jail cell? The answer is found in **Philippians 4:13** – *I can do everything through him who gives me strength* (NIV). The truth is we cannot be content in our own strength, but God can enable you to be strong and content no matter what you may be facing. Hallelujah!

i thought so

Proverbs 23:7 – *For as he thinks in his heart, so is he* (AMP).

What you think about will ultimately drop into your heart, and then it will come out of your mouth and in your actions. If you are having a difficult time controlling what you say or do, you need to take inventory of your thoughts. As Joyce Meyer says, "You need to begin thinking about what you think about."

Every morning when you wake up, your sinful nature and your Spirit man wake up with you. You then have a choice to make. Are you going to fix your mind on how you feel, or are you going to focus your attention on God? Many people immediately begin to think about how tired they are and that they'd rather stay in bed. They dwell on how awful their job is, or how they can't stand the sight of themselves in the mirror. These are not thoughts God desires you to think about. Thinking like this sets you up for failure.

When unpleasant thoughts begin to bombard our minds, the Bible implores us to take those thoughts captive and make them obedient to Christ (**2 Corinthians 10:5**). But you may ask, "How do I do this?" If you start to think about how tired and worn out you are, say something like, "The joy of the Lord is my strength. Hallelujah! I'm so thankful for another day of life." Focus on how good God is, not on how tired you are.

If you constantly think about how much you hate your job, begin to give thanks that you even have a job. If you can't stand the sight of yourself in the morning, thank God that you are fearfully and wonderfully made (**Psalm 139:14**). Ask God to help you see yourself the way He does.

Your thoughts are very powerful. They not only shape your perspective on life, but they dictate your behavior. **Romans 8:5** – *Those who live according to the sinful nature have their minds set on what that nature desires; but those who live in accordance with the Spirit have their minds set on what the Spirit desires* (NIV). I want to encourage you today to fix your mind on the Spirit. Don't allow negative thoughts to shape who you are.

present yourself approved

People crave approval. Approval brings assurance and a sense of accomplishment to a person. Being approved of means to be appreciated and supported. While there's nothing inherently wrong with wanting the approval of others, our self-worth should not be defined by whether or not people approve of us. We cannot please everyone all of the time.

Now, I don't recommend that you purposefully try to offend people either. Do not live your life to spite others. Your goal should be to please God and seek His approval, and the above verse teaches us how to do so.

If you want God's approval, you must study His word diligently and handle it appropriately. I believe that often times this verse is passed off as written specifically to those called into full-time occupational ministry. The truth is you may never stand behind a pulpit, but He still expects you to study the Word (in context) and apply it to your life.

Many believers don't even read their Bibles except on Sundays. Others skim over a few passages sporadically during the week, and some read His word like a storybook. To study actually means to apply your mind in an effort to learn. Christlikeness is learned behavior, and the Bible is the instruction manual.

Would you want a surgeon to operate on you if he'd never been to medical school? Not hardly. You certainly wouldn't approve of that. One day Jesus will return for God's children, not those who *pose* as His children. Have you studied how to be His child yet today? Purpose to be approved by Him.

wisdom calls aloud

> **Proverbs 4:5, 7** – 5 *Get wisdom, get understanding; do not forget my words or swerve from them...*7 *Wisdom is supreme; therefore get wisdom. Though it cost all you have, get understanding* (NIV).

The message here is very clear: Get wisdom. In other words, an effort has to be made for us to become wise. We have to get it. Being wise is a choice. I have heard many believers say things such as, "Wow, that person is so wise. He has great insight. I wish I had that kind of understanding."

Wisdom does not result from wishful thinking. Getting wisdom is not difficult. In fact, God has made it very simple for us to gain wisdom. It is available to everyone. **Proverbs 1:20** – *Wisdom calls aloud in the street, she raises her voice in the public squares* (NIV).

Wisdom is calling aloud to you. It is not reserved for an elite group of believers, nor is it hidden. Wisdom is clearly visible and attainable, but many people remain ignorant. But why? I believe the answer is found in the very next verse. *At the head of noisy streets she* (wisdom) *cries out* (**1:21**).

Many people's lives are too noisy and chaotic to hear the voice of wisdom. Is your life so out of balance that it causes you to make poor decisions? The Holy Spirit is the voice of wisdom on the inside of a believer. Distractions muffle His voice. You must discipline yourself, and respond to the voice of wisdom. If you don't, calamity will overtake you (**Proverbs 1:25-27**).

Perhaps today you are frustrated because you have acted too hastily. Maybe your life is governed by your feelings. If you are consistently making poor judgment calls, get wisdom. Ask God to help you. The Bible says that wisdom, knowledge and understanding come from the mouth of the Lord (**Proverbs 2:6**). He's been talking. It's time for you to listen.

> **James 1:5** – *If any of you lacks wisdom, he should ask God, who gives generously to all without finding fault, and it will be given to him* (NIV).

accountability

> **Acts 5:1-4** – 1 *Now a man named Ananias, together with his wife Sapphira, also sold a piece of property.* 2 *With his wife's full knowledge he kept back part of the money for himself, but brought the rest and put it at the apostles' feet.* 3 *Then Peter said, "Ananias, how is it that Satan has so filled your heart that you have kept for yourself some of the money you received for the land?* 4 *Didn't it belong to you before it was sold? And after it was sold, wasn't the money at your disposal? What made you think of doing such a thing? You have not lied to men but to God"* (NIV).

What was the crime in this story? Ananias thought he was pulling a fast one on the apostles and the church, but he was really lying to God. He wanted the church to think he and his wife were giving the full amount received from their purchase, when they had actually kept back some for themselves.

If you read on in Acts 5, you will see that this story has a tragic end, but there is a lesson to be learned. Read verse 2 again: *With his wife's full knowledge he kept back part of the money for himself.* This entire situation could have been avoided if Sapphira had held Ananias accountable. Rather than stopping her husband from making a fatal mistake, she partnered with him in sin.

You need someone in your life that will ask you the tough questions and tell you the hard truths, but your accountability partner cannot be someone who struggles with the same things you do. Otherwise, you will wind up condoning each other's sins instead of spurring one another on to holiness. A true accountability partner will point you to the heart of God no matter what, even if it comes at the expense of your relationship.

If you do not have someone who truly holds you accountable, ask God to bring that person into your life. When He does, be open and honest. Accountability is key to freedom.

> **Proverbs 12:15** – *The way of a fool seems right to him, but a wise man listens to advice* (NIV).

a craving

Imagine you've been stranded in the desert, and you're starving for food and drink. It's been a couple of days since you've eaten a meal, and your body is in desperate need of nourishment. You feel disoriented, as your body is about to give out. You stumble hopelessly, as your mind begins to play tricks on you. Suddenly, out of nowhere, a helicopter appears on the horizon and comes to your rescue.

The chopper lands, and your rescuers hurry into action and whisk you aboard the aircraft. They attach you to various machines and begin to check your vital signs. They pump fluids into you through an IV, and you start to feel human again. Once back in the city, you're taken to a nearby hospital to recover. You're checked into a private room, given some fresh clothes, and you lay down to get some rest.

A few minutes pass, and a nurse enters with a tray of food...*hospital* food. You uncover the plate to find an undercooked chunk of Salisbury steak, a spoonful of lukewarm mashed potatoes, something that resembles broccoli and a dry piece of chocolate cake. Without hesitation, you gratefully begin to inhale the meal in its entirety. Your strength returns, and you pay no mind to how undesirable the meal was you've just consumed. You didn't pick and choose to eat the more attractive portions of food, and you don't ask the nurse to take it back and bring out something new. You are content and fully satisfied.

This is the kind of insatiable hunger God desires for you to develop for His word. Many times we want to be selective when applying God's word to our lives. We want to dismiss the hard truths that convict and challenge us to change, and we want to embrace messages that tickle our ears. His word is beneficial to your life, and you need to develop a craving for all of it. **Proverbs 27:7** – *To the hungry even what is bitter tastes sweet* (NIV).

meditate

Do you want to know how to be in the center of God's will and be prosperous and successful? Sure you do. The key to knowing the heart of God and finding success is found in this verse: Meditate on His word day and night.

Most Christians understand they should spend time in God's word and in prayer on a daily basis. Many Sunday school classes are based on a daily relationship with the Lord, and countless messages have been preached on devoting part of your daily schedule to Christ. I'm not going to ask you, "Do you spend time with God on a daily basis?" You already know you should be doing that. The question I want to ask you today is, "Do you spend *quality* time with Him on a daily basis?"

The Bible says to meditate on God's word everyday. The word *meditate* is defined as to engage in thought or contemplation; reflect. I'll confess there's been numerous times I'm guilty of just skimming through the pages of my Bible and giving God a thoughtless "shout out" in prayer. I can only imagine the heartbreak I've caused my Maker. His sole purpose for creating us was for intimate fellowship with Him. Yet, countless times I have been flippant in the time slot I've allotted Him.

I challenge you, not only to read over His word, but also to study it, reflect on it and apply it to your life. Commit His word to memory, and search for deeper meaning. As you open your Bible today, don't settle for what's on the surface. Ask the Holy Spirit to give you a fresh revelation of who He is. I pray that your time with God will no longer be treated as a quota you have to meet.

six treasures

Isaiah 33:5-6 – 5 *The LORD is exalted, for he dwells on high; he will fill Zion with justice and righteousness.* 6 *He will be the sure foundation of your times, a rich store of salvation and wisdom and knowledge; the fear of the LORD is the key to this treasure* (NIV).

The above verses speak of six treasures God offers to the believer: justice, righteousness, salvation, wisdom, knowledge and a sure foundation. God's desire is for these promised treasures to be unlocked in the life of every believer, but there are many Christians who live their lives absent of these riches.

Maybe you are confused as to why you don't have the joy that accompanies salvation or the wisdom to discern God's will. Perhaps you crumble when the storms of life rage because your foundation is unsure. For many believers these treasures remain securely locked in God's treasure chest, but Isaiah revealed the key to releasing these treasures in your life: The fear of the Lord.

For you to have the fear of the Lord, you must first understand what it is. In his book, The Fear of the Lord, John Bevere says, "The fear of God includes, but is not limited to, respecting and reverencing Him, for we are told to tremble at His presence. Holy fear gives God the place of glory, honor, reverence, thanksgiving, praise and preeminence He deserves."

Fearing God has nothing to do with being scared of Him and everything to do with standing in awe of Him. We're not to fear God because of what He can do for us, but rather because of who He is. When you truly revere God, He takes priority over everyone and everything else in your life. Many people covet the promises of God, but they do not give Him the time of day.

Pray today that you will have a holy fear of the Lord. Repent for the times you've expected His treasures to be released in your life without giving any effort of your own. May you fear the Lord and inherit His promises today!

Galatians 6:7 – *Do not be deceived: God cannot be mocked. A man reaps what he sows* (NIV).

He's got His eye on you

Psalm 33:18-19 – 18 *But the eyes of the LORD are on those who fear him, on those whose hope is in his unfailing love,* 19 *to deliver them from death and keep them alive in famine* (NIV).

I've heard it said many times over the course of my life, "You may be able to fool everyone else, but you can't fool God. He sees everything, and He'll get you." Especially, if you've grown up in church, you've probably heard something along these lines before. Statements like these portray God as waiting anxiously to strike you down for wrongdoing. Yes, it is true that He sees everything we do, but that's not such a bad thing.

In fact, it's quite comforting to know I can never stumble off God's radar. Look at the above promises God makes to those who fear Him. He has His eyes on those who trust in His unfailing love, and He delivers them from death and keeps them alive in famine. Hallelujah!

Notice He does not promise to keep those who fear Him from ever going through a famine. He says He will deliver them from death and keep them alive *during* famine. The word *famine* is most commonly used to describe a drastic, wide-reaching food shortage. It is actually a drastic shortage or dearth. Given this definition, it's safe to say that a person can experience a famine in pretty much any area of life.

Maybe today as you read this you are going through some sort of shortage in your life. Perhaps you are experiencing a personal famine in your finances, family or faith. No matter your circumstance, you have the promise of deliverance if you have a holy fear of the Lord. His eyes never come off of you, and He will never give you more than you can handle. Even in the midst of great famine, stand in awe of God. He will see you through.

Psalm 23:4 – *Even though I walk through the valley of the shadow of death, I will fear no evil, for you are with me; your rod and your staff, they comfort me* (NIV).

it's okay to hate

Proverbs 8:13 – *To fear the LORD is to hate evil; I hate pride and arrogance, evil behavior and perverse speech* (NIV).

I absolutely love this verse. I was always taught never to say the word *hate*, and I was not supposed to hate anything or anybody. I've actually said the same sort of things to my sons, Noah and Jack. While this is a good moral standard for your relationships and behavior, it is not supposed to be applied to your feelings toward sin.

Those who fear the Lord hate sin. When you have a sincere reverence for Jesus Christ, you will be a selfless person. You will not tolerate evil behavior in your life, or in the lives of those you surround yourself with. You will stand up for what you believe in and refuse to blend in. Words of encouragement will be on the tip of your tongue because you have crucified the sinful nature. You will hate evil because you know sin hurts the heart of God, not because it can get you into trouble.

On the contrary, those who do not fear the Lord, tolerate sin. Sin is looked at as an unavoidable part of life. These people use God's grace as a cover-up for their wrongdoing. They would rather sweep their transgressions under the rug, as opposed to repenting and making a life change.

Do you fear the Lord? You can find out really fast by doing a quick survey of how you entertain yourself and how you behave around others. What kind of media do you allow into your home, your iPod or DVD player. What are the subjects of your conversations? I challenge you to examine your life today. Ask the Holy Spirit to reveal those areas where you have been too lenient when it comes to sin. My prayer is that you will hate, not tolerate, sin.

2 Corinthians 7:1 – *Since we have these promises, dear friends, let us purify ourselves from everything that contaminates body and spirit, perfecting holiness out of reverence for God* (NIV).

I know something you don't know

It's human nature to want to know everyone's secrets. When someone says, "I know something you don't know," our flesh crawls with excitement, and our natural inclination is to find out what it is he is talking about. Usually, a secret is some sort of juicy gossip. The person the secret is about probably doesn't want the information to become public knowledge, so they confide in someone "who won't tell". When the secret finally leaks out, feelings are hurt, trust is compromised and friendships end.

Not so with God's secrets. Friendships don't end when God spills His guts. In fact, friendship begins with God when He starts sharing secrets with you. Another version of **Psalm 25:14** says: *The LORD is a friend to those who fear him* (NLT). I don't know about you, but I want to be a part of God's inner circle.

I want to know all there is to know about our Maker. He is an infinite God with limitless wisdom. His knowledge and expertise far outweighs anything I could learn from a textbook. I want Him to be able to trust and confide in me. I don't ever want to compromise my relationship with Him. My prayer is that He would reveal a new aspect of who He is to me everyday. What's the key to this kind of friendship? You guessed it...the fear of the Lord.

I challenge you to live a life worthy of receiving God's trust. So many times we just expect God to show us *this* or speak to us about *that*, but we don't give him the honor and respect He deserves. When you fear Him, it builds trust in your relationship with God. When trust is established, He shares His secrets with you. Then supernatural friendship can begin.

the fear of man

The fear of man is the opposite of the fear of the Lord. A holy fear of God brings absolute freedom to the believer, but fearing man leads to bondage. People who fear man are constantly reinventing themselves in order to be accepted. They are trapped in a never-ending struggle to appease others and are overwhelmed by the fear of rejection.

John Bevere once said, "You will serve whom you fear." This makes perfect sense. The fear of man will cause you to attempt to please man. When you fear God, your motivation will be to please Him.

Maybe you are reading this, and you're caught up in trying to please people. It could be your best friends or a certain crowd you want to belong to. You may be trying to achieve a particular social status or fit into a mold Hollywood portrays as acceptable. If so, you're likely facing a major identity crisis. Those who fear man do not know who they are in Christ.

The person who fears the Lord finds his identity in Him. The fear of the Lord leads to intimacy with the Father. Remember, He shares His secrets with those who fear Him, and those who know God intimately are secure in themselves.

If you have an unhealthy fear of man today, I challenge you to crucify your desire to please people. There's nothing wrong with being at peace with those around you, but you will fall into a trap if pleasing others takes priority over pleasing God. I pray you are delivered from the endless cycle of reinventing yourself, and that you will find true freedom in the fear of the Lord. May you aim to please the Master today and everyday!

Ecclesiastes 2:26 – *To the man who pleases him, God gives wisdom, knowledge and happiness, but to the sinner he gives the task of gathering and storing up wealth to hand it over to the one who fears God* (NIV).

no vacancy

Luke 17:5-6 – 5 *The apostles said to the Lord, "Increase our faith!"* 6 *He replied, "If you have faith as small as a mustard seed, you can say to this mulberry tree, 'Be uprooted and planted in the sea,' and it will obey you"* (NIV).

Five times in the book of Matthew, Jesus addresses His disciples as having "little faith". In **Matthew 16:8**, Jesus came up on a conversation between the disciples and said to them, *"You of little faith, why are you talking among yourselves?"* There is a valuable lesson to be learned from this encounter.

Like spirits attract, and when they come together, they feed off one another. The disciples lacked faith as individuals, and their faith suffered even more as they sat and discussed their shortcomings. Jesus recognized what they were doing and rebuked them.

Maybe today your faith is on life support. The last thing you need is to surround yourself with naysayers and those of lesser faith. Mark 5 tells the story of Jesus and Jairus' daughter. This synagogue ruler went to Jesus when his daughter fell ill and asked Him to come to his home. While Jesus was in transit to Jairus' house, the little girl died. Jesus went anyway.

Jesus arrived on the scene and found everyone weeping and wailing loudly. Full of faith, Jesus ignored them all and said, *"Why all this commotion and wailing? The child is not dead but asleep"* (**Mark 5:39**). The first thing Jesus did was make a declaration of faith. Then what happened? They laughed at Him.

Undeterred, Jesus put them all out (**Mark 5:40**). He silenced those around Him who lacked faith. They were busy wallowing in their unbelief, and Jesus would have nothing of it. If you are surrounded by naysayers today, put up a no vacancy sign and separate yourself from them. Your faith depends on it.

John 14:12 – *"I tell you the truth, anyone who has faith in me will do what I have been doing. He will do even greater things than these, because I am going to the Father"* (NIV).

47

tunnel vision

Hebrews 12:2 – *Let us fix our eyes on Jesus, the author and perfecter of our faith* (NIV).

My family has gone on vacation a couple of times to the Smoky Mountains in Tennessee. One of the things we enjoyed the most was driving up through Pigeon Forge, past Gatlinburg and into the Great Smoky Mountains National Park. The scenery is absolutely gorgeous, with rivers and streams weaving alongside the highway and panoramic views every few hundred feet. There's no place like it on earth.

As we traveled deep into the national park, we drove through several tunnels. We'd roll down our windows and yell to hear the echoes. Though it was enjoyable for the whole family, the purpose of a tunnel is for so much more than entertainment.

Tunnels exist as a means to go through an obstruction. In our case, the tunnels we drove through in Tennessee were built to allow people to pass through an area of mountains that would have otherwise been impassable. When you go through a tunnel, you cannot see the obstacle you are going through. You can only see what's on the other side. If the tunnel were to be removed, the road would be buried beneath dirt and rock.

The same is true in the spirit realm. Perhaps you are facing a mountain today as you read this. Natural instincts will lead you to try and find a way around the obstacle, but God may be calling you to walk through your circumstance in faith. The only way to pass through to the other side is by fixing your eyes on Him and His word because He is the author and perfecter of your faith.

This will give you the tunnel vision necessary to go through any obstacle. When your eyes are centered on Jesus, all you can see is Him. Trials and tribulations may be all around you, but you cannot be overwhelmed as you focus on Him. When you take your eyes off of Him, you will either aimlessly wander or be crushed by your circumstance. Fix your eyes on Jesus today!

Proverbs 23:26 – *Let your eyes keep to my ways* (NIV).

48

help me!

Mark 9:24 – *Immediately the boy's father exclaimed, "I do believe; help me overcome my unbelief!* (NIV)

Have you ever found that it's sometimes easier to believe for someone else's miracle than your own? Why is that? It's because you have nothing to lose when you're believing for someone else. If God doesn't come through on their behalf, it is of little or no consequence to you. On the other hand, when it comes to believing for *your* breakthrough, you have everything to lose.

I know when my family, spiritual wellbeing, finances, etc. are riding on my faith, many times all I can think about is, "What if God doesn't come through for me?" This is the exact scenario played out in Mark 9. If you'll recall, a man came to Jesus and asked if He could help his son who was tormented by an evil spirit. Jesus answered in verse 23, *"Everything is possible for him who believes."* The boy's father responded in verse 24, *"I do believe; help me overcome my unbelief!"*

For the longest time I was puzzled by this statement. I could only see it as an oxymoron. He believes, but he doesn't believe...? It didn't make sense to me. So I asked the Holy Spirit to help me understand. Here's the revelation I received: This man believed Jesus was able to heal his son. He had no doubt heard the testimonies of those Jesus had already ministered to. Many people had received deliverance because of Jesus. He just did not know whether Jesus was going to do it for *his* son or not.

I believe many Christians have this same mentality. They know God is a miracle worker, they have seen Him move and they've heard the testimonies, but for some reason they lack the faith for their own miracle. I challenge you to believe and not doubt for whatever you have need of today. May your cry become, "Lord, I believe; help me overcome my unbelief!"

Mark 9:25-26 – 25 *"You deaf and mute spirit,"* he said, *"I command you, come out of him and never enter him again."* 26 *The spirit shrieked, convulsed him violently and came out* (NIV).

49

you don't have to beg

> **1 John 5:14-15** – 14 *This is the confidence we have in approaching God: that if we ask anything according to his will, he hears us.* 15 *And if we know that he hears us—whatever we ask—we know that we have what we asked of him* (NIV).

Have you ever noticed that people normally beg for things they're not supposed to have? Think about it. Heidi and I usually do not allow our children to drink soda during the week. Soft drinks are a weekend luxury. Occasionally, our oldest son will ask for a Coke before Friday arrives. Our automatic response is, "Sorry, but no. You have to wait until the weekend."

Generally he accepts our answer and walks away, but sometimes he's not quick to give up. He'll pooch out his bottom lip, tilt his head, bat his big, puppy dog eyes, and then the begging ensues. "Daddy, may I *please* have some Coke?" I'll admit, it's very difficult to tell my children no. Nine out of ten times I'll manage to stand by the rules, but every once in a while I'll give in.

On the flipside, he never has to beg me for something he knows he's allowed to have. The same is true with our heavenly Father. God's children do not have to beg Him for anything that lines up with His perfect will. You do not have to plead with Him to fulfill His word in your life. All you have to do is ask according to His will and believe what the Word says, and it will be done. That's it. Take it or leave it. You either believe God is who He says He is, or you don't. The Bible is true, or it isn't. You decide.

Take healing for example. **Isaiah 53:5** says, *"And by his stripes we are healed"* (NKJV). We *are* healed! When Jesus died and rose again, He purchased our healing once and for all. Why would He go through the crucifixion only to have us beg Him for the healing He's paid for? It just doesn't make sense.

I challenge you today to stop begging for God's will and word to be fulfilled in your life. If you do not know His will, ask Him. If you do not know His word, read it. Remember the words of Jesus: *"Whatever you ask for in prayer, believe that you have received it, and it will be yours"* (**Mark 11:24**, NIV).

clothed with compassion

Colossians 3:12 – *Therefore, as God's chosen people, holy and dearly loved, clothe yourselves with compassion, kindness, humility, gentleness and patience* (NIV).

Have you ever put on another person's shoes before? Maybe you accidentally put on someone's shoe that was similar to yours but the wrong size. Perhaps you thought it would be funny to swap shoes with somebody else. Odds are you have worn another person's shoes at some point in your lifetime. Whether voluntarily or accidentally, putting somebody else's shoes on usually makes for an awkward experience.

Our boys enjoy wearing Mommy and Daddy's shoes. They'll put them on and pretend to be us, or they will chase each other around the house. I use the word *chase* very loosely because they usually wind up tripping over their feet and falling into the furniture or into one another. Needless to say, the intrigue of wearing Mommy and Daddy's shoes wears off very quickly. It becomes more of a nuisance than anything, and they wind up kicking our shoes off somewhere and doing something else.

The Bible tells us in **Colossians 3:12** to clothe ourselves with compassion. *Compassion* is a feeling of deep sympathy and sorrow for another who is stricken by misfortune, accompanied by a strong desire to alleviate the suffering. Compassion is all about putting yourself in somebody else's shoes. This isn't always easy to do, and it can be quite awkward at times. Nevertheless, God requires it of us.

Compassion is so much more than just feeling sorry for someone. Compassion implies action. Put yourself in the other person's shoes and attempt to help him or her by thinking about how you would want to be treated if your situations were reversed. Human tendency is to cast judgment when people are afflicted, but I challenge you today to extend a helping hand.

Matthew 14:14 – *When Jesus landed and saw a large crowd, he had compassion on them and healed their sick* (NIV).

clothed with kindness

Colossians 3:12 – *Therefore, as God's chosen people, holy and dearly loved, clothe yourselves with compassion, kindness, humility, gentleness and patience* (NIV).

Being kind is the equivalent of being helpful. They are one in the same. Kindness has nothing to do with a person's intentions, and it cannot be pried out of someone. It is a character trait that must be cultivated on a daily basis, or it will never take root.

I believe it's very significant that the words *clothe yourselves* are used in this verse. Think about this with me. Why do we put on clothing? To cover our bodies. Our bodies are not naturally clothed, so we have to put on clothes every morning when we get up. I'm not trying to insult your intelligence here.

Our flesh is no different. Nobody's flesh is naturally kind, so you and I have to put on kindness everyday when we get up. If you don't consciously clothe yourself in kindness, you might have flashes of promise here and there, but you will never be consistent. Kindness is *helpful* action.

Many people have said to me, "I'd love to help you out," but then there's no follow through. Those who are genuinely kind do not make empty promises; they simply lend a helping hand where there is need. Kind people have a servant's heart. They are selfless individuals who put the needs of others above their own. They are a rarity because being kind requires effort, and it's less strenuous to be selfish.

I encourage you today, and everyday, to put on kindness. It's a trait that not many people truly possess, but it is one that God expects from those who love Him. Offer to help someone today at your school or workplace. Serve your leaders, or do something unexpected around the house. Your kindness level should always be increasing. Read **2 Peter 1:5-8**.

2 Peter 1:8 – *For if you possess these qualities in increasing measure, they will keep you from being ineffective and unproductive in your knowledge of our Lord Jesus Christ* (NIV).

clothed with humility

Colossians 3:12 – *Therefore, as God's chosen people, holy and dearly loved, clothe yourselves with compassion, kindness, humility, gentleness and patience* (NIV).

I made a discovery as I was studying humility. It may not be a groundbreaking one, but it was very helpful to me: Humility is directly tied to self-control, and here's how.

You probably know that pride is the opposite of humility. Pride is thinking of yourself more highly than you should; it's arrogance. **Romans 12:3** says: *Do not think of yourself more highly than you ought, but rather think of yourself with sober judgment* (NIV). If humility is the opposite of pride, this verse indicates that thinking of yourself with sober judgment is equivalent to walking in humility. So I looked up the word *sober*.

The dictionary offers numerous definitions for the word sober, but they all point to one thing: self-control. Pride will dominate your life unless you learn self-control. I have often wondered why so many people struggle with arrogance. It's because we have to discipline ourselves to be humble, and a lot of people just don't put forth the effort. Pride comes naturally, so without self-control, humility is impossible.

Zephaniah 2:3 says to seek humility. Humility cannot be imparted into you by a humble person. You must search for it, and then put it on. Being a person of godly character is no easy task, and it goes against our human nature. In fact, self-control is another attribute **2 Peter 1:5-8** encourages us to have in increasing measure.

One of the most humbling stories in the Bible is found in Luke 7. In the face of ridicule, a woman poured a jar of expensive perfume on the feet of Jesus and wiped them with her hair. Her humility was evident through this act of worship. Humble yourself before God today, and think of yourself with sober judgment.

1 Peter 5:5 – *All of you, clothe yourselves with humility toward one another* (NIV).

clothed with gentleness

Some might say that kindness and gentleness are one in the same, but I disagree. If you'll remember, kindness has to do with helpful *action*. A person can do random acts of kindness with a wrong attitude. For instance, I've picked up trash around the church grounds before while grumbling to myself about how messy people are. I did a kind act, but with a bad attitude.

Gentleness speaks of one's nature, the motive behind a person's actions. Gentleness is never rough or violent, but is honorable and respectful, even when it is done wrong. Gentleness is a fruit of the Spirit, and once again, it is not a natural characteristic of our flesh.

1 Timothy 6:11 says: *Pursue righteousness, godliness, faith, love, endurance and gentleness* (NIV). If you pursue and clothe yourself in gentleness, there is a good chance that your immediate reaction to adversity will be gentle.

A gentle answer turns away wrath, but a harsh word stirs up anger (**Proverbs 15:1**). I'll be the first one to tell you this verse is true. I have responded both gently and harshly to conflict, and I've found a gentle answer tends to calm things down and a harsh one magnifies the situation.

As you pray today, ask God for the gift of gentleness. Ask Him to mold your nature to match His. My prayer is that your kindness would be backed by a gentle spirit and not an indifferent one. If you face difficulty at some point today, I pray you confront it with gentleness. Refuse to allow anger to rule your life.

clothed with patience

If patience is a virtue, I have to admit it's a virtue I have lacked the majority of my life. I believe building patience is a constant work in progress for everyone. It's one of those processes that you cannot afford to take even one day off from. If you do, it is as if you set yourself back months.

It's not possible for a human to reach "patience perfection", but that does not give us a free pass to quit the process altogether. Many people liken their impatience to their personality, and they write off the possibility of ever changing. Others attribute their impatience to our high-paced society.

Here are my feelings on the subject: A person who refuses to build patience is selfish. Furthermore, the Christian who is not striving to be patient is living outside the will of God. Listen to this: The opposite of patience is laziness. **Hebrews 6:12** – *We do not want you to become lazy, but to imitate those who through faith and patience inherit what has been promised* (NIV).

One of the characteristics a patient person possesses is persistence. Many people abandon the call of God because they lack the patience to see His will fulfilled in their lives. Relationships fall apart because the two sides are not willing to endure the rebuilding process. People lash out in anger because they do not make patience a focal point in their lives.

I want to encourage you today to take the patience process one step at a time. My patience level is higher now than it once was, but I have to make a conscious effort to work at it daily. You will not go from impatient to patient overnight; so don't beat yourself up when you stumble. It's all a part of the process.

Proverbs 19:11 – *A man's wisdom gives him patience; it is to his glory to overlook an offense* (NIV).

step 1: separation

Romans 12:2 – *And do not be conformed to this world, but be transformed by the renewing of your mind, so that you may prove what the will of God is, that which is good and acceptable and perfect* (NASB).

The first step to knowing God's will for your life is to separate yourself from the world. Allow me to rewrite this verse so you can better understand what's being said: Do not become similar to the world in nature, form or character.

There is a worldly pattern that Christians are to have nothing to do with. It's a combination of qualities, acts and tendencies God wants us to avoid, but unfortunately, avoiding such things is no easy task. In fact, it is human nature to desire the exact opposite. Our flesh wants to blend in with the crowd, but God is very specific about His feelings on this matter. **1 John 2:15** – *Do not love the world or anything in the world. If anyone loves the world, the love of the Father in not in him* (NIV).

So many Christians are clueless as to what God's will is because they have an unhealthy relationship with the world. You cannot hear God's voice clearly when your mind is polluted by the lusts of the flesh.

Have you ever been talking with someone on your cell phone, and all of a sudden the connection goes fuzzy or starts cutting in and out? There's actually a dead zone on the interstate that causes my cell to drop calls every time. If you're anything like me, such instances irritate you to no end. It is especially annoying when I am in the middle of a serious conversation.

Interference is virtually unavoidable when it comes to the cellular world, but you can do something about the bad connection between you and God. If you cannot hear His voice clearly today, you need to evaluate your life and cut out the worldly patterns you have conformed to. God never drops calls.

Romans 7:18 – *And I know that nothing good lives in me, that is, in my sinful nature. I want to do what is right, but I can't* (NLT).

---

step 2: transformation

Romans 12:2 – *And do not be conformed to this world, but be transformed by the renewing of your mind, so that you may prove what the will of God is, that which is good and acceptable and perfect* (NASB).

The second step to knowing God's will for your life is to be transformed by the renewing of your mind. To transform means to undergo a change in form, appearance or character. In this case, Paul was talking about a transformation from a worldly pattern to a godly one. We need to understand that heathens are not the only people who live worldly lifestyles. Many Christians mask their worldliness with a Bible, but their lives are in desperate need of a makeover.

This kind of change can only happen if we renew our minds. How do you renew your mind? Four words: The word of God. Rather than patterning yourself after the world, you have to conform your mind to His word. Godly principles must take the place of earthly mindsets. Worldly compromise should be replaced with a sincere desire for holiness.

Renewing your mind is an everyday decision, and God expects every believer to undergo this transformation. Making a change from worldliness to godliness is a grueling process, but it is absolutely vital to knowing God's will for your life.

If you do not take anything else from this message today, please remember this. Your actions will never change until your way of thinking does. Your mind will not change unless it is constantly fed God's word. Memorize the Word, apply it to your life and watch as you conform more into His image on a daily basis. Glory to God!

Ephesians 4:22-24 – 22 *You were taught, with regard to your former way of life, to put off your old self, which is being corrupted by its deceitful desires;* 23 *to be made new in the attitude of your minds;* 24 *and to put on the new self, created to be like God in true righteousness and holiness* (NIV).

step 3: prove it

> **Romans 12:2** – *And do not be conformed to this world, but be transformed by the renewing of your mind, so that you may prove what the will of God is, that which is good and acceptable and perfect* (NASB).

The third step to knowing God's will for your life is to prove what the will of God is. After you stop conforming to the world and renew your mind, the NIV says that you will be able to test and approve what God's will is. This tells me that even after you've made the decision to walk in holiness, the will of God will not always be spelled out for you word for word and line by line.

You will have a better idea of where He's leading you, but you still have to prove what His good, pleasing and perfect will is. The first thing you need to know about the word *prove* is that it is a verb. I learned in grade school that verbs are action words. Proving what the will of God is requires faith, which is an action.

James 2:26 says, *"Faith without deeds is dead."* In other words, unless our faith is accompanied by action, we have no faith at all. We can believe something is the will of God all day, but in order to *prove* it's His will we have to walk it out by faith.

There's a truth in **Romans 12:2** that is often overlooked. We can receive deliverance from the world, renew our minds, take the steps necessary to live a holy life and still live outside the will of God. Many Christians have godly morals and even know God's will, but they do not step out in faith to do it. They are good people with great intentions, but they have become comfortable.

I challenge you today to step out in faith. Test and approve what God's will is for your life. You may misstep every now and then, but God is gracious and sees your heart. Do not get caught waiting around for His will to come to pass. Most of the time He is waiting on you.

> **Hebrews 11:8** – *By faith Abraham, when called to go to a place he would later receive as his inheritance, obeyed and went, even though he did not know where he was going* (NIV).

are we there yet?

Have you ever gone on a long, car trip with small children? If not, maybe you have been the small child on a long, car trip. I'm "lucky" enough to have experienced it both ways. When I was little, my parents chauffeured my sister and me all over the United States from Carrollton, Texas. There are not too many states that I have not been to because of our marathon family trips.

We drove to Yellowstone in Wyoming, Disney World in Orlando, Seattle, D.C., Las Vegas and more. We even drove to Toronto and Vancouver in Canada! The car rides were less than desirable, and my sister and I probably blurted out, "Are we there yet?" hundreds of times.

I can't complain, though. I have had the rare opportunity to see Mount Rushmore and the Grand Canyon. I've snow skied in both Colorado and New Mexico. I have seen the Golden Gate Bridge and walked Myrtle Beach in South Carolina. Reaching the final destination was always the highlight of my childhood travels, but I did not fully appreciate the thousands of miles we drove in order to get there. I just wanted to be there fast. Some trips were smooth and easy, but others were long and exhausting.

The same is true as we travel down the road to God's will. Many times you will enjoy mountaintop experiences, but other times God will lead you through valleys. Perhaps you are suffering today as you faithfully follow God's direction. Maybe you've recently asked Him, "Am I there yet?" I want to encourage you not to give up. Keep in mind it is on the road to His will that your character is built. Lastly, enjoy the trip and be willing to endure because the final destination is worth it.

learning from Judas (pt.1)

> **Matthew 27:3-5** – 3 *When Judas, who had betrayed him, saw that Jesus was condemned, he was seized with remorse and returned the thirty silver coins to the chief priests and elders.* 4 *"I have sinned," he said, "for I have betrayed innocent blood." "What is that to us?" they replied. "That's your responsibility."* 5 *So Judas threw the money into the temple and left. Then he went away and hanged himself* (NIV).

I believe the end of Judas' life is widely misunderstood. A lot of people tend to picture him only as a deceitful traitor who killed himself, but he wasn't solely the heartless betrayer he's known for. In fact, there are vital lessons about forgiveness to be learned from the moments leading up to his suicide.

This entire episode unfolds with Judas handing Jesus over to the chief priests for thirty silver coins. Jesus was later brought before the Roman authorities and eventually sentenced to death. Judas got word of the judgment and the reality of his sin sunk in.

Like Judas, many people get caught up in the moment and do not think about the consequences of their actions. They focus in on the "thirty silver coins" and lose all reason. Many times they do not recognize the severity of their sin until faced with a reality check, much like the one Judas encountered.

As you read this today, perhaps you have traded friendship with Jesus for the temporary pleasures of sin. If so, may this serve as your reality check! I pray that you would be made aware of your transgressions and prepare to deal with them.

Sometimes things slip in undetected, but I pray the Holy Spirit illuminates all that is hidden and brings it to the surface. We serve a merciful God, and He gives you every opportunity to confront your sin. May your hard heart be made sensitive today.

> **Psalm 19:12-13** – 12 *Who can discern his errors? Forgive my hidden faults.* 13 *Keep your servant also from willful sins; may they not rule over me. Then will I be blameless, innocent of great transgression* (NIV).

learning from Judas (pt.2)

> **Matthew 27:3-5** – 3 *When Judas, who had betrayed him, saw that Jesus was condemned, he was seized with remorse and returned the thirty silver coins to the chief priests and the elders.* 4 *"I have sinned," he said, "for I have betrayed innocent blood." "What is that to us?" they replied. "That's your responsibility."* 5 *So Judas threw the money into the temple and left. Then he went away and hanged himself* (NIV).

After Judas was made aware of his transgression, he confessed his sin. He said, "I have sinned for I have betrayed innocent blood." This is a very significant step in receiving forgiveness of sins. It is not enough to acknowledge our sin. We have to own up to it and then make it right.

Look at the progression. Judas realized the severity of his sin, confessed it and then made restitution by giving back the thirty silver coins. This may be hard for some of you to swallow because you've only known Judas as a suicidal traitor, but I believe Judas genuinely wanted to make things right. He made more of an attempt to receive forgiveness than a lot of Christians do today.

He actually cut ties with the source of his betrayal; he gave back the silver coins. A lot of Christian circles teach that recognizing your sin and confessing it are all you need to do to be forgiven. People accept this way of thinking because it costs them nothing. They do not swallow their pride or repent. They say a sinner's prayer while keeping one foot in the world.

I strongly believe Judas was ready to change. Can you imagine how pride swallowing it must have been for him to walk back into the temple and give the elders their money back? He wanted nothing to do with the ransom he had received to betray Jesus. You can only experience true forgiveness when you give up the worldly passions that cause you to sin. So give them up today.

> **Luke 3:3** – *He went into all the country around the Jordan, preaching a baptism of repentance for the forgiveness of sins* (NIV).

learning from Judas (pt.3)

Matthew 27:3-5 – 3 *When Judas, who had betrayed him, saw that Jesus was condemned, he was seized with remorse and returned the thirty silver coins to the chief priests and the elders.* 4 *"I have sinned," he said, "for I have betrayed innocent blood." "What is that to us?" they replied. "That's your responsibility."* 5 *So Judas threw the money into the temple and left. Then he went away and hanged himself* (NIV).

After betraying Christ, Judas was ready to make things right. He realized what he had done was wrong, he confessed his sin and he made restitution. I believe Judas desired to change. He was ready to receive forgiveness, but we all know the story does not end with him being restored. My question is, "Why?"

The answer is two-fold. The first reason Judas didn't find what he was looking for is found in verse 3: *he was seized with remorse.* In other words, he was taken captive by deep and painful regret for what he had done. He was overwhelmed with guilt. Judas could not escape the fact that he was the mastermind behind the death of the Son of God.

Listen to me. Satan has a counterfeit for every authentic work of God. Guilt is his counterfeit for the conviction of the Holy Spirit. The devil uses guilt to shame a person. He wants to implant the thought into your mind that your sin cannot be pardoned. Even a person, like Judas, who is genuinely sorry for his mistakes, will not allow himself to be forgiven because of guilt.

I want you to understand something today. God does not condemn you for your wrongdoing. He wants you to be aware of your sin and change your lifestyle, but guilt and humiliation are not tactics He uses. Judas was unable to accept forgiveness because he was overcome with shame. My prayer is for you to lay down your guilt today and be washed in the blood of the Lamb.

John 3:17 – *For God did not send His Son into the world to condemn the world, but that the world through Him might be saved* (NKJV).

learning from Judas (pt.4)

> **Matthew 27:3-5** – 3 *When Judas, who had betrayed him, saw that Jesus was condemned, he was seized with remorse and returned the thirty silver coins to the chief priests and the elders.* 4 *"I have sinned," he said, "for I have betrayed innocent blood." "What is that to us?" they replied. "That's your responsibility."* 5 *So Judas threw the money into the temple and left. Then he went away and hanged himself* (NIV).

The second reason Judas did not find the forgiveness he sought is found in **Matthew 27:4**. Judas went to the church in search of help. He laid his heart on the line, and look at their response: "What is that to us? That's your responsibility."

Judas must have been devastated. He was ashamed and desperate. He went to the church looking for answers, but they rejected him. My heart broke as I studied this tragedy. I could not help but think about how many times this same story has played out in churches all across the world.

How quick we are to judge! It's human nature to stereotype people because of their sins, and I'll admit I have done it out of ignorance many times myself. It is not our job to judge the sins of others, and I thank God I was not written off when I was at my worst. We are not to condone sin, but we need to love sinners where they are. They need to be lead to a place of repentance and restoration, not condemned or made to feel unwelcome.

My prayer for you today is that your heart would be softened towards those who don't know Christ. May you recall the time when you were lost in sin and desperate for change. Pray for your tendency to rank the sins of others to no longer be a part of your life. Sin is sin, and it all separates us from God. The earthly consequences of sin vary, but Jesus' blood has cleansed them all.

> **Matthew 7:1-2** – 1 *"Do not judge so that you will not be judged.* 2 *For in the way you judge, you will be judged; and by your standard of measure, it will be measured to you"* (NASB).

learning from Judas (pt.5)

Matthew 27:5 – *So Judas threw the money into the temple and left. Then he went away and hanged himself* (NIV).

Judas was overcome with guilt. He longed for forgiveness, but he was rejected by the church. Frustrated and confused, he threw his ransom at the feet of the chief priests and ran from the temple. But where did he go?

He fled to the same place so many lost and offended people run to: isolation. It's in the place of isolation where Satan takes control of the battle. It was in the place of isolation where Judas went from genuinely seeking deliverance to giving up completely. It's the place where hurt people go to escape, but end up being tormented to the point of breaking. Judas killed himself in the place of isolation.

As you have read the story of Judas, maybe you've realized your current condition is much like his. You have sinned and grieved the heart of God. Perhaps you have been overcome with guilt and searched for answers, only to be rejected by those you trusted. Maybe a pastor or church leader has even brushed you aside. The enemy will do everything he can to try and isolate you in your sin. He will make you feel wretched and unworthy, and he'll even use Christians to assist him.

If you find yourself in Judas' shoes today, this message is for you. Do not lose hope! His grace is sufficient for you! Do not go to the place of isolation and agonize over your faults. Instead turn to Him in your hour of need, and ask Him to surround you with people who are nonjudgmental and who truly love God.

I pray that you find refuge in God Almighty today. May the burden of guilt you carry be lifted off your shoulders now, in Jesus' name. You are set free in Him today, and you are released from the torment of your past sin. Glory to God!

Psalm 55:22 – *Our LORD, we belong to you. We tell you what worries us, and you won't let us fall* (CEV).

abiding by or abiding in?

Jesus said that His true followers will abide in His word. Before going any further, you need to understand there is a distinct difference between abiding *by* His word and abiding *in* it. The dictionary offers a couple different definitions for the word *abide*. The first of which is to put up with or tolerate.

This is the attitude of someone who abides *by* God's word. They view the Bible as a list of rules and regulations. They are annoyed with the idea of someone else governing their lives, even if that someone else is Jesus Christ. Many look at His word with contempt, but they tolerate it because they think abiding by the rules will get them into heaven.

Sometimes they have a great knowledge of the Word, but their relationship with the Lord is surface level at best. These people specialize in finding fault in others. They are generally unfulfilled and void of joy. They are religious.

Abide is also defined as to have one's abode; dwell; reside. Not coincidentally, the word *abide* in **John 8:31** comes from the Greek word *meno* meaning to stay in a given place or dwell. True disciples make God's word their dwelling place, their place of residency. They have a daily relationship with the Word; it's their source of livelihood.

Don't get me wrong. Devoted followers of Christ make it their goal to abide *by* the Word also. God wants you to listen to Him. One of the major differences between the two is the attitude behind the action. Examine yourself today. Are you someone who tolerates God's word, or are you one who celebrates it? If you are begrudgingly "following the rules," repent and ask Him to forgive you. As you'll find out, there are great benefits to abiding *in* His word.

no more violence

Psalm 17:4 – *As for the deeds of men, by the word of Your lips I have kept from the paths of the violent* (NASB).

The first benefit of abiding in God's word is violence will no longer be a part of your life. Violence is intense by nature. When I hear the word *violence*, I initially think of blood and guts, but it's not limited to only physical brutality. The above verse was not written to single out murderers or those who enjoy inflicting physical pain on others.

By definition, violence is any uncontrolled, strong or rough force. It is characterized by cruelty and aggression. Violence manifests in action, speech and attitude. It causes a person to react to adversity with swift and harsh judgment. Anger and hostility rule a violent person's life, but abiding in His word keeps you from violence.

So many people live their lives in a constant state of turmoil because they do not live in the word of God. His word is a part of their lives, but they have not made it their lifeline. The opposite of violence is peace. There is peace for the person who makes the Word their dwelling place.

Perhaps you find yourself consumed by violence today. Maybe your anger gets the best of you, and your immediate response to difficulty is to lose self-control. Your aggression can be replaced with gentleness today. Maybe you have a tendency to speak negatively or harshly to others. Abiding in God's word will change your outlook in every area of life.

I pray that you will be set free today as you make a concerted effort to pattern your life after the word of God. May peace dwell in your home, your relationships and your workplace. May He keep you from the paths of the violent.

Proverbs 15:1 – *A gentle answer turns away wrath, but a harsh word stirs up anger* (NIV).

holiness made possible

Psalm 119:11 – *I have hidden your word in my heart that I might not sin against you* (NIV).

The second benefit of abiding in God's word is walking in holiness is made possible. Whether you agree with me or not, God expects holiness from His people. He spoke to the church in **Leviticus 19:2** when He said, *"Be holy because I, the LORD your God, am holy."*

Think about this. God is holy, and He wants us to be like Him. Our lives are supposed to be a reflection of who He is. Unfortunately, in large part, the church has portrayed a distorted image of Christ to the world. Why? There's not enough of an emphasis placed on living a holy life. Many Christians view holiness as an okay concept, but an unattainable goal. So they do not make it a priority.

Holiness is not a suggestion. God does not give you the option of being holy or not; we are to be holy because He is. This raises the question: How can a fleshly human be like a holy God? I'm glad you asked. Holiness is only possible if the Word is hidden in your heart, and the Word can only live in your heart if you abide in it. You must see yourself as holy by faith.

There is a difference between holiness and legalism. Legalistic Christians resent holiness. Those who value holiness love God's word. They make His word their priority because they desire to be like Him.

Take a minute to examine yourself. Is holiness a focal point of your life, or do you find yourself making excuses for your inconsistencies? Please understand that you will never be perfect because you are not God, but you are to be *perfecting* holiness out of reverence for Him (**2 Corinthians 7:1**). Make His word your dwelling place today, and holiness will become a reality in your life. Thank You, Lord.

Psalm 119:133 – *Direct my footsteps according to your word; let no sin rule over me* (NIV).

restoration

Psalm 119:25 – *My soul cleaves to the dust; revive me according to your word* (NASB).

Have you ever just felt lifeless and hollow? As you are reading this, maybe you find yourself spiritually dead and in need of being revived. Before I give you the key to restoring life to your relationship with the Lord, I want to talk about the root of your condition.

Did you know that the word *cleave* actually means to remain faithful? Given this definition, the above verse can be rewritten as: My soul remains faithful to the dust. It is for this very reason that so many Christians are dried up spiritually. There is no life in dust.

Please understand that the Scripture is not talking about rolling around in the dirt. In fact, God says in **Genesis 3:19**, *"For dust you are and to dust you will return."* If you and I are dust, then this is what **Psalm 119:25** is actually saying: My soul remains faithful to myself. Now we're getting somewhere.

A relationship with God dies because the individual becomes solely dependent upon himself, the dust. Everyone's story is different, but the lesson to be learned is usually the same. Most Christians fall away from God because they stop relying on Him and focus on themselves. It's here where the third benefit of abiding in God's word comes in: Dwelling in the Word revives you.

The root of spiritual death is selfishness, but His words revive. If you find yourself cleaving to the dust today, seize this opportunity to repent from your self-reliance. His word has the power to take someone empty and restore him to right standing with God. Maintaining a healthy and vibrant relationship with God is only possible if you become dependent on the Word. Let go of the dust, and remain faithful to His word.

John 6:63 – *"The Spirit gives life; the flesh counts for nothing. The words I have spoken to you are spirit and they are life"* (NIV).

the sword of the Spirit

The fourth benefit of abiding in God's word is you will have an unstoppable weapon to fight with. Imagine you are recruited and become a part of the United States Armed Forces. You go through rigorous tests challenging both your physical and mental toughness. You complete your training, and you are eventually deployed to fight somewhere overseas.

Upon your arrival, you are immediately called to action. Your training has prepared you for this moment. You board a helicopter and are taken to the battlefield. You jump from the chopper ready to engage the adversary. Explosions and gunfire are heard all around you. Instinctively, you reach for your weapon only to find you don't have one. You have gone to battle without your weapon! Because of your huge blunder, it doesn't take long for you to be overtaken by your enemies.

This tragic tale plays out all too often in the lives of many Christians. They prepare themselves in every area imaginable, but they have no relationship with God's word. They run to the frontlines ready to fight, but are quickly dismantled because they have nothing to fight with. The word of God is absolutely vital in fighting the enemy.

Those who abide in God's word have an invaluable weapon at their disposal. Not only does it provide a means in which to attack, but it also offers protection to those who possess it. The Word strikes fear into the opposition, and it gives confidence to those who make it their priority. The word of God gives us the strategy to overwhelm the enemy successfully.

Maybe you are engaged in a battle that is hopeless in your own strength today. Lay down your game plan and take heed in His word. Do not go to war without your weapon.

no forged weapon

> **Isaiah 54:17** – *"No weapon forged against you will prevail, and you will refute every tongue that accuses you. This is the heritage of the servants of the LORD, and this is their vindication from me," declares the LORD* (NIV).

The word *forge* is defined as to form or make by concentrated effort. This means that Satan makes a concentrated effort and forms specific weapons in which to attack you with. He designs them with your weaknesses in mind.

Your enemy won't normally attack you where the walls are well fortified. He strategically pinpoints your character flaws, and then he attacks with a weapon crafted solely for bringing *you* down. The devil is no respecter or persons; he does not care what your social status or title is. He hates you with a passion, and his purpose is to separate you from God.

It's important for you to understand this because there are many Christians who have an unbalanced view of the devil. Some give Satan way too much credit, but there are others who pretend he doesn't exist. He is very real, and he is a worthy opponent. He is not a dummy, and he has devoted his entire existence to destroying the human race. He has a game plan, and he is a master at executing that plan. He feasts on those who are unprepared, and he has ravaged the lives of countless people.

Even so, you can stand on God's words, "No weapon forged against you will prevail." This does not mean you won't be battered and bruised, tired or afflicted. It means you will not be overcome by the devil's schemes. The word of the Lord will not return to Him empty, but its fulfillment in your life depends on your obedience. You must do your part by abiding in the Word and applying it to your life. As long as you guard yourself, continuously build your spirit and pursue holiness, you cannot be destroyed by the enemy's schemes.

> **Isaiah 59:19** – *When the enemy comes in like a flood, the Spirit of the LORD will lift up a standard against him* (NKJV).

true and false

Isaiah 54:17 – *"No weapon forged against you will prevail, and you will refute every tongue that accuses you. This is the heritage of the servants of the LORD, and this is their vindication from me," declares the LORD* (NIV).

An *accusation* is a charge of wrongdoing, an imputation of guilt or blame. Accusations lead to a judgment, or a verdict. They will either be proved true or false. I tell you this because it's important for you to understand there is a huge difference between being accused and being held accountable.

Accountability is meant to point you to the heart of God. There will be times the person who holds you accountable tells you truth that is not easy to swallow. Our flesh flares up when faced with hard truth, and we will often times try to deflect attention from us by pointing out the flaws in others. This is not what it means to refute every tongue that accuses you. Accountability is godly, healthy and necessary.

This verse is talking solely about those who will try to cast judgment on you because of your transgressions. No person on this earth has the right to judge your sin. The devil is our accuser, and his purpose is to overwhelm us with guilt. God will judge our sin, and no one else can hand out a guilty verdict. That is the promise the Lord makes here.

For the longest time I thought this verse was only referring to *false* accusations made against us. If anyone tries to judge us unjustly, we have the God-given authority to refute them. This is true, but the Lord doesn't say we will only prove false accusers to be in the wrong. He says we will refute *every* accusation. As long as you repent and are covered with the blood of Jesus, your accusers will be proven wrong. No one has the right to shame you or cast judgment on you. God alone is the righteous judge.

Psalm 58:11 – *"Surely the righteous still are rewarded; surely there is a God who judges the earth"* (NIV).

71

our heritage

Isaiah 54:17 – *"No weapon forged against you will prevail, and you will refute every tongue that accuses you. This is the heritage of the servants of the LORD, and this is their vindication from me," declares the LORD* (NIV).

Two promises: No weapon forged against you will prevail, and you will refute every tongue that accuses you. The awesome thing about these promises is they came directly from the mouth of God. They are absolute truth, but not everyone has the right to them. God's promises are for everyone, but they are always conditional. They are the heritage of the servants of the Lord.

You have no legal or spiritual right to any of God's promises unless you are His servant, period. A *heritage* is something that comes or belongs to one by reason of birth; an inheritance. We must be truly devoted to Christ to share in His promises. Man can be fooled, but God knows who His children are. You cannot con Him into sharing His inheritance with you.

A true servant remains faithful even when things go south or don't make sense. If we stick by Him, then we have access to His promises. **Romans 8:17** – *Now if we are children, then we are heirs—heirs of God and co-heirs with Christ, if indeed we share in his sufferings in order that we may also share in his glory* (NIV).

God has a legacy He wants to leave with each of His kids. It is divine and fruitful. It is without lack, and it is constant. It causes us to be more than conquerors, and it grants us access to the very throne room of God. It's a legacy that is to be passed from generation to generation to generation. I challenge you today to serve God passionately and unconditionally. His promises give you the hope you need to persevere against the weapons forged against you and the tongues that accuse you.

Psalm 37:18-19 – *18 The LORD knows the days of the blameless, and their inheritance will be forever. 19 They will not be ashamed in the time of evil, and in the days of famine they will have abundance* (NASB).

vindication

I have never been charged with a crime, so I have not stood before a judge with my life in the hands of a panel of jurors. I can only imagine the emotional torment one must feel in such a position. Whether guilty or not, the nerves of the defendant are no doubt shot as he waits for the verdict to be handed out. Then, after what seems like an eternity, he finally hears the words he's been praying for, "We find the defendant not guilty on all charges."

All of a sudden, the tables are turned. Doubt and disbelief transform into jubilee and ecstasy. The defendant has been found not guilty! Fear of captivity is replaced by a newfound sense of freedom. The plaintiff's accusation has been proven false. Case closed. Life is not over for the accused. The defendant has new life and a fresh start ahead of him.

New life begins at the moment of vindication. It is because of this fact that I believe human beings are so quick to try and defend themselves. When faced with an accusation, it is only natural to feel like a caged animal. Even when charges made are false, the "backed into a corner" feeling is undeniable. Under such circumstances, we instinctively come out swinging to prove our innocence. Why? We fear for our freedom when faced with a charge.

Accusations confine, but you do not have to fight your battles. When you are a servant of the Lord, vindication is His. The blood of Jesus purchased your freedom once and for all. If you are bound by charges, true or false, take your case to the Judge. Repent for your transgressions and stand on His word. All charges made against you have been dropped in Jesus' name!

from victory to defeat

> **Exodus 13:17-18** – 17 *When Pharaoh let the people go, God did not lead them on the road through the Philistine country, though that was shorter. For God said, "If they face war, they might change their minds and return to Egypt." 18 So God led the people around by the desert road toward the Red Sea* (NIV).

There is a recurring theme in the church today that is demonstrated in the story of the Israelites deliverance from Egyptian bondage (If you're not familiar with the story, I recommend you go read **Exodus 13-15**). It is a tale of God's people experiencing tremendous victories, only to return to despair shortly thereafter.

The lives of many Christians today follow the same pattern, but why? It's a matter of trust, or the lack thereof. Over the next several days, we are going to diagnose seven symptoms of someone who has lost trust in God. Using the Israelites' story, we will not only identify possible areas of distrust in your life, but you will be given the remedy for them as well.

After being enslaved by the Egyptians for 430 years, Pharaoh finally granted the Israelites permission to leave. It was an awesome time in Israel's history! They were set free from captivity and had the promise of a new land full of God's presence and blessing. Life was good, and their faith level was at an all-time high. However, their enthusiasm was short-lived.

God led the Israelites to the bank of the Red Sea, and Pharaoh's heart was hardened so that he pursued them from behind. With mountains on each side, Israel was trapped. It's at this point that we can identify the first symptom: Those who have lost trust in God cannot understand how a loving God could lead them into an impossible situation.

Perhaps this is your mindset today. Maybe you've recently experienced a breakthrough in your life, only to have it followed by great adversity. You can't understand how God could give you great victory and then lead you to a place of defeat. Trust in Him! You have not met your demise; allow Him to shape your character.

crippled

Exodus 14:10 – *As Pharaoh approached, the Israelites looked up, and there were the Egyptians, marching after them. They were terrified and cried out to the LORD* (NIV).

The second symptom of those who have lost trust in God is they are crippled by fear. After being led into an impossible situation, the Bible says the Israelites were terrified. They were scared to death and trapped, so they cried out to the Lord in desperation.

When you begin to lose trust in God, many times peace is replaced by fear. Peace and fear cannot coexist. Maybe you used to be an optimist, but now you look at the glass as half empty. It is impossible to keep perspective when fear grips your life. Fear will cause you to dwell on worst-case scenarios and cry out to God frantically, just as Israel did.

I imagine their cry sounded something like, "God, do You see us down here? What are You doing? We thought You were on our side. How could You do this to us?!" Perhaps you find yourself uttering these same words when faced with adversity. If so, you need to take your emotions captive.

2 Timothy 1:7 declares, *"For God has not given us a spirit of fear, but of power and of love and of a sound mind"* (NKJV). You need to understand that God will often times lead you into a trial, but He does not give you fear. Fear is a self-inflicted emotion that only you can control. Emotions are selfish. You decide how you are going to respond when adversity strikes.

Speak the Word over yourself and declare His promises when you face troubles. If you do so, your faith level will increase, and you can walk through your situation in peace rather than in fear. Glory to God! He has not given you a spirit of fear!

Psalm 46:10 – *"Be still, and know that I am God"* (NIV).

I can't see!

Exodus 14:11a – *They said to Moses, "Was it because there were no graves in Egypt that you brought us to the desert to die"* (NIV)?

The third symptom of people who have lost trust in God is they can't see a way out. The Israelites were gripped so tightly by fear that they had already sentenced themselves to death. They saw no way out of the mess they were in. In their eyes, God had led them to the bank of the Red Sea to die.

Maybe your current circumstance has reached a point of hopelessness. Maybe you have zeroed out your bank account, and your relationships are falling apart. You've passed the point of no return, and you have sentenced your situation to death. Many Christians have put their seemingly hopeless circumstances in a casket and are making funeral arrangements, but why? How is it that the most devout believers can come to a place where they can't see a way out? They take their eyes off of the promise.

The Israelites fixed their eyes on what was temporary; they totally lost sight of the new life God had promised them. When you take your eyes off of Jesus, you become blinded by your circumstance. Your difficulty is ever before you, and you eventually won't be able to see a way out. Focusing on the temporary will only breed despair and heartache.

Listen to the words of Paul in **2 Corinthians 4:16-18** – 16 *Therefore we do not lose heart. Though outwardly we are wasting away, yet inwardly we are being renewed day by day. 17 For our light and momentary troubles are achieving for us an eternal glory that far outweighs them all. 18 So we fix our eyes not on what is seen, but on what is unseen. For what is seen is temporary, but what is unseen is eternal* (NIV).

These verses offer two keys to getting your eyes off of your situation and raising your level of trust in Him. First, you need to view your troubles as light and momentary. Second, you must get your priorities straight. I challenge you to quit majoring on what is temporary, and fix your eyes on the eternal. Don't totally disregard your circumstances, but make God your priority.

what have *you* done?

Exodus 14:11b – *"What have you done to us by bringing us out of Egypt?"* (NIV)

The Israelites turned on Moses, "What have *you* done?" they accused. They challenged Moses' authority and blamed him for their predicament. The fourth symptom of people who have lost trust in God is they lose trust in God's delegated authority.

One of the tragic things about losing trust in God is it causes you to become leery of everyone who is in authority. When you doubt, you question God and those who represent Him. Many times we are quick to point the finger at others when things don't go as we'd like them to. More times than not we wind up blaming those God has established to lead us.

Please understand the authorities that have been established by God will never be perfect, but it is not your place to expose their shortcomings when they falter. Just because you believe someone in authority has wronged you, just as the Israelites did with Moses, does not give you the right to slander him.

I want to ask you a question. What man or woman of God are you forbidding to speak into your life because you've lost trust in Him? Godly men and women are strategically placed in your life to encourage and hold you accountable. Losing trust in God causes you to push these people away and hold them at an arm's distance. The enemy wants to use the trials of your life to cause you to isolate yourself from those God can use to help you.

I encourage you today to let your pastor, youth pastor, Sunday school teacher, boss or parent off the hook. If you have truly been led to ruin by an authority figure in your life, seek godly counsel, approach the issue in a biblical manner and keep your heart pure. The person you are pushing away may be the very instrument God desires to use to set you free.

Romans 13:2 – *Consequently, he who rebels against the authority is rebelling against what God has instituted, and those who do so will bring judgment on themselves* (NIV).

familiarity

Basically, Israel said to Moses, "We would rather go back to being slaves than trust you and your God." Serving God had proven to be too difficult, so they wanted to return to familiarity. The fifth symptom of people who have lost trust in God is they cling to what is familiar.

Bondage is what Israel had grown accustomed to. The work was hard under Pharaoh, but their basic needs of survival were met. They had a place to sleep, food to eat and their lives were not on the line. Though they were slaves and often mistreated, they were safe because they were valuable workers. With the Red Sea before them, Pharaoh's army behind them and mountains on either side, slavery was looked pretty good.

Maybe you find yourself in this same position today. Trusting God has not been easy for you and returning to your old lifestyle seems rather appealing. A relationship with God is not always comfortable. There can be peace in every situation, but your personal comfort is not guaranteed anywhere in Scripture.

Trusting God *now* is the key to overcoming your past. If you are ever going to move on from what's familiar, you must step out of your comfort zone. When you make a decision to trust God, rest assured that adversity will come. And when it does, you are going to want to run back to familiarity.

Like the Israelites, some people will forfeit the will of God and cling to something that's undesirable but familiar. This kind of mindset forms from an unhealthy relationship with the past. Many people walk hand-in-hand with dysfunctional relationships, financial problems and so on because it's easier than trusting God for victory. Cut ties with your past and hold fast to God today. Stick it out, and endure the process. It will lead you to victory!

the grass is greener

Exodus 14:12b – *"It would have been better for us to serve the Egyptians than to die in the desert!"* (NIV)

We have probably all said something like this at one time or another. My family has walked through some trying seasons, and I'd be lying if I told you I haven't thought of "amending" God's will for my life. There have been times when veering from the path God has marked for us looks more appealing than staying on it. It's in those difficult seasons that Satan will do everything he can to make a worldly lifestyle look more attractive than a godly one.

The sixth symptom of those who have lost trust in God is they think the grass is greener on the other side. The Israelites were so low that they actually wanted to serve their enemies. Serving the Egyptians seemed far easier than serving God.

Perhaps you find yourself in this same struggle. I've heard some Christians say such things as, "I'm tired of seeing the heathen blessed while I struggle," or "Why should I trust God when it only leads to hardship?" Maybe you have recently said something along these lines, and you think the grass looks greener on the other side.

In times of crisis, the enemy works overtime propagating himself and his kingdom. The devil makes a good living off of disgruntled Christians. He's a master manipulator and is skillful at public relations. He knows when you're at a low point, and that's when he swoops in and waves the benefits of worldliness in front of you. You must be on your guard, and do not be ignorant of his devices.

I want to encourage you today to remain faithful to what God has called you to do. Serving your enemy may offer temporary benefits and comfort, but the eternal security that comes from trusting God is priceless.

Psalm 20:7 – *Some trust in chariots and some in horses, but we trust in the name of the LORD our God* (NIV).

right song on the wrong side

> **Exodus 15:1-2** – 1 *"I will sing to the LORD, for he is highly exalted. The horse and its rider he has hurled into the sea. 2 The LORD is my strength and my song; he has become my salvation. He is my God, and I will praise him, my father's God, and I will exalt him"* (NIV).

After exemplifying virtually no trust in God whatsoever, what happened to the Israelites? They were obliterated by the Egyptians, right? Absolutely not. In fact, quite the opposite occurred; God performed one of His greatest miracles! He caused the Red Sea to part, and Israel crossed on dry land. Once the Israelites were safely across, the Lord buried Pharaoh's army in the sea. Because of His great mercy God spared Israel that day, and they proceeded to sing the praises recorded in Exodus 15.

The Israelites danced and worshiped before the Lord because He delivered them from Egypt. But as they rejoiced, I believe the heart of God was broken. The seventh symptom of people who have lost trust in God is they sing the right song on the wrong side (David Wilkerson has a great sermon on this).

Israel did not praise God until after they had crossed to the other side of the Red Sea. God allowed their safety to give them another chance to trust Him. Their deliverance cost them absolutely nothing, and their worship was a slap in His face.

The song Israel sang was not the problem; it's where they sang it. God does not want us to praise Him only when we get what we want or what we think we deserve. He wants us to sing in the midst of our trials and rejoice in our sufferings. Trust develops in the midst of the storm, not when it is sunny.

I challenge you to sing to your circumstance today. Don't wait to praise God until after the storm passes because another one is coming right behind it. If you learn to trust Him, I guarantee He will see you through. Sing the *right* song on the *right* side.

> **Psalm 18:3** – *I call to the LORD, who is worthy of praise, and I am saved from my enemies* (NIV).

sing to your chains

Maybe you think it's crazy to sing to your circumstance. One day Paul and Silas were minding their own business on the way to the place of prayer, and they were met on the road by a servant girl who was possessed by an evil spirit. She followed them around for days causing disturbances until Paul finally had enough. He commanded the spirit to leave her, and it did.

The girl's masters were enraged, and they took Paul and Silas before the magistrates and pleaded their case. Paul and Silas were severely beaten, bound and eventually thrown into prison. What was their crime? Doing the work of the Lord. Now in prison, these men of God were faced with the same dilemma you may be facing today. They had a choice to make. They had to decide whether or not they would trust God, even though they were imprisoned because of Him. I ask you: Will you still trust Him when His perfect will leads you to persecution?

The above verses tell us that Paul and Silas began to sing while shackled in their cell. As they glorified God in the midst of their trial, I can see the hand of the Lord reaching down from heaven and shaking the foundations of that prison. They did not wait for God to deliver them before they praised Him. In fact, they sang to God without knowing whether He'd rescue them or not. Deliverance was not the motive behind their praise. Paul and Silas were set free because they trusted God wholeheartedly despite of their unfavorable circumstance.

I encourage you to sing to your circumstance today! Dare to trust God no matter what, and He will never let you down.

Psalm 9:2 – *I will be glad and rejoice in you; I will sing praise to your name, O Most High* (NIV).

they're listening

Acts 16:25 – *About midnight Paul and Silas were praying and singing hymns to God, and the other prisoners were listening to them* (NIV).

Paul and Silas were not alone in prison. There were others being held captive that day. The Bible says the other prisoners listened as these two Christian men glorified their God in chains. What a testimony!

Listen to me. Our world is in the midst of a global crisis like never before. People are bound by fear because of disease, natural disasters and economic collapse. Those without God are searching desperately for relief of some kind, and many are watching to see how the church responds.

Just as Paul and Silas' fellow inmates watched to see how they'd respond to being imprisoned, the world is watching to see how you react to crisis. The unsaved of this generation don't want to see another miracle. Modern medicine and science produce miracles everyday. They do not want to hear Christians tell them everything will be alright if you ask Jesus into your heart. They need to see God's people walk peacefully through the valley of the shadow of death. The unsaved do not benefit when Christians obliviously float through life's trials pretending they don't exist. They need to see God-fearing saints who praise and trust God as they boldly walk through adversity.

How do *you* respond to trials? What do the lost of this world see as they watch you face difficulty? What do they hear coming from your mouth as they listen? Somebody is watching you, listening to you. Your response to crisis may be the testimony that causes someone to turn to Christ or reject Him. Do you praise or curse Him when the going gets tough? Think about it today. There's more than just your soul on the line.

Psalm 35:28 – *I'll tell the world how great and good you are, I'll shout Hallelujah all day, everyday* (MSG).

it's about souls

Acts 16:29-30 – 29 *The jailer called for lights, rushed in and fell trembling before Paul and Silas.* 30 *He then brought them out and asked, "Sirs, what must I do to be saved?"* (NIV)

Singing the right song on the right side provoked the jailer in this story to give his life to Jesus. This man was accountable for the prisoners, and when they were set free by the power of God, he was devastated. **Acts 16:27** – *The jailer woke up, and when he saw the prison doors open, he drew his sword and was about to kill himself because he thought the prisoners had escaped* (NIV). He was distraught and ready to end his life because he knew he'd be held responsible for their escape, but God stepped in.

The jailer fell before Paul and Silas and said, "What must I do to be saved?" What a turn of events. The jailer was prepared to take his own life, but because Paul and Silas trusted God he was saved instead. In fact, the jailer and his entire family received salvation!

Who knows how the story would have ended if Paul and Silas had not been obedient and sang praises to God during their trial? I'd venture to say that the outcome would have been much different. Paul and Silas might have very well rotted in prison, and the jailer and his family may not have ever come to know Christ.

Maybe you've struggled recently as you've read through the accounts of the Israelites and Paul and Silas. Perhaps you've questioned, "How do I praise God and trust Him in the midst of my greatest time of need? What's the benefit in doing so? There's no reason for me to sing to God!" If you've found yourself saying such things, you need to ask yourself the following question. Is my personal comfort more valuable than another person's soul?

If you have lost trust in God, ask the Holy Spirit to show you the root of your distrust. Once He does so, repent and fall back into the arms of Jesus. Learn to trust Him unwaveringly.

Psalm 9:10 – *Those who know your name trust in you, for you, O LORD, do not abandon those who search for you* (NLT).

disappointment in relationships

Proverbs 13:12 – *Hope deferred makes the heart sick, but a longing fulfilled is a tree of life* (NIV).

This message has been burning in my heart, and if you find yourself lacking intimacy with God, this verse may be the key to your breakthrough. Hope deferred makes the heart sick. What a sad truth. To better understand the meaning of this statement, let's look at another version of this verse: *Unrelenting disappointment leaves you heartsick* (MSG). Disappointment comes in a variety of sorts, but the person who is continually disappointed winds up brokenhearted.

The first area I want to deal with is disappointment in relationships. There are countless people who have experienced broken relationship after broken relationship. As a result, they've closed themselves off to the idea of intimacy with anyone. They will allow a person to come "only so close" before they withdraw.

Many people have been cheated on, stabbed in the back or abused by those they have been in relationship with. Children are mistreated by their parents, spouses are unfaithful, best friends gossip and slander one another, pastors betray their flocks and the list goes on. When not dealt with, these types of experiences will be carried over into every new relationship.

Those who have deferred hope in relationships eventually wind up harboring unforgiveness toward those who have wronged them. They become bitterly offended and filter *all* of their relationships through that offense. This truth tragically includes their relationship with God.

Perhaps you find yourself separated from God today. Could it be that you have unforgiveness toward someone? Unforgiveness puts a wedge between you and God. You may be justified in your offense, but you will not experience intimacy in any relationship until you deal with unforgiveness.

Matthew 6:15 – *"But if you do not forgive men their sins, your Father will not forgive your sins"* (NIV).

disappointment in yourself

The second area I want to deal with is disappointment in yourself. People become disappointed with themselves for many different reasons. Failures in school, in the workplace or in relationships cause many to lose hope. The guilt and shame they carry because of such failure leaves them imprisoned unable to forgive themselves.

Forgiving yourself is often times more difficult than forgiving someone else. Intimacy with God is largely dependent on your ability to forgive yourself. You have to allow the blood of Jesus to wash away your shortcomings. **Micah 7:19** – *You will again have compassion on us; you will tread our sins underfoot and hurl all our iniquities into the depths of the sea* (NIV). God has compassion on you and He wants to throw your sins away, but you have to let go of them first.

Maybe you have been torturing yourself because of past failures. It's time to let yourself off the hook. Do not just blow off your shortcomings, though. Learn from them. When you fall short, don't beat yourself up. Become a better person. I pray that you will believe in and trust yourself again. To *defer* means to put off or postpone. Perhaps you have put your personal dreams and expectations on hold. If so, I encourage you to pray the following prayer over yourself:

"Lord Jesus, You are awesome. I surrender my entire self to You. I give You all of my failures and shortcomings. Wash me in Your precious blood. I want to be completely free. Take away my guilt and shame; make me whole again. Restore my hope, and help me to trust myself once more. The joy of the Lord is my strength, and I will walk in unspeakable joy. Thank You, Lord, for giving me the ability to dream again. I love You. Amen."

disappointment in God

> **Proverbs 13:12** – *Hope deferred makes the heart sick, but a longing fulfilled is a tree of life* (NIV).

The third area I want to deal with is disappointment in God. This may be the most difficult relationship for hope to be restored to. God is always ready to take you back, but human beings are notoriously stubborn creatures. Many people lost hope in God years ago and have held decade-long grudges against Him ever since. They no longer have any godly expectations, and they blame Him for whatever reason.

If you are one of those people, listen to me carefully: It's not God's fault, so get over it. Please do not misunderstand me. I'm not trying to downplay the personal pain and rejection you might be feeling. I understand that feelings are very real, but *you* manufacture and manage your feelings, not God. God does not change, and His word is eternal. He is not capable of lying, and He has never let anyone down, ever.

Many times people lose hope in God because of unrealistic expectations. Others misinterpret unanswered prayers as rejection. As the old Garth Brooks song says, "Some of God's greatest gifts are unanswered prayers." Looking back over my life, I am very thankful now that I did not get everything I prayed for.

God has a perfect plan for our lives, and His ways are sovereign. Do not lose hope when God doesn't work things out the way you would like Him to, or when it seems like your prayers are falling on deaf ears. He is always working on your behalf, and He hears everything you say.

Hebrews 11:1 – *Now faith is being sure of what we hope for and certain of what we do not see* (NIV). What do you hope for? Do not suspend your dreams because you are mad at God for something He didn't do. Give Him your grudge; you really don't want it anyway.

> **I Peter 5:7** – *Give all your worries and cares to God, for he cares about you* (NLT).

germ-infested restrooms

Proverbs 13:12 – *Hope deferred maketh the heart sick: but when the desire cometh, it is a tree of life* (KJV).

The Bible says that unrelenting disappointment makes the heart sick. Those who have lost hope in relationships are no different. They literally become heartsick. That's why it is so difficult for relationships to be restored. Allow me to explain.

Have you ever stopped at a rest area off the side of the highway? Odds are you have, but if not, you have surely gone into some skeptical truck stops or gas stations in your lifetime. I've traveled thousands of miles on interstates across the country, and I've found myself in some nasty, germ-infested restrooms. You know what I'm talking about: the ones where you have to hold your breath and tiptoe around not to step in something.

In those situations I do my best not to touch anything, and I've even used paper towels to turn knobs and open doors. Sometimes I won't wash my hands because I know they will only be dirtier after doing so. There are others who go to even greater extremes to avoid germs. Why do we do this? We don't want to get sick. Most people are not voluntarily going to make themselves ill, so they are very careful to stay away from germs.

This is exactly why broken relationships stay broken. Disappointment after disappointment causes people to become heartsick. They do not want to get sick again, so they avoid intimacy in relationships like they would avoid a nasty restroom.

Relationships are a gift from God, but He never intended for them to be a source of disappointment. Healthy relationships bring life and encouragement. They are meant for intimacy and accountability. Don't allow rejection or offense to rob you of this beautiful gift from God. If you do, you will remain heartsick, and you will never know what intimacy with God is like.

Ephesians 3:19 – *And to know the love of Christ, which passeth knowledge, that ye might be filled with all the fullness of God* (KJV).

trees of life

We have learned that chronic disappointment makes the heart sick, but all it takes is one fulfilled desire to restore hope. The Bible teaches that a desire fulfilled is a tree of life. What an awesome truth! No matter how many failures you have faced, it is amazing how refreshing one victory can be.

Think of it this way. Let's say you have been longing for a certain family member to come to know God. After months or even years of prayer, he finally receives salvation. You get word of your loved one's conversion, and joy floods your heart. In that moment a tree of life is planted.

From then on, you are able to draw faith and encouragement from that tree. When faced with a relationship or situation that threatens to steal your hope, you are able to look at that tree of life and know God can meet your need because He did it before. The tree of life serves as a testimony of God's goodness and faithfulness. Its fruit is enough to get you through to the next victory.

Even greater is the fact a new tree is planted every time a desire is fulfilled, but hope deferred cuts these life-giving trees down. I want to encourage you today to not lose hope. No matter how dismal the circumstances are surrounding your life and relationships, dare to trust God and fight the good fight of faith. Draw strength from the good works God has done previously in your life. Those testimonies are there to help propel you to the next victory!

great, not gray

> **Hebrews 12:1** – *Therefore, since we are surrounded by such a great cloud of witnesses, let us throw off everything that hinders and the sin that so easily entangles, and let us run with perseverance the race marked out for us* (NIV).

I believe that if you can grasp the meaning of this verse, it will be an encouragement to you as you walk through life. I pray for you to be revived as you are enlightened by its message. God's word brings life and liberty. May you be strengthened today, in the name of Jesus!

Many times Christians, and people in general, walk through life as if a gray cloud is looming overhead. The unsaved usually don't know any better, but believers have no excuse for having such an attitude. The writer of Hebrews states that we are surrounded by a *great* cloud, not a *gray* cloud. A great cloud surrounds you whether you like it or not, but you decide if you are going to acknowledge its existence.

The Bible calls this cloud a great cloud of witnesses. Who are these witnesses that make up this cloud? Read Hebrews 11. The great cloud that surrounds you is made up of heroes of the faith. The testimonies of Abel, Noah, Abraham, Isaac, Jacob, Rahab, Joseph and others have been recorded for you to draw encouragement from.

If you find yourself struggling today, go back through your Bible and read the accounts of those listed in Hebrews 11. Learn from their mistakes, and be blessed by their stories. All of them went through trials, but they persevered to the end. They made no excuses, and they fulfilled the destiny God had for each of them. When things are tough, you will be tempted to abandon the path God has marked for you. But instead of forfeiting your destiny, draw strength from the great cloud of witnesses.

> **Philippians 3:14** – *I press on toward the goal to win the prize for which God has called me heavenward in Christ Jesus* (NIV).

throw off everything

The world is a tough place to live in, so why do we insist on making it even harder on ourselves? Many Christians make matters more difficult because they carry around excess baggage with them. The journey is hard enough to make with no luggage, but it is near impossible with all the checked bags and carry-ons we try to take with us.

Hebrews 12:1 instructs us to throw off everything that hinders and the sin that so easily entangles. Things that hinder and sin that entangles are two separate "bags" that we are going to deal with. Let's look first at the things that hinder. Many of the bags we carry are not sin, but they do hinder us just the same.

More times than not these bags are full of garbage from your past. I am not talking about the sins of your past; I am not addressing sin yet. I'm talking about past hurt or guilt that you carry around with you. Maybe you experienced some form of physical, emotional, verbal or sexual abuse, and you still carry the pain from that trauma. Pain and guilt are not things God intends for you to live with the rest of your life.

There are also certain character flaws that become hindrances and knock people off track. While disorganization, poor time management and forgetfulness (there are other things as well) are not necessarily sins, they hinder many Christians as they pursue the will of God for their lives. You don't have to accept the inconsistencies in your character. Reprioritize and make it a point to strengthen your weaknesses. Throw off everything that hinders!

throw off the sin

Hebrews 12:1 – *Therefore, since we have this great cloud of witnesses, let us throw off everything that hinders and the sin that so easily entangles, and let us run with perseverance the race marked out for us* (NIV).

After throwing off everything that hinders, it's now time to get rid of the sin. The phrase *easily entangles* jumps out at me when I read this verse. It does not take very much sin at all to get us all twisted and tangled up. This makes it all the more important for us to deal with sin immediately.

Sin has no spiritual ranking. The same fate awaits both the murderer and the little white liar. Earthly consequences for sin vary, but the heavenly consequences are the same. No matter what form it comes in, sin that is not dealt with will separate us from God forever.

Many Christians will occasionally allow certain "small" sins to slide. They sweep them under the rug. When Heidi and I first got married, I was not very hip on cleaning. Once in a while she would ask me to help her around the house, and I'd usually be over the floors. I wanted to be done as quickly as possible, so I would sweep whatever was on the floor under a nearby rug. My method of cleaning was "out of sight, out of mind." As long as no one could see the dirt, it was as if it wasn't there. I was a genius. The only problem was that the dirt *was* still there!

It didn't take long for Heidi to figure out what I was doing. The apartment looked clean, but it was still dirty. And because I did not sweep properly the first time, I created more work for myself. The same is true when it comes to our sin. Do not allow your transgressions to pile up under some spiritual rug. You know they are there, God knows they are there, and you will eventually be found out. If you desire holiness, you will not want any sin in your life for even a moment. Shake out your rugs today!

1 John 1:9 – *If we confess our sins, he is faithful and just and will forgive us our sins and purify us from all unrighteousness* (NIV).

run, run, run

> **Hebrews 12:1** – *Therefore, since we have this great cloud of witnesses, let us throw off everything that hinders and the sin that so easily entangles, and let us run with perseverance the race marked out for us* (NIV).

Every human being is in a race. It is not a competition against one another; it's the race of life. Your race will take you down different paths and through different trials than mine, but our final destinations are meant to be the same. God's desire and perfect plan is for all of mankind to one day reach the finish line and fall into the arms of Jesus. Unfortunately, many people have fallen just short of the finish line, or they have chosen to run away from God completely.

I don't know what stage of the race you are in today, but I want to encourage you with two things. Number one, you are to *run* the race. I used to absolutely hate running. I knew it was hard, and I had no desire to start doing it. Many Christians have been saved for years, but they have never left the starting gate. They are afraid to start the race because they know it will be difficult. It's much more comfortable to remain a baby Christian because you get free milk and diaper changes. If this is you, get a move on!

Number two, you are to run the race with *perseverance*. When I finally decided to start running, I wasn't good at it at all. Most of the time I would start out in a full sprint and then be exhausted moments later. I would have to stop to catch my breath, and I sometimes injured myself. Many Christians do this too. They get fired up for God and take off running. They don't prioritize or set boundaries. They don't slow down long enough to receive practical teaching. There is no balance to their lives, and they wind up burned out.

Once I learned how to pace myself, I was able to build up my endurance and run with perseverance. Pace yourself with prayer, and read God's word on a daily basis. Do *only* what God has called you to do, and you won't burn out. You will not only run the race, but you will do so with perseverance. Glory to God!

the race is marked

One of the major reasons why people have such a hard time running the race is they are not running the race that has been marked out for them. God has a specific plan that He's designed for each person to follow. I am going to discuss two reasons why I believe people run the wrong race, and you can decide whether or not you fit into one of the categories.

First of all, people run the wrong race because they are confused. *Confusion* is defined as disorder; lack of clearness or distinction. A person is confused when he or she cannot clearly define what is right and what is wrong. Confusion has no place in the life of a believer. The word of God clearly outlines right and wrong. If a Christian is confused, it is because his or her life is out of order. Maybe today you are not sure whether you are running the right race or not. Make God your priority again, and He will show you where to run. God is not the author of confusion.

Secondly, people run the wrong race because they are disobedient. The fact of the matter is many Christians are not running the race marked out for them because they would rather run somebody else's race. So that's what they do. Their race is either too difficult or the other person's seems more beneficial. Knowing what is right, but not doing it, is disobedience.

My wife recently ran a half-marathon. There were markers posted along the way to let the runners know how far they had run and to assure them they were on the right path. God gives us peace, as a marker in the spirit, to assure us that we are on the right path. If you are not at peace today, backtrack to where you were the last time you felt His peace and go from there.

disciplined for holiness

Hebrews 12:10-11 – 10 *Our fathers disciplined us for a little while as they thought best; but God disciplines us for our good, that we may share in his holiness.* 11 *No discipline seems pleasant at the time, but painful. Later on, however, it produces a harvest of righteousness and peace for those who have been trained by it* (NIV).

When I was a kid, there wasn't anything I dreaded more than being disciplined by my dad. Don't get me wrong, my dad is not a scary person by any means, and it was not the punishment I was afraid of. I hated facing my dad when I had done something wrong because I knew I had let him down.

Whether it was getting bad grades or lying, and I was a pro at both, he would discipline me to make sure I would not do what it was I had done ever again. I didn't enjoy the punishment at the time, but I realized as I grew older that my dad was just trying to keep me on the right path. I never liked giving him the keys to my car or going without television for days on end, but I respected his discipline and attempted to change because I trusted him and wanted to be like him.

God disciplines us in much the same way. When we venture out from His perfect will, He gently corrects us through His word and sometimes through others. Many times His chastening is extremely uncomfortable, but He always has our best interest at heart. God's desire is for us to share in His holiness because He loves us beyond measure. He enables us to be holy when we walk according to His purposes.

As I mentioned, I tried to change my actions and behavior when disciplined because I trusted my dad and loved him so much. I wanted to be like him, so I was willing to listen. For God's discipline to be effective in your life, you have to trust and love Him enough to want to change. It will sometimes be difficult to endure, but the promised harvest of peace is a nice perk.

John 14:27 – *"Peace I leave with you; my peace I give you"* (NIV).

make every effort

Hebrews 12:14 – *Make every effort to live in peace with all men and to be holy; without holiness no one will see the Lord* (NIV).

Is your life in a state of turmoil today as you read this? Are your relationships falling apart right before your eyes? If you answered "yes" to either of these questions, peace probably seems like a lost cause. I want to encourage you to pay careful attention because this is a word from the Lord for you.

The Bible commands us in **Hebrews 12:14** to make every effort to live in peace with all men. There are three things you need to understand from this statement. First of all, the word *effort* is defined as an earnest or strenuous attempt. Nobody can put forth an effort for you in anything. You have to make an attempt at peace. Most people lack peace in their lives because they lack the discipline necessary to possess it.

Secondly, we are told to make *every* effort to live in peace. Many people will say, "But I have tried to live at peace. I made an effort, and it just didn't happen for me." They give up and grow accustomed to the chaos surrounding their lives. If your life is not filled with peace in every area, then you must be willing to endure and exhaust every option in order to obtain it. If you are not experiencing the peace of God, then there's something you have not tried yet. Ask the Holy Spirit what to do next.

Lastly, God's will is for us to be at peace with *all* men. This doesn't necessarily mean that you will befriend everyone, but all of your relationships can be void of unforgiveness, bitterness, envy, hatred, offense, etc. You're even to live at peace with your enemies (**Matthew 5:43-45**).

I challenge you to examine yourself today. Are there any areas of your life, including your relationships, that are in a state of unrest? If so, turn to God's word, and ask Him to direct you to the peace you long for.

Philippians 4:7 – *Then you will experience God's peace, which exceeds anything we can understand. His peace will guard your hearts and minds as you live in Christ Jesus* (NLT).

95

make every effort *again*

Hebrews 12:14 – *Make every effort to live in peace with all men and to be holy; without holiness no one will see the Lord* (NIV).

The word *holiness* in this verse comes from the Greek word meaning "separation unto God". Think about this for a minute. We are encouraged to make every effort to live our lives separated unto God. We have to purpose in our hearts to be holy, and then we have to be willing to do whatever it takes to walk in holiness on a daily basis.

Walking in holiness is a process. It's having the attitude of Christ Jesus in **Matthew 26:39** when He said, *"Yet I want your will to be done, not mine"* (NLT). For His will to be done in your life, your will has to die. You must crucify the sinful nature (**Galatians 5:24**). Paul said in **1 Corinthians 15:31**, "I die every day." Holiness is a daily death to your flesh. Separation unto God is not possible in your own strength. You have to make room for the Holy Spirit to work out *His* holiness in your life. The Lord tells us in **Exodus 31:13** that He is the one who makes us holy.

God's desire is for us to be holy as He is holy. He has no character defects or hidden sin. God already is perfectly holy. **2 Corinthians 7:1** challenges us to *purify ourselves from everything that contaminates body and spirit, perfecting holiness out of reverence for God.* The key word in this verse is *perfecting.* Once again, holiness is a day-by-day process we are to be perfecting.

I want to encourage you to ask the Holy Spirit right now to examine your heart, even the hidden places you may be unaware of. Ask Him to reveal those things that are unpleasing to Him. Maybe you have some shameful habits you've kept in secret. Lay them at the feet of Jesus. Perhaps your attitude needs adjusting or the motives of your heart are impure. Repent right now. Now allow Him to purify you completely.

Isaiah 35:8 – *And a highway will be there; it will be called the Way of Holiness. The unclean will not journey on it; it will be for those who walk in that Way; wicked fools will not go about on it* (NIV).

blind to who God is

Hebrews 12:14 – *Make every effort to live in peace with all men and to be holy; without holiness no one will see the Lord* (NIV).

I love my wife Heidi more than anyone on the planet. Everyday is a new day of discovery in our relationship. I enjoy learning new things about her and finding out what makes her, her. As I thought about this verse, I asked myself what it would be like if someone came up to me and said, "Today is the last day you will ever learn anything new about your wife. From this moment on, what you know now is all you will ever know."

I would be devastated. I would still be in a relationship with her, but it would be one that could only go so far. Eventually, our relationship would become stagnant as intimacy fades. One of the reasons relationships crumble is because the people involved stop making new discoveries about each other.

The same is true in your relationship with God. The Bible says that without holiness no one will see the Lord. I struggled for the longest time with the meaning behind this statement, and this is what the Lord showed me. The person of Jesus Christ is far too awesome for any human to ever know everything there is to know about Him. Lifetimes have come and gone, and we are yet to even begin to scratch the surface of who God is.

The intimate details of His character are reserved for those who walk in righteousness. They make a new discovery about their Maker on a daily basis. But once someone veers from the path of holiness, he can no longer see the Lord. His walk with God becomes stagnant, and he ceases to learn anything new about Him. This person will only know what he knew about God before; no new discoveries will be made. What a pitiful relationship to be involved in.

If you desire to know God more intimately and you want Him to show Himself to you in new ways, make holiness your aim.

Matthew 5:8 – *"Blessed are the pure in heart, for they shall see God"* (NASB).

childhood to adulthood

Heidi and I have two little boys. When they were newborns, they could not do anything for themselves. We fed them, burped them, changed them and cleaned up after them. As they have grown older, they've instinctively started to do certain things on their own. Other things we have taught them to do.

It's natural for children to become more independent as they grow older. Our boys are both in school now. They are by no means self-sufficient, but they can do a lot of things without our help. They eat, use the restroom and wipe (sometimes), brush their teeth and get dressed on their own. They still rely on Heidi and me for a lot, but not near as much as they did when they were babies.

Childhood is preparation for adulthood. Good parents want to see their kids become successful, functioning adults, so they encourage and train them while they are young to become more independent. Then one day the child grows up, gets a job, moves out and hopefully fulfills his or her purpose in life.

On the flipside, however, there are some children who never grow up. It is a lot easier to depend on others to meet their needs, so they purpose to remain a children forever. It is unnatural for an adult to behave and reason like a child. Unfortunately, it is commonplace in the world, as well as in the church.

There are many adult Christians today who still have not moved on to maturity. I am not talking about people who first get saved later in life. I'm talking about people who have been in the church for years and still behave like children, or even babies. There are different levels of spiritual maturity, and we all have areas in our character that need work. I encourage you to examine yourself as we move forward together. Let's go on to maturity!

whatever is true

I believe one of the main reasons why Christians do not mature in their faith is they haven't stopped thinking like children yet. Think about it. Your mindset is what causes you to reason, relate and react the way that you do. Your emotions and problem-solving ability are all linked to the way you think. If a person has the mind of a child, he or she is going to act like one. In order to go on to maturity, we have to start thinking maturely.

1 Corinthians 14:20 – *Brothers, stop thinking like children. In regard to evil be infants, but in your thinking be adults* (NIV). What do adult, or mature, Christians think about? **Philippians 4:8** gives us a breakdown.

Paul first tells us to think about whatever is true. The word *true* in this verse comes from the Greek word meaning true in conduct; sincere and upright. The truth also conforms to reality. It is genuine and not deceitful or confusing. Someone who only thinks about what is true does not speculate. He or she gathers all the facts before judging whether something is true or false.

A godly individual has no business thinking about things that are not true. Doing so is a waste of time. It is not healthy for you to even listen to statements or accusations that are false. There will be people that come across your path who speak lies about everything from religion to relationships, and believing those lies will bind you. That's why it is so important for you to know the truth, and if you don't know what the truth is, take time to find out.

Don't be gullible. If you entertain fallacy for an extended period of time, you will eventually believe it to be truth. Nobody purposes in their heart to believe lies, so be on your guard.

whatever is noble

Think about whatever is noble. The word *noble* in this verse comes from the Greek word *semnos*. It is actually translated as the English word *honest*. The definition of *semnos* is dignity; a majestic and awe-inspiring quality that invites and attracts.

I have learned that we eventually become whatever it is that we think about. If you think happy thoughts, odds are you are a happy person. If you view the glass as half empty, you are likely a negative person. If you want to be a noble person, you have to think about whatever is dignified, majestic or awe-inspiring, and then live that way. Noble thoughts are centered on God and His word. He is dignified, majestic and awe-inspiring. When you fix your mind on Him, you will want to be like Him.

Nobility is an attractive quality. People are drawn to individuals that are honest in thought and deed. On the other hand, people tend to avoid those who are dishonest and who have poor character. Many unsaved people are turned off of God because a lot of Christians do not think, look or act godly. Their thinking is carnal, and they do not meditate on whatever is noble.

Be careful not to become snobbish in your thinking, though. Being noble does not mean you look down at those who are not. The noble Christian leads by example. I encourage you today to evaluate your way of thinking. Maybe you think about things that are good, but they are not noble.

I challenge you to begin focusing on the person of Jesus Christ, His majestic and awe-inspiring qualities. You will become more like Him, and people will be attracted to Him through you.

whatever is right

> **Philippians 4:8** – *Finally, brothers, whatever is true, whatever is noble, whatever is right, whatever is pure, whatever is lovely, whatever is admirable—if anything is excellent or praiseworthy—think about such things* (NIV).

The King James Version of this verse says to think on whatsoever things are just. In other words, the words *right* and *just* are interchangeable in this verse. To be just is to be correct in judgment. We are to think about what is good and proper. This is what it means to think about whatever is right.

There are many well-meaning people who have poor judgment. Poor judgment comes as a result of not knowing the difference between right and wrong. Many people never realize their dreams because they make foolish decisions, or poor judgment calls, trying to fulfill them.

Take for instance a little boy who dreams of flying. Full of vigor and expectation, he glues paper wings to his back and climbs onto the roof of his house. He carefully positions himself at the edge of the roof, extends his arms and takes a flying leap. The end result is less than desirable. His dream is shattered, and he is left injured and confused. He thought for sure his plan would work, but he went about fulfilling his dream all wrong.

I know this is an extreme example, but the lesson learned can be applied to everyday life. Maybe you find yourself at a standstill today. All you have to show for your dreams is a laundry list of bad decisions and poor judgment calls. It is hard to do the right thing when you don't know what it is.

Psalm 119:125 – *Give discernment to me, your servant; then I will understand your laws* (NLT). Ask God to give you discernment everyday when you pray. It is one of the gifts of the Spirit spoken of in 1 Corinthians 12. He wants you to know and do what is right.

> **Proverbs 3:21** – *My son, preserve sound judgment and discernment, do not let them out of your sight* (NIV).

whatever is pure

Philippians 4:8 – *Finally, brothers, whatever is true, whatever is noble, whatever is right, whatever is pure, whatever is lovely, whatever is admirable—if anything is excellent or praiseworthy— think about such things* (NIV).

The word *pure* in this verse comes from the Greek word meaning freedom from defilement or impurities; innocent. The dictionary defines *pure* as free from anything contaminating. Given these definitions, one might think, "Lord, have mercy. The majority of my thoughts are impure!" If this is you, do not be disheartened. You're not alone, and your thinking *can* be changed.

In order to purify your thoughts, it is important to first identify where the impure thoughts originated from. They can stem from a variety of sources such as the way you entertain yourself, past experiences, addictions, etc. You need to ask the Holy Spirit to help you pinpoint the cause of the impurity, and then repent and rid yourself of it.

Impure thoughts do not ever come from God. They are a product of your fleshly, sinful nature. If you are not thinking about whatever is pure, then you are feeding your sinful nature somehow. What do you listen to or watch on television or at the movies? Maybe you participate in unclean conversations with friends or coworkers. Perhaps you have been mistreated or abused in your past and haven't forgiven yet. Bitterness and resentment cause impure thoughts of revenge and malice. Lust leads to unhealthy, sexual fantasies, and the list goes on.

Thoughts eventually lead to action, whether pure or impure. **Romans 8:5** – *Those who live according to the sinful nature have their minds set on what that nature desires; but those who live in accordance with the Spirit have their minds set on what the Spirit desires* (NIV). If you are struggling with impure thoughts, crucify the sinful nature with its desires. Then your thinking will change.

Galatians 5:24 – *Those who belong to Christ Jesus have crucified the sinful nature with its passions and desires* (NIV).

102

whatever is lovely

The word *lovely* is defined as charmingly or exquisitely beautiful; of a great moral or spiritual beauty. The Greek definition is something acceptable or pleasing. Christians run into problems when their idea of what is lovely differs from God's. Many times we find things acceptable and pleasing that God finds repulsive and offensive. We must learn to think about what God considers morally and spiritually beautiful.

If you don't know where to start, begin by getting into that secret place where God is. Anywhere God dwells is beautiful because *He* is beautiful. Make this your prayer, *"How lovely is your dwelling place, O LORD Almighty! My soul yearns, even faints, for the courts of the LORD; my heart and my flesh cry out for the living God"* (**Psalm 84:1-2**, NIV). His dwelling place is lovely, and our thoughts wander from lovely to ugly when we live outside of His presence.

God desires intimacy with you, and that relationship is formed and developed in His presence. The most intimate times I have with my wife are face-to-face, not over the phone or in written notes to one another. The most meaningful moments in our relationship have come when it's just the two of us together.

Relationships suffer when the individuals involved do not spend enough time together. If your thoughts are immoral or unpleasing, get back into God's presence. Look upon His face because He is lovely. When you become intimate with Him, you will begin to think about how beautiful He is. Thank You, Jesus!

Psalm 27:4 – *One thing I ask of the LORD, this is what I seek: that I may dwell in the house of the LORD all the days of my life, to gaze upon the beauty of the LORD and to seek him in his temple* (NIV).

whatever is admirable

> **Philippians 4:8** – *Finally, brothers, whatever is true, whatever is noble, whatever is right, whatever is pure, whatever is lovely, whatever is admirable—if anything is excellent or praiseworthy— think about such things* (NIV).

Something that is admirable is first-rate. It is top of the line. The dictionary defines the word *admirable* as inspiring approval, reverence or affection. What, or who, do you consider admirable?

I used to admire a certain professional basketball player. In fact, I was pretty obsessed with him. I watched every game of his I could, and I would record the ones I missed. I bought his jerseys, collected his basketball cards and memorized his stats. I knew where and when he was born, what schools he attended and many other factoids. I also made it a point to tell anyone who would listen how awesome of a basketball player he was. I even pretended to be him when I played. I thought he was the greatest ever. He inspired me, and my admiration for him pushed me to be a better basketball player.

I admired this man's basketball abilities, but his personal life did not promote godliness. I wanted to play ball like him, but I had no desire to imitate his lifestyle. You can learn valuable lessons from individuals who do not serve God, but I encourage you to admire people, things and accomplishments that push you to become a more godly person. You should aim to be Christ-like in your thinking.

Become obsessed with knowing God. Admire Him, and fix your mind on how holy and awesome He is. Develop a fascination for His word and meditate on it. Purpose in your heart to pattern your life after Jesus Christ today. Read about Him, memorize the story of His life and learn His character traits. It is safe to admire His abilities *and* His lifestyle.

> **Hebrews 12:28** – *Let us show gratitude, by which we may offer to God an acceptable service with reverence and awe* (NASB).

if anything is excellent

> **Philippians 4:8** – *Finally, brothers, whatever is true, whatever is noble, whatever is right, whatever is pure, whatever is lovely, whatever is admirable—if anything is excellent or praiseworthy—think about such things* (NIV).

I believe the word *excellent* is widely misused. It is defined as possessing outstanding quality or superior merit; remarkably good. Given this definition, how many people or things do we label as excellent that do not possess outstanding quality or superior merit? The answer: too many to count.

The truth is the definition of *excellent* is going to vary from person to person, but Paul lists seven things that are excellent and profitable in **Titus 3:1-2** – 1 *Remind the people to be subject to rulers and authorities, to be obedient, to be ready to do whatever is good,* 2 *to slander no one, to be peaceable and considerate, and to show true humility toward all men* (NIV). If you desire to be excellent, you must purpose in your heart and mind to live according to these verses. Examine yourself as I go through them.

It is not uncommon for me to hear Christians bad mouth and ridicule anyone from bosses to pastors to the President and so on. If you do not agree with those God has established over you, submit to their authority anyway and pray for them.

Partial obedience is disobedience. Are you doing something God has not asked you to do? Perhaps you are avoiding something He *has* told you to do.

You have to put yourself in position to do whatever is good. Many people wind up doing or saying things they regret because they set themselves up for failure. Set yourself up for success.

Now let me ask you some questions. Do you slander or gossip about others, or do you uplift with your words? Are you at peace with everyone you are in relationship with? Do you put the needs of others above your own? Would the people in your life describe you as humble? If you are lacking in any of these areas, I encourage you today to commit yourself to excellence.

if anything is praiseworthy

Philippians 4:8 – *Finally, brothers, whatever is true, whatever is noble, whatever is right, whatever is pure, whatever is lovely, whatever is admirable—if anything is excellent or praiseworthy— think about such things* (NIV).

Something that is praiseworthy is deserving of approval, a person or idea that should be commended. Heidi and I were recently at an outdoor music festival. Nine or ten artists performed over the course of the two-day event, and there were over forty-five thousand people in attendance. There were five musical acts the day we attended, but only one of them blew me away.

I have set through many concerts in my lifetime. I have heard bands that should rethink their careers, and I have heard others who are absolutely awesome. I had anticipated this certain individual's set all afternoon. I knew he would not disappoint, but he totally exceeded my expectations. His guitar playing was second to none, he sang beautifully and he related well to the audience. It was the greatest musical performance I have ever experienced in a concert setting. He put on an amazing show.

When he was finished, the crowd roared their approval and applauded (myself included). He was to be commended; his performance was definitely praiseworthy.

I want to challenge you today to think about that which is praiseworthy. Keep alert, and look for opportunities to applaud the people who surround you. If one of your children does something exceptional, voice your approval and appreciation. If a coworker or subordinate resolves a pressing issue at work, commend him or her. How many times a day do we miss out on blessing others for their accomplishments?

We often do not notice the positive things in life because we become so focused on the negative. Readjust your thinking today, and give praise where praise is due.

2 Corinthians 10:18 – *For it is not the one who commends himself who is approved, but the one whom the Lord commends* (NIV).

wholesome thinking

2 Peter 3:1 – *Dear friends, this is now my second letter to you. I have written both of them as reminders to stimulate you to wholesome thinking* (NIV).

It says in this verse that Peter wrote two entire books of the Bible with the purpose of reminding Christians to think wholesomely. I find it disturbing that God's people have to be reminded to think healthy thoughts, but I will be the first to admit I fall short time and time again. Why? More times than not, we are setting ourselves up for failure. Let me explain (Keep in mind that the word *wholesome* is defined as nourishing or nutritious).

At the beginning of every new year, hundreds of thousands of people purpose to lose weight and become healthier. Statistics indicate that the vast majority of them will fail. Some will last longer than others, but most fall short of their goals. Many set out to change their bodies, but they fail because they do not discipline themselves or adjust their lifestyles accordingly.

They want physical health, but they do not consistently exercise. They voice the need to eat more nutritiously, but their cabinets are full of everything unhealthy, and fast food is so much easier than cooking. Most do not have someone to hold them accountable, and they wind up miserable and more out of shape than they were to begin with.

The same concept is true for those who vow to be more wholesome in their thinking. You can purpose in your heart today to change the way you think, but you will fail if you do not make proper adjustments to your lifestyle.

Get rid of things that promote impure thoughts, and cut out demeaning conversations. Turn off television and radio programs that condone violence, cursing or sexual sin. Allow God to mold the way you think. Sometimes we just need a friendly reminder.

1 Corinthians 14:20 – *I'm getting exasperated with your infantile thinking. How long before you grow up and use your head—your adult head?* (MSG)

a warning to the idle

> **1 Thessalonians 5:14** – *And we urge you, brothers, warn those who are idle, encourage the timid, help the weak, be patient with everyone* (NIV).

It is important for us to understand that Paul wrote this message to Christians, not the unsaved. Paul says that idle believers should be warned. When a warning is issued, it is usually because there is impending danger. Severe weather warnings are for areas that could possibly be affected by tornadoes or thunderstorms. They encourage people to take the appropriate actions necessary to keep themselves safe.

If you are currently idle in your faith, or if your life is at a standstill, let this serve as a warning to you. The alarm is sounding, danger is looming, and you must take action now!

Being idle is the exact opposite of working. One can have the appearance of being busy, but still be inoperative. **2 Thessalonians 3:10-11** – 10 *For even when we were with you, we gave you this rule: "If a man will not work, he shall not eat."* 11 *We hear that some among you are idle. They are not busy; they are busybodies* (NIV).

The Bible says an idle person is equivalent to a busybody. Interestingly enough, a busybody is a person who pries into or meddles in the affairs of others. He or she is a gossip and blabbermouth. Idlers talk a big game and can look as if they are working, but they accomplish little to nothing. They leech onto those who are doing the work. They expect things to get done, but they have no intention of ever lifting a finger.

I want to encourage you to examine yourself today. Do you need to get a job? Actively pursue one. Are you fulfilling a role in your local church? Become involved. Do not be content with mooching off of those who are doing the work. Otherwise, the Word says you will not eat.

> **1 Timothy 5:13** – *And not only do they become idlers, but also gossips and busybodies, saying things they ought not to* (NIV).

encouragement for the timid

Another word for *timid* is *fearful*. **2 Timothy 1:7** – *For God has not given us a spirit of fear, but of power and of love and of a sound mind* (NKJV). There are many people who walk through life full of fear. They worry about everything from the economy to their health. They are scared of being burglarized, or they constantly feel like someone is out to get them.

Listen to me carefully. God does not give you fear; *you* cause yourself to be fearful. Living in fear will cause you to shut down. In fact, fear is one of the major reasons why people become idle. If you are bound by timidity, I want to encourage you with the word of God today. He has given you power, love and soundness of mind!

I am not talking about just any power. God has given you *dunamis* power making you able and capable. This power gives you strength to oppose the spirit of cowardice, or fear. You are not to give in or relent to your fears. Go on the offensive, and take your fears captive. Hallelujah!

The love He gives you comes from the Greek word *agape*. It is the unconditional love that God has for the human race. His love for you causes Him to always do what is best for you, even if it is not necessarily what you want Him to do. His limitless love for us was the reason behind Jesus being sent to die in our place. But He not only gives us this love, He gives us the ability to love others in the same way.

Lastly, He gives you soundness of mind, or self-discipline. Fear will cause you to be a scatterbrain, but God has given you the ability to think soberly. I encourage you to believe what God says about you today. Refuse to be bound by timidity.

1 Chronicles 22:13 – *Be strong and courageous. Do not be afraid or discouraged* (NIV).

help the weak

1 Thessalonians 5:14 – *And we urge you, brothers, warn those who are idle, encourage the timid, help the weak, be patient with everyone* (NIV).

I love to wrestle with our two boys. When I get down on my knees, it signifies to them that it's "go time". I immediately become some kind of villain and the object of their wrath. They go into superhero mode, and the battle is on. My goal is to have fun and not to hurt either of them, but we do not share the same goal.

At ages 8 and 6, I can still take them, but sometimes they get a good shot in and really hurt me. I will roll around on the floor moaning in agony, and they think it's great. Rather than asking if I am okay or offering to help me out, they recognize my weakness and move in to finish me off. Where I come from they call this "kicking them while they're down."

It is a shame how many people seem to have adopted this same mindset in the church today. Instead of seeking to help those who have been weakened, they tend to nitpick and fault find. God has said for us to help the weak, not judge them for how we think they got that way.

Think of how you would feel if your situations were reversed. Perhaps you *are* in a weak state right now. Maybe you need encouragement because of mistakes you have made or because of life's trials. How do you want to be treated? I'll tell you what you don't want. You don't want someone to come along saying, "I told you so. You shouldn't have done that, now you are getting what you deserve."

Matthew 7:12 – *"Therefore, treat people the same way you want them to treat you"* (NASB). In other words, if you are at a weak point in your life right now, help someone else who is down. If you do, it will only be a matter of time before you receive the help you need.

Psalm 41:1 – *Blessed is he who has regard for the weak; the LORD delivers him in times of trouble* (NIV).

be patient with everyone

Waiting is easy when the circumstances are favorable. I do not have a problem waiting for someone when I am reclined in my favorite chair, sipping my favorite drink, watching my favorite show. I can wait all day under those kinds of circumstances and never get upset, but that is not being patient.

Patience is long-suffering (emphasis on the words *long* and *suffering*). Patience is required when you are tired and at your wits end. It is the ability to endure under less than favorable conditions for an extended period of time. Patience builds character, and there are some situations and people that will push you to the limit.

Even so, we are instructed to be patient with *everyone*. This is no easy task. Odds are you have someone in your life that gets on your last nerve. This individual has the ability to push your buttons and get under your skin. He or she brings out the worst in you without even trying. You know who I'm talking about.

Perhaps it is a coworker or your boss. Maybe it is a classmate or someone you minister to. Sometimes it is even a relative. I know my patience is tried most by people who act ignorantly, but they really know better. I will admit there are certain people I would just like to slap some sense into, but all that would do is make my hand sore.

I believe God strategically places people in your path to aid in building your character. I encourage you today not to avoid people whose personalities clash with yours. Patience is a fruit of the Spirit, and the true fruit of our lives comes to the surface during times of adversity. Life presents plenty of opportunities for us to practice patience. Embrace them.

Romans 12:12 – *Rejoice and exult in hope; be steadfast and patient in suffering and tribulation; be constant in prayer* (AMP).

payback

Revenge comes natural. It is a built-in part of the human psyche. Even from birth, our instincts tell us to repay wrong for wrong. If you have ever observed small children, you know exactly what I am talking about.

I have witnessed my fair share of nursery-sized "throw downs," and they usually start the same way. Our two sons are perfect examples that seeking revenge starts early. Picture little Jack minding his own business, playing basketball. Rather than digging through the toys and getting his own ball, older brother Noah swoops in, snatches Jack's ball and runs away.

Usually a scream, a chase and a punch follow. Jack yells, runs Noah down and wallops him. A brief brawl ensues, and both of them wind up hurt. Unfortunately, many people never grow out of this kind of behavior. When somebody does them wrong, they get angry and plan their revenge. And more times than not, the act of revenge is worse than the original offense.

I am about to say something that may make you want to seek revenge against me. Revenge is always wrong. This idea goes directly against what society teaches us today. Most people are taught to pay back those who do them wrong. Malice is rewarded and not seeking revenge is portrayed as wimpy.

Try repaying evil with good today. Do not practice what society preaches because revenge leaves a trail of bodies behind it. Dare to trust God at His word. So much pain could be avoided if God's people would learn to respond gently to wrath. I challenge you today to be kind to everyone, even those who do you wrong.

bits and rudders

Your tongue is the bit or rudder that directs the course of your life. You shape your world with your words. What you say has the ability to propel you down the path toward God's will or cause you to wander in the wilderness.

You might ask, "How is it that words pack such a powerful punch?" Jesus answers this question in **Matthew 12:34** – *"For out of the overflow of the heart the mouth speaks"* (NIV). What comes out of your mouth is a direct reflection of what is stored up in your heart. You say what you think, and you think about what you desire. Every time you open your mouth you alter the course of your life.

Those who lie or speak negatively all the time are allowing their tongues to lead them down a path to destruction. On the other hand, speaking the Word has the ability to restore hope in the midst of tragedy. This principle is true when it comes to how we speak to others as well. Our words either uplift or tear down those who hear them.

I want to encourage you today to speak positively to everyone and in every situation. If you truly desire the purposes of God in your life, your speech will reflect that desire. If you find the tone of your speech to be harsh or angry, perhaps there is a root of bitterness somewhere in your heart.

My mom used to say, "If you don't have anything good to say, don't say anything at all." I'll say this to you. If you don't have anything good to say, speak the word of God!

Psalm 35:28 – *And my tongue shall speak of Your righteousness and of Your praise all the day long* (NKJV).

a world of evil

James 3:5-6 – 5 *Consider what a great forest is set on fire by a small spark.* 6 *The tongue also is a fire, a world of evil among the parts of the body. It corrupts the whole person, sets the whole course of his life on fire, and is itself set on fire by hell* (NIV).

James is obviously describing the tongue of someone whose life is not governed by the Holy Spirit. He paints a picture here of the tongue in its fleshly state. The tongue is naturally a world of evil. That is why most babies come out screaming bloody murder instead of cooing (just kidding).

As I thought about this passage, I wondered to myself, "How many people, who claim to be Christians, have a tongue that has been set on fire by hell?" I don't know about you, but having my mouth set on fire by hell does not sound too appealing.

The tongue is like a small spark capable of igniting an entire forest. I wonder how many forest fires I have started with my words. I shudder at the thought. How often do you engage in gossip? All it takes is two people to spread a rumor. An initial conversation takes place, and then it can spread like wild fire from person to person. Truth gets twisted, and soon enough everyone is talking. A great forest is set ablaze.

There is a Spirit-inspired fire that purifies, but I am talking about a fire that destroys everything it touches. How many marriages are consumed by hurtful words? One spiteful remark can set the course of any relationship on fire. Many people avoid intimacy because they have been burned so many times.

Is your tongue set on fire by hell? Are you corrupting yourself, and the world around you, with your words? Ask the Holy Spirit to help you today. Think before you speak; do not stereotype. Let your tongue be an instrument God uses to put out fires. I pray for there to be healing in your words. Hallelujah!

Psalm 39:1 – *I said to myself, "I will watch what I do and not sin in what I say. I will hold my tongue when the ungodly are around me"* (NLT).

zap!

I am amazed when I think about the different kinds of animals man has tamed. Some of the fiercest beasts the world has ever known will listen to humans and do as they are commanded. It is quite remarkable. People charm venomous snakes, perform tricks on the backs of killer whales and play with Bengal tigers. Bald eagles land on the shoulders of their trainers, and dogs can be taught to do just about anything.

When I was a teenager, my parents got a new dog for the family, a Beagle named Bailey. I remember they brought her home with a cone on her head, and my dad immediately began to train her. She was still a puppy, but her previous owners had housebroken her. My dad's goal was to train her to stay out of the bedrooms and the dining room. Other than that, she had pretty much free reign of the house.

Animals typically train best if they are punished for poor behavior and rewarded for positive behavior (the same can be said of most humans). Dad opted to use a shock collar and doggie treats to train Bailey. So it began. The four of us would go into a room Bailey was not allowed in and call for her.

She would come running, and as soon as she'd step foot onto the carpet of the bedroom, my dad would zap her. She would yelp, and we would repeat the process for all the rooms she was banned from. Bailey was a smart dog, so she figured it out after the initial shocks. We went back through each room, called her and then rewarded her with a doggie treat when she didn't come in.

If you have a problem speaking negatively, come up with a punishment and reward system to help break you of it (key word *help*). If you say something derogatory, put a quarter in a jar for each offense. When your habit is broken, reward yourself and buy something with the quarters. A dog perhaps…

no man can tame it

You can implement some kind of punishment and reward system to help train your tongue, but that alone will not get the job done. In fact, no one can master the tongue on his own. The Bible teaches that no man can tame the tongue. No matter how hard we try, taming the tongue is not something we can do in our own strength.

James calls the tongue a restless evil, full of deadly poison. Another word for *restless* is *edgy*. Something, or someone, that is on edge is usually very unpredictable. In its natural state, the tongue is an unpredictable, deadly evil. It is very dangerous, and if we try to handle it on our own, we will just wind up defeated and constantly frustrated. Not to mention, we will be discouraging and hurtful to others.

I have vowed many times to change the way I communicate. It's not usually *what* I say; it is the *way* I say it. Tone of voice is my downfall, and I tend to fail in this area when speaking to my wife. I do not intend to use a poor tone because I know it can be hurtful, but it comes out anyway. Sometimes I can be sarcastic or harsh without even realizing it. It comes naturally.

Time and time again I have promised to make an adjustment, but I continuously fall short. Why? Unless I ask the Holy Spirit to help me, my promises are empty because I cannot tame my tongue. I have to make an effort, but my efforts are ineffective unless I partner with the Holy Spirit.

If your tongue is out of control today, stop trying to do something only God can do. Ask and allow Him to tame your tongue. What is impossible for man is easy for God.

praise and cursing

James 3:9-10 – 9 *With the tongue we praise our Lord and Father, and with it we curse men, who have been made in God's likeness.* 10 *Out of the same mouth come praise and cursing. My brothers, this should not be* (NIV).

Both praise and cursing should not come out of the same mouth, but all too often they do. Many Christians give God lip service while talking down to their fellow man. God is not flattered by our compliments, and His approval cannot be bought. In fact, His heart is grieved because of such behavior.

The person who praises God while cursing man is a liar. He lives a double life. He appears to have it together as he lifts up the name of the Lord, but he secretly slanders others. He is a double-minded man, unstable in all he does (**James 1:8**). You cannot truly praise God and curse the people He loves. God will not be mocked (**Galatians 6:7**).

James 3:11-12 explains: 11 *Can both fresh water and salt water flow from the same spring?* 12 *My brothers, can a fig tree bear olives, or a grapevine bear figs? Neither can a salt spring produce fresh water* (NIV). A mouth that genuinely praises God cannot curse men, and a mouth that curses men cannot genuinely praise God.

I thank God that His mercies are new everyday. It is impossible for a man to live perfectly. There will be times we speak negatively about someone else, but if we love God and aim to please Him, we will immediately feel the conviction of the Holy Spirit and fall to our knees in repentance.

Be honest with yourself today. Perhaps you backbite and gossip in between weekly worship services. If you do, repent and receive His forgiveness. Your praise will be genuine once your heart is pure toward others. Thank You, Jesus!

Job 27:4 – *My lips will not speak wickedness, and my tongue will utter no deceit* (NIV).

anger

I believe it is very important to point out how Jesus compares murder and anger in the above verses. We can get angry and not sin (**Psalm 4:4**), but the anger Jesus speaks of in Matthew 5 refers to a person who harbors malice. Murder and anger have very different earthly consequences, but Jesus teaches us that both the murderer and the one who remains angry with someone will face the same judgment.

The eternal severity of these two sins is the same. They will both separate us from God forever. It is for this reason that I want to teach on anger. Killing someone is obviously wrong, but many people give their anger problem a free pass. They will say, "Rage runs in my family" or "It's my personality."

Anger may not always be sinful, but *unresolved* anger always is. My goal over the next few days is for you to better understand anger and how it impacts your life. I want to introduce to you a story in **Numbers 20:1-12**. From this passage I am going to point out seven truths about anger that will help you deal with it before and after it becomes sinful.

Moses had been entrusted by God to lead Israel into the Promised Land. The mass exodus featured millions of people and their egos. This made the trip less than desirable on numerous occasions, especially for Moses. In this particular instance, Israel complained to Moses about a water shortage. Moses finally had enough. His frustration boiled over into anger, his anger eventually became sin and his sin wound up costing him something very precious. Be honest with yourself today as we begin this study. Does anger have a hold on you?

residual frustration

Numbers 20:10-11 – 10 *He and Aaron gathered the assembly together in front of the rock and Moses said to them, "Listen, you rebels, must we bring you water out of this rock?" 11 Then Moses raised his arm and struck the rock twice with his staff* (NIV).

Moses was mad. He yelled at the Israelites, and then he beat a rock with his staff. But why was he so upset? Israel was complaining again. In **Numbers 20:2-6** you can read how the Israelites moaned and groaned about there being no water. They went on and on about how Moses had led them into the desert to die. Unfortunately, this was not the first time they had whined.

The Israelites were an ungrateful bunch that frequently grumbled against Moses. Their complaints were constant even though God gave them great victories. Moses listened to their nagging, but he finally had enough and blew his top.

This brings me to the first truth you need to know about anger. Anger results from residual frustration. Moses allowed Israel's complaints to pile up one on top of the other, and it broke him. He lost his temper.

There are many well-meaning Christians who are irritated and dangerously frustrated in their personal lives. Maybe your nerves are depleted because of the current economic crisis, or the boss is riding you at work. Perhaps your teenagers are rebelling, school is demanding or the baby is crying again! Frustration is mounting, tension is building and an emotional tirade is looming. Now take a deep breath. Frustration does not have to birth anger.

Perhaps you have been lashing out as Moses did. You may not be smacking people or objects with sticks, but your words may be hurtful at times. I encourage you to deal with frustrations as they come. Do not hold everything in until you are at a breaking point. Exchange the nagging pressures of life for the peace of God. You, and those around you, will be glad you did.

1 Corinthians 10:13 – *And God is faithful. He will not allow the temptation to be more than you can stand* (NLT).

119

a lack of self-control

Proverbs 25:28 – *Like a city whose walls are broken down is a man who lacks self-control* (NIV).

Anger is a product of a lack of self-control. There are many talented and anointed men and women of God who do not have self-control. They have charisma, but no character. Their lack of control opens them up to attack and causes them to be prone to outbursts. Show me a person who lacks self-control, and I will show you a person whose walls are broken down around him. When the walls come down, we become vulnerable.

The walls came crashing down in Moses' life, and he lost all sense of reason. It caused him to react irrationally and say hurtful things. The walls in our lives protect us from physical, emotional and spiritual attacks. They also keep us from acting out foolishly. Anger is just one of those foolish acts.

Self-control is a learned behavior. It does not just happen, and it cannot be imparted into you by somebody else. Self-control requires daily effort, and that is why many people have a shortage of it. **2 Peter 1:5-8** lists several qualities that we are to possess in increasing measure. One of which is self-control.

I used to battle serious anger problems. I was aware of my issue, but I could not get victory over it for some reason. I would continuously lash out and say things that were inappropriate. I never cursed or anything like that, but my words would be hurtful at times. After outbursts I would feel guilty and want to change, but it was not until I disciplined myself that change began.

Developing self-control is a process. To this day I continue to endure that process. I have to add to my self-control daily. There are times when I stumble and cracks form in my walls, but I repair them and fight back with the word of God. I encourage you to do the same. If self-control is a quality you lack, start the daily journey toward change today. Don't let anger get the best of you.

James 1:19 – *Everyone should be quick to listen, slow to speak and slow to become angry* (NIV).

anger breeds disobedience

As mentioned earlier, it is okay to get angry, but when our anger becomes sin, we have a problem. Moses demonstrates this point perfectly.

Moses had seen the hand of the Lord at work time and time again on behalf of the Israelites, but here they complained against God again. Moses was sick and tired of Israel taking God for granted. He took their ridicule personally and got angry. He was justified in his anger, but because he lacked self-control, his anger became sin. He disobeyed God.

The Israelites were thirsty, so God told Moses to speak to the rock and then water would pour out for them to drink. Instead, out of his frustration, Moses struck the rock twice.

Many times we have legit reasons for being angry, but the minute we lose control and lash out, we step out of God's will. **Psalm 37:8** – *Refrain from anger and turn from wrath; do not fret—it leads only to evil* (NIV). Giving into anger will lead you down a path to destruction. Anger many times causes us to ignore God's command and take a path of our own making.

Maybe you know all too well what it is I am talking about today. You are upset and have been disobedient, and you may even have legitimate reasons for being angry. If you have acted out and ventured away from God's will, this is your opportunity to get back on track.

I encourage you to repent and receive forgiveness. The best way to correct disobedience is to obey. Do what it is He has commanded you to do. Get your life back on course today.

James 1:20 – *For man's anger does not bring about the righteous life that God desires* (NIV).

reverting to the past

> **Exodus 2:11-12** – 11 *One day, after Moses had grown up, he went out to where his own people were and watched them at their hard labor. He saw an Egyptian beating a Hebrew, one of his own people.* 12 *Glancing this way and that and seeing no one, he killed the Egyptian and hid him in the sand* (NIV).

During Israel's journey to the Promised Land, Moses was a humble man with godly intentions. He knew the voice of the Lord, and he walked closely to Him. But that was not always the case. As you just read in Exodus 2, Moses struggled with anger earlier in his life. He became so angry one time that he murdered an Egyptian guard who was mistreating a fellow Hebrew.

After the murder, God handpicked and anointed Moses to be the leader of Israel's deliverance. With that anointing came the ability to deal with difficult circumstances in a godly manner. Time passed, and Moses led Israel out of bondage. They faced many hardships as they traveled, but Moses was a model of patience. The Israelites complained, and Moses brought their requests to the Lord. He seemed to have left the past behind him.

Some time later, God gave Moses the chance to prove his character. Unfortunately, he flopped. Moses was armed with a word from the Lord, he was anointed to handle the situation properly, but his anger caused him to revert back to his old way of handling things.

Our true character is revealed when we are under fire. All is well with our attitude as long as life is going as we think it should, but it is only a matter of time before our character will be put to the test. Times of testing show us what we are made of.

Maybe today you are close to giving up on living a godly lifestyle. God has brought you through so much! Do not revert back to your past because you are angry. He has anointed you to do what is right. Cast your cares on Him, and let Him guide you.

> **1 Timothy 2:8** – *I want men to pray with holy hands lifted up to God, free from anger and controversy* (NLT).

a sign of distrust

Numbers 20:12 – *But the LORD said to Moses and Aaron, "Because you did not trust in me…"* (NIV).

Sergio Scataglini once said, "When we move in fleshly anger, we reveal that we are trusting in ourselves rather than God." I have found this to be true in my own life.

I began playing basketball when I was in elementary school. I was tall, slim and had a lot of natural talent. My dad taught me how to shoot, and I picked it up very quickly. I played in school all the way through high school, and I also participated in organized city and church leagues. I couldn't get enough.

When I was a senior in high school, I played for a very small school, and I was pretty good. Our team wound up going to the state championship that year, and I was named the league's Most Valuable Player. I was the stuff!

I remember certain games during the course of the season that our team would be trailing, and I'd get very upset. Winning was all that mattered, and I *really* could not stand losing to a team we should beat. So I would completely throw out the coach's game plan because I decided his way was not working, and I tried to take the game over. Sometimes the face of the game would change because of my efforts, but many times it was a fat disaster.

My anger caused me to lose trust in my coach, the head of our team. I thought my way was better than his, even though he eventually led us to the championship game. I lost sight of the big picture because of my anger. The same thing happened to Moses when he hit the rock instead of speaking to it. His rage caused him to take matters into his own hands. How foolish we are!

Perhaps today you have taken matters into your own hands. Maybe you think your ways are more effective than His. I pray anger does not violate the trust between you and God. Do not forget that He sees the big picture.

Proverbs 29:8 – *Mockers stir up a city, but wise men turn away anger* (NIV).

anger misrepresents God

Up to this point in our story, God had shown Himself to be holy and faithful. He was committed to Israel. Even though they were unfaithful numerous times, God remained faithful to them. The Israelites knew Him to be gracious and patient. He was a God who provided and cared for them. He was slow to anger, and He chose Moses to represent Him to the people.

The Bible says that Moses did not trust God and dishonored Him in front of the assembly. Moses was disobedient and brought discredit to the integrity of God right in front of His people. What a poor demonstration of God's character!

When we act out in anger and frustration, we are misrepresenting God to the lost and those around us. I'm ashamed to think about how many times I have let my frustration get the best of me in front of others, my family included. Unfortunately, our families and those closest to us often see the worst side of us.

I hate to think about how many times I have ruined my witness because I lost my cool. Somebody is always watching. Our actions and reactions are a testimony to those who surround us. And when you are a Christian, you represent Jesus Christ. Our lives are meant to be a reflection of who He is. When I came to this realization, I began to act and respond differently.

I challenge you to change the way you view yourself. A lot of people live their lives as if they have a small circle of influence and that their actions do not affect many people. You need to begin seeing yourself as God's representative, and you must understand that your response to adversity makes a great impact on those around you. A lot of people have a distorted image of who God is, so it is time for us to paint a better picture.

don't forfeit God's promises

Let's go back to Exodus 3 and briefly look at the day Moses was called to be Israel's deliverer. The Lord appeared to Moses in a burning bush and began to speak to him about the misery of His people. God was moved with compassion for the Israelites, and He told Moses he would be their leader (vs. 10).

Then in **Exodus 3:17** God made a promise, *"And I have promised to bring you up out of your misery in Egypt into the land of the Canaanites, Hittites, Amorites, Perizzites, Hivites and Jebusites—a land flowing with milk and honey"* (NIV). God told Moses he would be the one to lead Israel into the Promised Land. What an awesome promise!

Unfortunately, God has the right to break His promises. I realize this statement may go against your view of our loving Savior, but in **Numbers 20:12** the Lord says to Moses and Aaron, *"You will not bring this community into the land I give them."* Why would God break His promise? Doesn't that go against His very nature?

Disobedience will ultimately cause us to forfeit the promises of God. God is not a liar, and He never makes empty promises. But the fulfillment of His promises in our lives hinge on our obedience.

If you have wandered down a path of disobedience today, I want to encourage you to refocus. There is no earthly treasure or relationship worth trading God's promises for. He has wonderful things in store for those who follow after Him wholeheartedly. May you inherit the promises of God today!

a new creation

2 Corinthians 5:16-17 – 16 *So we have stopped evaluating others from a human point of view...*17 *This means that anyone who belongs to Christ has become a new person. The old life is gone; a new life has begun!* (NLT)

When it comes to changing your lifestyle, you are your own worst enemy. Maybe in the past couple of weeks you have committed to drop anger (or some other flaw) and pursue righteousness. The journey to holiness is tough enough without you beating yourself up along the way. Which raises the question: Why are we so hard on ourselves?

It is very difficult to stop evaluating ourselves from a human point of view. Once you have come clean, repented and rejected the sin in your life, you have to begin looking at yourself differently. God's desire is for us to see ourselves the way He sees us, and He sees us as forgiven. His blood eliminated our sin and made us worthy to be received by Him.

Our problem is we constantly remind ourselves of our past transgressions, and we cannot believe a genuine change has taken place in us. It is important to understand Paul's teaching in **2 Corinthians 5:14** – *Either way, Christ's love controls us. Since we believe that Christ died for all, we also believe that we have all died to our old life* (NLT).

When you relinquish control and allow Christ's love to control your life, your old life dies. Your anger, rage, malice, bad attitude, lust, etc. all dies, and *you* are the only one capable of resurrecting your old self.

It is time for a change of perspective. When a caterpillar becomes a butterfly, it no longer thinks or acts like a caterpillar. If it did, it would continue crawling around and never fly. You belong to Christ, and you are a new person. Your old life, with its passions and pleasures, is dead. Today your new life begins!

2 Corinthians 5:15 – *He died for everyone so that those who receive his new life will no longer live for themselves* (NLT).

joy = strength

Nehemiah 8:10 – *"Don't be dejected and sad, for the joy of the LORD is your strength!"* (NLT)

Another version says, *"And be not grieved and depressed"* (AMP). There are too many Christians who are miserable and downcast. Depression is draining. Many believers are tired and lifeless because they continuously wallow in self-pity. Feeling sorry for ourselves wears us out physically, emotionally and spiritually, but Nehemiah declares, "The joy of the Lord is your strength!"

If you are worn out and tired today, all you need is a dose of His joy. You may say, "Well, that's great and all, but I do not have anything to be joyous about. My life is terrible." If that is you, you need an attitude adjustment.

In all actuality, you probably have many things to rejoice over, but one thing is certain. If you are in relationship with Jesus, no matter what you face, you can always find joy in your salvation. Hallelujah! Pray as David did in **Psalm 51:12**, *"Restore to me the joy of Your salvation, and sustain me with a willing spirit"* (NASB).

Satan knows that if he can steal our joy, he can break our will. And once our will is broken, it is only a matter of time before we are overcome with sadness. Then we are rendered useless to the kingdom of God, and the enemy has us right where he wants us…tired and depressed.

Maybe today you are swimming in a sea of self-pity. You're dejected and worn out. I challenge you to look past your misery and focus on what the word of God says about you. I pray that the joy you felt at the time you came to know Jesus would be restored to you! Allow His joy to strengthen and uphold you right now. Depression has no hold; you are a child of God. Glory to His name!

Psalm 13:5 – *But I trust in your unfailing love; my heart rejoices in your salvation* (NIV).

rejoice in the Lord

Notice the *righteous* are being told to rejoice in the above verse, and the upright in heart are encouraged to sing. It is a simple command, but after reading it over a few times, I felt there was a deeper meaning. So I asked the Holy Spirit to give me a fresh revelation. Here is what I learned.

I have often wondered why it is that so many believers have a difficult time rejoicing. I will honestly admit that I have faced this same dilemma multiple times myself. Church services are regularly full of lemon-faced Christians who are unhappy with life. When it comes time to praise God and rejoice for all the great things He has done, the best they can muster up is a blank stare. They live dull lives free of joy.

The Bible calls for the righteous and upright to rejoice and sing. It says this because I believe those are the only people who really have anything to rejoice and sing about. Those who purpose to live holy lives, and who strive to know God intimately, have much to be thankful for.

The benefits of holy living are plentiful. That is why you will see certain people dance, sing and make fools of themselves in the presence of the Lord. They are overcome with joy because of what God has brought them through. They have left their old lifestyles behind to pursue Him, and they cannot help but rejoice because of the freedom that comes with righteousness.

When I find myself unable to rejoice, it is often times caused by an inconsistency in my character. Sin puts a wedge between us and God. Sinful behavior is selfish. When there is unresolved sin in our lives, we cannot rejoice because our aim is not to please Him. If you are unable to rejoice today, pursue righteousness. Repent of your sin and live uprightly. Now rejoice!

this is the day

This particular verse has been sung for years and years. It has been written into hymns, as well as contemporary Christian music. Many artists and worship leaders have entertained and led people into the presence of God by singing this verse, but do we really understand it? I want to share with you two truths found in this verse.

First of all, this is the day the Lord has made. Tomorrow is the day the Lord has made, and the day after that is the day the Lord has made. He has made every day from now until eternity. He has made both the good days and the bad days. Days of plenty and days of lack were both made by Him. He made the days we would like to forget and the ones that are memorable. Nothing ever has, and nothing ever will, catch God by surprise.

Let this truth be an encouragement to you. God always knows what is going on with us throughout the course of each day. He has handwritten every day. God cares for you so much that He is always watching over you.

Secondly, we make a daily decision whether or not we are going to rejoice and be glad in the day He has made. Some days will be wonderful and others will bring great suffering. It is easy to rejoice when things are going well, but we must choose to praise Him when life throws us a curve.

I don't suggest you begin saying, "Lord, thank You for this awful day. I just love how everything keeps going wrong. I could use a few more days like this." That's not rejoicing. Rejoicing during a trial sounds more like, "Lord, You are faithful! Even in the midst of my difficulty, I will praise You because I know You will see me through! Glory to God!" Remember God has made every day. Make up your mind to rejoice today no matter what.

Philippians 4:4 – *Rejoice in the Lord always. I will say it again: Rejoice!* (NIV)

rejoice in suffering

---

1 Peter 4:12-13 – 12 *Dear friends, do not be surprised at the painful trial you are suffering, as though something strange were happening to you.* 13 *But rejoice that you participate in the sufferings of Christ, so that you may be overjoyed when his glory is revealed* (NIV).

If you follow Christ, you will suffer. In fact, you will likely walk through many seasons of suffering. The Bible warns that tribulation is inevitable, but many times we are still caught off guard. Scripture even tells us that our trials will be painful. Even so, it is hard for us to wrap our minds around this concept. How could a loving Father willingly lead His people through adversity?

When unfortunate things start happening to us, we tend to fool ourselves into thinking, "Nobody knows what I am going through. My sufferings are unique." Pain hurts, and when we are hurting, we can become narrow-minded. But there are other people just like you and me. They face great opposition, and Jesus certainly knows what it means to suffer. You are not alone.

I grew up in church, and I have always been in church. I came to know Christ at a very young age, and I have never turned away from Him. My elementary and junior high years were great. Nobody really cared if you were a Christian or not; everyone pretty much got along. That all changed when I got into high school. Some of the most painful trials I have ever faced came between grades nine and twelve. Being ridiculed by my peers for doing the right thing was devastating.

It was during those years, though, that I grabbed a hold of **1 Peter 4:14** – *If you are insulted because of the name of Christ, you are blessed, for the Spirit of glory and of God rests on you* (NIV). I can rejoice now because I am blessed, and I bear His name (**1 Peter 4:16**). He knows what you go through, and you should celebrate because His glory is about to be revealed. Hallelujah!

James 1:2 – *Consider it pure joy, my brothers, whenever you face trials of many kinds* (NIV).

---

promises for the sorrowful

If you find yourself grief-stricken today, this message is for you. No matter the source of your sorrow, I pray that you are encouraged by the word of the Lord. Jesus makes three promises to the sorrowful in this verse. Allow His words to bless and uplift you. He is your glory and the lifter of your head (**Psalm 3:3**).

The first promise Jesus makes is, "I will see you again." There is coming a day when we will see Jesus face to face. **1 Corinthians 13:12** – *Now we see but a poor reflection as in a mirror; then we shall see face to face. Now I know in part; then I shall know fully, even as I am fully known* (NIV).

As it is now, we can only know Him in part, but we will soon know Him fully. We will know Him as well as He knows us! When Jesus returns, we will be like Him because we will see Him as He is (**1 John 3:2**). Glory!

The second promise He makes is, "Then you will rejoice." Maybe today you are at the lowest point of your life. Be encouraged; you will rejoice again! There is an old Darrell Evans song that says, "I'm trading my sorrows. I'm trading my shame. I'm laying it down for the joy of the Lord." Make this your song today. **Psalm 30:5** says: *Weeping may endure for a night, but joy comes in the morning* (NKJV). Praise God!

The third promise Jesus makes is the best, "No one can rob you of that joy." The devil will try, and he will send people to try, but nobody can steal your joy. Joy is like a gift you receive. You choose to accept it and open it up. It is yours, and you decide whether to share it, hoard it or give it away. But nobody can rob you of it. How awesome!

Are you consumed by sorrow today? Grab a hold of these promises, and remember nobody can take them away from you.

Revelation 19:7 – *Let us rejoice and be glad and give him glory!* (NIV)

the house of mercy

John 5:2-4 – 2 *Now there is in Jerusalem near the Sheep Gate a pool, which in Aramaic is called Bethesda and which is surrounded by five covered colonnades. 3 Here a great number of disabled people used to lie—the blind, the lame, the paralyzed—and they waited for the moving of the waters. 4 From time to time an angel of the Lord would come down and stir up the waters. The first one into the pool after each such disturbance would be cured of whatever disease he had* (NIV).

I want to talk to you today about a pool called Bethesda, or in Hebrew—the house of mercy. It was located near the temple, and it was there that God would mercifully heal the infirmed. Bethesda was surrounded by five covered porches where the sick and diseased gathered in hope of being healed.

Occasionally, an angel would come and stir the waters of the pool. The first person into the pool would be gloriously healed. I imagine it was a place of great expectation. When I read this story, I can't help but see a parallel between Bethesda and the church today. I believe God's intent is for every church to be a house of mercy. The church is meant to be a place where the lost and hurting can come to find refuge.

Unfortunately, many churches today have a shortage of God's presence. It has been a long time since the pool has been stirred, and because of this spiritual drought, expectations are low. One thing is certain, though. There is no shortage of people who need healing. The world is dying, and churches cannot afford to be on life support.

It is time to invite the presence of God back into our churches! Start praying and believing for Him to stir the waters in your local church. The sick and diseased are gathering. All they need now is a house of mercy where the healing power of God resides. Come stir the waters, Lord Jesus. Come!

Psalm 79:8 – *May your mercy come quickly to meet us, for we are in desperate need* (NIV).

132

the blind

John tells us there were three types of disabled people who gathered at the pool of Bethesda—the blind, the lame and the paralyzed. These people no doubt had great physical need, but I want to continue to draw from the parallel between Bethesda and the church. I believe the three physical disabilities mentioned here represent the grave spiritual condition of many people in the church today.

The first group referred to is the blind. There are countless Christians who are spiritually blind. They lead, and they are being led. Many are pastors, as well as patrons. They teach and attend Sunday school regularly, and some of them have even grown up in church. But those who have lost their vision all face this same glaring reality: If they have not fallen into a pit already, they will soon enough. Jesus said in **Matthew 15:14**, *"If a blind man leads a blind man, both will fall into a pit"* (NIV).

Let me first speak to those who are in leadership of some kind. Whether you are the boss of your company, the pastor over a ministry, or the man of your house, you have been entrusted by God to lead those He has placed under you. You cannot afford to wander aimlessly without seeking vision and direction from the Holy Spirit. Your decisions influence more than just your life.

I also want to address those who are under authority. It is your responsibility to submit to the vision of the leadership God has established over you. Once you think you know better than your boss, pastor or parents, you remove yourself from under God's covering. You become blind and vulnerable. I encourage you today to get into the pool. Ask God to give you vision and to help you support the vision of the leader He has set up over you.

the lame

John 5:3 – *Here a great number of disabled people used to lie—the blind, the lame, the paralyzed—and they waited for the moving of the waters* (NIV).

The second group of disabled people is the lame. To be lame means to be weak or inadequate. If somebody's leg or foot is lame, he or she walks with a limp or with great difficulty. A lame body part is still usable, but it does not have full range of motion. This condition usually results from some sort of defect or injury.

I am an avid sports fan. I enjoy watching certain sports, but I love playing most of them. I play anything from football to soccer to baseball, but basketball has always been my first love. I have tweaked my ankle numerous times while playing basketball. It's not uncommon to step on another player's foot and roll my ankle. I'll come up a little lame, but I can usually continue to play.

It is extremely awkward to play through pain, and it limits my range of motion. I am not as explosive with a bum ankle. I cannot jump as high, move as quickly or run as fast. It affects my shooting, as well as my ability to defend.

Every believer is a vital part of the body of Christ. **1 Corinthians 12:12** – *The body is a unit, though it is made up of many parts; and though all its parts are many, they form one body. So it is with Christ* (NIV). Unfortunately, the body of Christ is a lame version of what it is supposed to be. Many Christians are playing hurt. Some of their injuries are self-inflicted, but others were of no fault of their own. They continue to press on, but their efforts are inadequate. They are beat up, and the church is limping around as a result.

If you are one of the spiritually lame today, I believe the angel of the Lord is stirring the pool right where you are reading this. You may need to take a step back to find rest. Playing through an injury is admirable, but it can also cause more damage.

1 Corinthians 12:26 – *If one part suffers, every part suffers with it; if one part is honored, every part rejoices with it* (NIV).

the paralyzed

The third group of disabled people is the paralyzed. *Paralysis* is defined as a loss or impairment of voluntary movement in a body part, caused by injury or disease of the nerves, brain or spinal cord.

Paralysis is a far more severe condition than being lame. The lame can still be somewhat useful, but the paralyzed are helpless. They are characterized by the inability to act. If someone is paralyzed from the waist down, he or she cannot walk. Another common side effect of paralysis is the loss of feeling in the impaired body part(s).

There are many people in the church today who are spiritually paralyzed. They are imperative parts of the body of Christ, but they have had a complete stoppage of productivity. For whatever reason, they have been rendered ineffective and are unable to fulfill their function.

Some Christians have become so calloused they are unable to even feel the presence of God. Their lives were once meaningful and full of promise, but now they are hollow and empty. A lot of them have been victimized by friendly fire. The wounds from pastors and other church leaders have left them helpless. They have lost the desire to serve.

Others were crippled by their own folly. Mistakes were made, and they have suffered unnecessary paralysis. Whatever the cause, the body of Christ has many parts that are not functioning. When one part is paralyzed, the entire body suffers.

Are you paralyzed today? Maybe you were wounded and have given up. Perhaps you are the cause of you own misfortune. Either way, it is time to go for a swim at the house of mercy.

1 Corinthians 12:27 – *Now all of you together are Christ's body, and each one of you is a separate and necessary part of it* (NLT).

do you want to get well?

One of the men at Bethesda that day had been sick for thirty-eight years. The Bible is not specific as to what his condition was, but many scholars believe he suffered from palsy because he had apparently lost the use of at least one of his limbs.

His infirmity made it near impossible for him to get into the pool by himself, and he had no one to help him. Look at what he told Jesus in **John 5:7** – *"Sir,"* the invalid replied, *"I have no one to help me into the pool when the water is stirred. While I am trying to get in, someone else goes down ahead of me"* (NIV). What a heartbreaking predicament.

Perhaps today you find yourself in a similar situation. You have been sick for a long, long time. Maybe you have accepted your condition as permanent and have lost hope. Everyone has abandoned you, and there is no one around to offer you a helping hand. You have tried everything you know how to do, but nothing works. Watch what happens next in this story.

Jesus saw the invalid lying there and asked him, "Do you want to get well?" It was the opportunity of a lifetime! Thirty-eight years of being passed over, and finally someone was showing interest. And the person showing interest was the very One who was able to give him the healing he so desired.

As you read this, I believe Jesus is standing before you. Others have overlooked you, but He sees you now, just as He saw the invalid. Though there is no one to help you, He holds your healing in His hands. He asks you today, "Do you want to get well?" Don't allow your doubt to rob you of your spiritual health. Thank You, Jesus, for Your mercy. Answer *yes* today.

hallowed be Your name

Matthew 6:9 – *"This, then, is how you should pray: 'Our Father in heaven, hallowed be your name...'"* (NIV)

What is the number one reason why prayers are not effective? The vast majority of people do not know how to pray. There are many books, sermons and seminars dedicated to teaching Christians how to pray, but a lot of people remain frustrated with their prayer life. If you are searching for answers today, I believe the next few days will be very enlightening.

First of all, Jesus says, "This is how you should pray." Jesus is an expert on everything, so it is important to pay attention when He tells us how to do something. He first teaches to address God as our Father in heaven. Many people pray, but it seems like they don't know who they are praying to.

In my experience, when I call someone by name, it gets his or her attention. When we call on God, He stops whatever He's doing and focuses on us. He never ignores us. We mean so much to Him, and He longs to spend quality time with us. When you say His name, He is quick to listen.

After we get God's attention, it's time to praise Him. Hallowed be Your name! Begin telling God how awesome and holy He is. Lift up His name and magnify Him. There is nobody like Him, and He is worthy to be reverenced as such.

Prayers often become self-centered, but we need to make them all about Him. He is not egocentric, but He needs to know we value Him more than the answer to our prayers. This is where so many people go wrong. They treat God like He is Santa Claus. They just want something from Him. He is not going to give us what we want just because we are a good people.

I challenge you to change the focus of your prayers. If you tend to be selfish, begin honoring God at the beginning of your prayer time. Make *Him* the center of your conversation, not you.

Psalm 66:20 – *Praise be to God, who has not rejected my prayer or withheld his love from me!* (NIV)

Your kingdom come

Matthew 6:10 – *"...your kingdom come, your will be done on earth as it is in heaven"* (NIV).

After you get His attention and lift up His name, pray for His kingdom to come. By doing this, you give God permission to set up His kingdom and be your Lord. You abdicate the throne of your life and gladly establish Him as your first priority.

I cannot stress enough the importance of establishing God's kingdom in your life. There are a lot of people who pray for His will to be done, but they have not made Him their Lord. If He is not the Lord of your life, then *you* are. You can pray for God's will to be done, but at the end of the day, you are still going to do whatever it is *you* want to do.

God looks beyond our cleverly crafted words and sees the motives of our heart. I encourage you to allow Him to govern your life. When His will takes precedence over ours, our prayers will no longer be selfish. We will become kingdom-minded, and our intention will be to please Him. You will no longer pray self-seeking prayers, but you will glorify Him and ask Him to show you His will. Many prayers are left unanswered because they are contrary to God's plan.

If you pray, "Your kingdom come, Your will be done on earth as it is in heaven," you are asking Him to set up His heavenly kingdom on the earth. So what does His kingdom look like? **Romans 14:17** – *For the kingdom of God is not meat and drink; but righteousness, and peace, and joy in the Holy Ghost* (KJV).

Paul was saying here that God is not concerned about our religious rituals, or praying out of obligation. God's kingdom is one of order. Praying for His will to be done on earth as it is in heaven means purposing to live a life full of righteousness, peace and joy in the Holy Ghost as long as you live on earth.

1 Peter 4:2 – *And you won't spend the rest of your life chasing after evil desires, but you will be anxious to do the will of God* (NLT).

our daily bread

Jesus taught us in Matthew 6 how we *should* pray. He is not suggesting we pray like this; He's telling us to pray like this. It is important for us to understand that we should pray this way every day. Make this prayer the blueprint of your daily quality time with the Lord. When we pray His word according to His will, our prayers will always be effective.

Next Jesus instructed us to tell God to give us our daily bread. Scholars are unsure as to what the Greek meaning of *daily bread* is in this verse, but I want to share with you **Matthew 6:11** from The Power New Testament: *"You must now give us today the things necessary for our existence."*

Making this statement is a confession of our total reliance on God. We must learn to depend on Him to supply everything we need for our physical, as well as spiritual, livelihood. He must be your source in every area of your life.

In Matthew 4, the devil went to Jesus in the desert and tempted Him. Jesus was tired and hungry, and Satan looked to take advantage of Him while He was vulnerable. The devil suggested that Jesus turn some stones into bread for food, but Jesus rebuked him. **Matthew 4:4** – *Jesus answered, "It is written: 'Man does not live on bread alone, but on every word that comes from the mouth of God'"* (NIV).

Even Jesus, who could have supplied whatever He had need of, confessed His dependency on God. You and I cannot be self-sufficient and expect to be productive on a daily basis. The enemy will try to fool us into thinking we can do things on our own. Don't believe him.

Maybe today you are burned out. Perhaps you have been trying to do things in your own strength, and it has left you broken and defeated. If that's you, tell God you need your daily bread.

forgive to be forgiven

Matthew 6:12 – *"And forgive us our debts, as we also have forgiven (left, remitted, and let go of the debts, and have given up resentment against) our debtors"* (AMP).

I chose this translation because I want to make sure you understand this portion of the Lord's Prayer. "Forgive me, as I have forgiven," is a very bold statement. Basically, there is no forgiveness for you if you have unforgiveness in your heart toward someone else.

Forgiving someone is so much more than simply saying, "I forgive you for such and such." Many people voice their forgiveness, and then go on to bad mouth their offender constantly. That is not forgiveness at all!

I remember a time when someone in church leadership sinned against me. At the time, I was under this person's authority. I was very hurt by the situation, and it took me a long time to actually forgive the person. There were many times I would say I had forgiven, but I really had not. I even convinced myself that all was well.

Unfortunately, every time this person came up in conversation, I would find myself talking about what had been done to me. If this person walked into the room I was in, a replay of the offense would go through my mind. My heart was full of resentment, and my prayers were ineffective because of it.

The Bible is very clear in **Romans 3:23** – *For all have sinned and fall short of the glory of God* (NIV). You are going to need and ask for forgiveness multiple times over the course of your life. If you go to God asking for forgiveness with unforgiveness in your heart, you will walk away still burdened by your sin.

If you are reading this today and you have resentment toward someone who has sinned against you, forgive. Let go of the offense, and never speak of it again.

John 20:23 – *"If you forgive anyone his sins, they are forgiven; if you do not forgive them, they are not forgiven"* (NIV).

lead and deliver

Matthew 6:13 – *"And lead us not into temptation, but deliver us from the evil one, for yours is the kingdom and the power and the glory forever. Amen"* (NIV).

This is one of the most exciting parts of Jesus' teaching on prayer. After we have totally submitted ourselves to Him, He becomes our leader and our deliverer.

Most people fall into sin because they do not pray this on a daily basis. Temptation is inevitable, but much of it could be avoided if we would allow the Holy Spirit to lead us. In **John 16:13**, Jesus says the Spirit will guide us into all truth. Rather than leading you into temptation, God leads you to righteousness. **Psalm 23:3** – *He guides me in paths of righteousness for his name's sake* (NIV).

1 Corinthians 10:13 – *No temptation has seized you except what is common to man. And God is faithful; he will not let you be tempted beyond what you can bear. But when you are tempted, he will also provide a way out so that you can stand up under it* (NIV). He will not allow you to be tempted beyond what you can handle, but those who are self-led will stumble upon temptations they are not prepared to deal with. When that happens, sin is often the result. Ask Him today to steer you away from temptation.

Maybe you are already enslaved by sin. If so, cry out to God because He is your deliverer! He will set you free from the evil one. No matter what you have done, or how many times you have done it, He has come that you may have life.

I want to encourage you today to ask God to lead you. I know that it is sometimes difficult to admit you are lost and need directions, but stop and ask anyway. His desire is for you to walk paths of righteousness, not temptation. He never sets you up for failure, but if you do fall, He is your deliverer. Glory to God!

John 10:10 – *"The thief comes only to steal, and kill, and destroy; I came that they might have life, and might have it abundantly"* (NASB).

help in weakness

I don't know about you, but there are certainly times when I don't feel like praying. I've heard many people say, "I just don't have time to pray. My schedule is full, and there is no time for me to fit prayer in." That is a lame excuse. We make time for what is important to us, but that is not what I want to address today.

I want to talk to you about the times when you are completely worn out and don't feel like praying. I am talking about the times when you are so physically and emotionally drained that you cannot conjure up a coherent thought, let alone pray. It's in those moments when the last thing you want to do is pray, but it's also in those moments that you need to pray the most.

You may find yourself in that position today. If so, I have great news for you. The Holy Spirit helps us in our weakness. **2 Corinthians 12:9** – *But he said to me, "My grace is sufficient for you, for my power is made perfect in weakness"* (NIV). When we are weak, He is strong!

It is very easy to get discouraged in your prayer life when you are exhausted. The Holy Spirit will help us, but we have to be willing to put forth genuine effort. We also need to make time to rest. If you are tired all of the time and don't ever feel like spending time with the Lord, there is something wrong.

The Spirit also helps us by giving us wisdom. Ask Him to help you evaluate your schedule. If you will take practical steps to better manage your time, you will not always feel drained. As you become a better steward, He will sustain you so that you can pray. Take a moment to thank Him for helping you today.

John 14:16-17 – 16 *"And I will ask the Father, and He will give you another Helper, that He may be with you forever; 17 that is the Spirit of truth..."* (NASB).

what now?

Romans 8:26 – *In the same way, the Spirit helps us in our weakness. We do not know what we ought to pray for, but the Spirit himself intercedes for us with groans that words cannot express* (NIV).

The Spirit not only helps us when we are weak, He intercedes for us when we do not know how to pray. Have you ever set down to pray and had no idea what to say? Sure you have. We have all been there at one time or another.

I know there has been many times when my mind wanders from here to there and everywhere, making it virtually impossible for me to pray anything rational. And there are other times when I run out of things to pray in English. It's in those moments that the Holy Spirit, our Helper, will come to our rescue if we let Him.

In Acts 2, Luke describes the day when the Holy Spirit came at Pentecost. About 120 people were gathered together in prayer, and suddenly a violent wind filled the place. Tongues of fire appeared over the heads of each person present, and then read what happens. **Acts 2:4** – *And they were all filled with the Holy Spirit and began to speak with other tongues, as the Spirit gave them utterance* (NKJV).

One of the gifts the Holy Spirit gives to each believer is the ability to speak in an unknown tongue (**1 Corinthians 12:10**). You and I have our own, unique prayer language. It is a dialogue between us and God that only He can understand.

A lot of Christians debate over whether or not speaking in tongues is relevant today. I believe that it is, but it is not required. Your salvation does not depend on whether or not you speak in a heavenly language, but doing so is very beneficial and it enhances your prayer life.

If you have a hard time knowing what to pray, ask the Holy Spirit for the gift of tongues. If you already have it, use it.

Mark 16:17 – *"And these signs will accompany those who believe: In my name...they will speak in new tongues"* (NIV).

143

sucker punch

Romans 8:26 – *In the same way, the Spirit helps us in our weakness. We do not know what we ought to pray for, but the Spirit himself intercedes for us with groans that words cannot express* (NIV).

Have you ever been to a foreign country where you could not speak or understand the native language? If you have, then you know it can be rather confusing and sometimes irritating. It makes you feel left out.

Every year some members of our church staff and congregation go to a leadership conference in Buenos Aires, Argentina. A few years ago, my wife and I had the privilege of going together. It was a great time. I knew a little Spanish while we were there, but it didn't matter. The locals spoke some sort of Spanish/Italian mix. Needless to say, I was confused.

There were times that I would catch a word here or there that I knew, but they spoke so fast I would still be lost. I did not know if they were talking about God, the weather or if they were making fun of me. Many times I just felt awkward.

Paul teaches us in Romans that the Spirit enables us to pray with groans that words cannot express, or tongues. When you speak in your heavenly language God is the only person who knows what you are saying. You don't even know, and Satan certainly doesn't know.

Every time you open your mouth and pray in an unknown tongue, you are sucker punching the devil. He gets blindsided from every angle, and he is left dazed and confused. Satan hates it when we pray in tongues because he has no idea what is going on. He is defeated every single time!

When you pray in your native language, the enemy understands you and is somewhat able to guard himself. But when you pray in tongues, he is defenseless. Take that, devil!

Romans 16:20 – *And the God of peace will soon crush Satan under your feet* (NASB).

pray God's will

Romans 8:27 – *And he who searches our hearts knows the mind of the Spirit, because the Spirit intercedes for the saints in accordance with God's will* (NIV).

I believe there are many Christians who do not know what it means to pray God's will. Some don't know how to and others just don't want to. There are two ways we can pray in order to know we are always praying God's will. The first one is a benefit of praying in tongues. The Spirit intercedes for us in accordance with God's will.

Every time you pray in your heavenly language you are praying the will of God. Guaranteed. No questions asked. The Holy Spirit never misspeaks. His prayers are always on time, and they are always beneficial to the kingdom of God and your life. What an awesome and precious gift to have, especially when you pray for your enemies.

Jesus teaches in **Matthew 5:44**, *"But I tell you: Love your enemies and pray for those who persecute you"* (NIV). I will be the first one to admit that praying the will of God over my enemies is extremely difficult to do in my own words. I usually find myself wanting to pray for them to get what they deserve. I'm sure you know what I mean. But when you allow the Spirit to speak through you, you will bless and not curse.

It is also hard to know how to pray for those who are in leadership over us, especially if we do not agree with them. Our first inclination is to pray that they will do what it is we want them to. That is rebellion. God expects us to honor godly and ungodly authorities alike. If you struggle with what to pray over the leaders in your life, speak in tongues and your prayers will be honorable.

Make sure to pray in your heavenly language daily. Doing so not only guarantees you will pray His will, but it also feeds and edifies *your* spirit. God is so good!

Jude 20 – *But you, dear friends, build yourselves up in your most holy faith and pray in the Holy Spirit* (NIV).

pray the Word

The second way to know we are always praying the will of God is to pray His word. The Bible says that all Scripture is God-breathed (**2 Timothy 3:16**), but we have to pray His word according to His will. A lot of people pray God's word according to *their* will. If we do so, our prayers will still be fruitless.

Another version of **Isaiah 55:11** says that His word will accomplish what *He* desires and achieve the purpose for which *He* sent it (NIV). When your desires and purpose match His, you will pray His word and His will for your life will be accomplished.

Not only does your desire and purpose have to line up with His when you pray the Word, but the timing has to be right as well. Many times we will try to rush God with our prayers. When we know God's will and word concerning our lives, we tend to get overly excited. We then start pushing God to give us something we are not ready for. **Ecclesiastes 3:1** – *There is a time for everything, and a season for every activity under the sun* (NIV).

Also keep in mind **Psalm 18:30** – *As for God, his way is perfect; the word of the LORD is flawless* (NIV). His ways are perfect, but ours are faulty. His word is flawless, but our words are defective. When you pray your will or His word according to your will, you prove that you trust yourself more than God. This is evidence that you do not have confidence in Him.

There are so many Christians who do not know how to pray. It is heartbreaking to me. They aimlessly jabber and stumble over their words because they have a need to sound super-spiritual. Be encouraged today. Pray in the Spirit, and pray His word.

those who love Him

> **Romans 8:28** – *And we know that in all things God works for the good of those who love him, who have been called according to his purpose* (NIV).

This is one of the greatest promises of God. He works everything out for our good. He has the ability to take tragedy and turn it into triumph. He takes the most dismal of circumstances and makes them work out for our benefit. We can always count on God to keep His promises, but the fulfillment of His word in our lives is conditional.

This particular promise has two conditions. Number one, He will work all things for our good *if we love Him*. I'm not talking about the shallow appreciation that many Christians have adopted toward God. Many people are fascinated by what God can do for them, but they have no relationship with Him. Their "love" for God is based on feelings.

The word *love* in **Romans 8:28** is translated the Greek word *agape*. Agape is the unconditional love that God has for His creation, and He enables us to love Him and others in the same way. Agape love is unnatural. A person cannot love anyone unconditionally in his own strength. This kind of love only comes from Him.

Those who truly love God will continue to trust Him even if He does not work things for their good. Their love for Him is not limited based on what He does or does not do. **Matthew 14:15** – *"If you love me, you will obey what I command"* (NIV). Jesus teaches here that our love for Him is directly tied to obedience.

God will work all things together for your good if you will obey Him. Maybe today you are facing a personal tragedy. If so, align yourself with the word of God. Prove that you truly love Him, and then watch as He goes to work on your behalf.

> **Genesis 50:20** – *"You intended to harm me, but God intended it for good to accomplish what is now being done, the saving of many lives"* (NIV).

according to His purpose

Romans 8:28 – *And we know that in all things God works for the good of those who love him, who have been called according to his purpose* (NIV).

If God is going to work all things for our good, we have to first love Him unconditionally. Secondly, we have to be called according to *His* purpose. There are a lot of people believing God to work things out for them, but they live their lives however they want to. Doing so is a recipe for disappointment.

A lot of Christians are saddled by chronic disappointment, and much of it is self-inflicted. We set ourselves up for failure when we expect God to fulfill His promises outside of His purposes. It is delusional to think this way.

Many people willingly make foolish decisions that are contrary to God's will, yet they still expect God to work everything out for them. But when He does not bail them out, they become depressed and act as if He has let them down somehow. God is merciful, but He is not dumb. Sometimes *we* will have to climb out of the hole we dig ourselves into.

He has placed a high calling on each one of our lives. **Ephesians 1:11** – *In him we were also chosen, having been predestined according to the plan of him who works out everything in conformity with the purpose of his will* (NIV). Allow me to rewrite this verse so you can better understand: Each of us is chosen by God. His plan is for us to receive an eternal inheritance, and He works everything out according to His purpose.

Nowhere in the Bible does it say that God will rescue you when you do your own thing with good intentions. He is compassionate and saves people from themselves all the time, but you cannot expect God to come to your aid when you are not conformed to His purposes. Live according to His will today.

Psalm 138:8 – *The LORD will fulfill his purpose for me; your love, O LORD, endures forever—do not abandon the works of your hands* (NIV).

148

conform to Him

A lot of people hear the word *predestination* and immediately think God created certain people to go to heaven and others to go to hell. This is a false doctrine many people have adopted, and it could not be further from the truth.

The Bible scarcely mentions predestination. When it does, it teaches that we were chosen to be like Christ and to conform to the will of God. **Ephesians 1:4-5** – 4 *For he chose us in him before the creation of the world to be holy and blameless is his sight. In love* 5 *he predestined us to be adopted as his sons through Jesus Christ, in accordance with his pleasure and will* (NIV).

Before you ever came to know God, He knew you. And He predestined you to be just like His Son, Jesus. Your life is meant to be a reflection of Christ's character. His desire is for every person to be holy. The Bible does not say anything about God having predetermined who will go to heaven and who will not.

But there are many who will argue, "If God has infinite knowledge, then He knows who is going to heaven and who is not." It is true that God knows everything, but He has also given humanity free will. God does not control how a person thinks, talks or acts. God is not a micromanager, and He has not purposed for anyone to spend eternity separated from Him.

The problem is humankind has chosen to live outside the will of God, while blaming Him for their indiscretions. They will reason, "He created me this way. He knew I was going to act like this, so why does it matter?" This is a lie from the pit of hell.

You will be judged according to how you choose to live your life. I encourage you today to be the person God predestined you to be. Conform yourself to His likeness and follow His will.

2 Peter 3:9 – *He is patient with you, not wanting anyone to perish, but everyone to come to repentance* (NIV).

called

Paul taught that God has called us, but what exactly does this mean? I receive constant calls and text messages on my cell phone daily. It often seems like someone is always trying to get a hold of me. The nature of each contact varies. Some conversations are casual and others are serious. One person may want something from me, and the next may offer to help me. But one thing holds true: Every person who calls me is trying to get my attention for one reason or another.

The same is true when God calls you. He is simply trying to get your attention. He wants to connect with you and speak to you on a personal level. The purpose of the call is to teach you and point you in the direction your life is supposed to go. He wants to show you who you are in Christ, but you have to answer the phone.

Every time my cell phone rings, the name or number of the incoming caller is displayed on the screen. If the name of the person calling appears, it means I know who it is. Having their contact information was important to me so I entered it into my phone. If just the number appears, though, odds are I do not know the person at all, or I have not spoken to him in a long time. Either way, I make the decision each time my phone rings whether I am going to answer it or not.

The same is true when God calls you. Maybe you know the voice of God. You have engaged in many conversations, but you still need to decide whether you are going to answer Him. Perhaps you don't know God's voice today. He has been trying to reach you, but you don't recognize His number because it has been so long since you have talked. God is calling. He desires to give you direction and purpose. Will you answer Him?

1 Peter 2:21 – *To this you were called, because Christ suffered for you, leaving you an example, that you should follow in his steps* (NIV).

justified and glorified

Romans 8:30 – *And those he predestined, he also called; those he called, he also justified; those he justified; he also glorified* (NIV).

A lot of people feel unworthy to answer the call of God. They take a look at their lives and see a laundry list of character flaws and shortcomings. Maybe you find yourself facing this same dilemma today. God has called you to be great, but you feel inadequate.

The truth of the matter is when God calls us, we *are* inadequate. But when we get over ourselves and choose to answer Him, He is the one who makes us worthy to receive the call. Once we make ourselves available to Him, He justifies us and equips us to do His will. **Hebrews 13:20-21** – 20 *And now, may the God of peace, who brought again from the dead our Lord Jesus,* 21 *equip you with all you need for doing his will* (NLT).

You must come to understand that we are all sinners saved by grace. Your sin is no different from anyone else's. **Romans 3:23-24** – 23 *For all have sinned and fall short of the glory of God,* 24 *and are justified freely by his grace through the redemption that came by Christ Jesus* (NIV). We are all sinners, but we are all justified freely because of Christ's work on the cross. Are you grasping this? God is so good!

Romans 8:30 also tells us that we will be glorified. He is not talking about puffing up your ego here. It is a promise of eternal glorification! Those who fulfill the purpose God has predestined for them will inherit eternal life. What an awesome promise.

I want to encourage you today. Your life is very significant to the kingdom of God. You were created to impact the world around you with the Gospel of Jesus Christ. Say, "Yes," to Him right now. You are worthy of the call you have received!

2 Thessalonians 1:12 – *We pray this so that the name of our Lord Jesus may be glorified in you, and you in him, according to the grace of our God and the Lord Jesus Christ* (NIV).

get some rest

Mark 6:31-32 – 31 *He said to them, "Come with me by yourselves to a quiet place and get some rest." 32 So they went away by themselves in a boat to a solitary place* (NIV).

I can't overstress the importance of getting an appropriate amount of rest. Nobody is superhuman, and everyone needs to take care of themselves. It sounds easy enough, but you'd be surprised how many people don't know how to rest. Perhaps you're one of them.

I want to highlight a few points from the above passage about the importance of resting. Let me first bring you up to speed on this story. Jesus sent out the disciples at the beginning of Mark 6, and they went about doing the work of the Lord. They preached that people should repent, drove out demons and healed the sick. The disciples then returned to Jesus and reported to Him all they had done and taught. Then one day so many people had come and gone that they all forgot to eat.

The first point I want to make is that even Jesus realized the significance of rest. He and the disciples had been working extremely hard, and Jesus instructed them to come with Him to get some rest. Jesus understood the value of resting, so He stopped everything and they went.

In order to rest properly, you have to first understand how important it is. Many people don't rest because they think its unnecessary or a waste of time. Some people decide to rest, but they can't because they just think about all the things that still need to be done. If you think about what needs to be done long enough, you'll eventually start trying to accomplish it.

You will never be fully restored with this kind of a mentality. God does not honor foolishness. Jesus expects us to rest because it's important to Him, and it's necessary to you. He took time for Himself, and today He's telling you to do the same.

Psalm 91:1 – *He who dwells in the shelter of the Most High will rest in the shadow of the Almighty* (NIV).

come with Me

> **Mark 6:31-32** – 31 *He said to them, "Come with me by yourselves to a quiet place and get some rest."* 32 *So they went away by themselves in a boat to a solitary place* (NIV).

Notice the first three words out of Jesus' mouth when He instructed the disciples to rest. He said, "Come with Me." There is no better place to find rest than in the presence of God. It's in His presence where we will be restored completely. There are a couple more lessons to be learned from this passage. I'll talk about one today and the second tomorrow.

I first want to talk about the importance of finding rest for our souls. Your soul is your mind, will and emotions. As I briefly touched on yesterday, there are some people who cannot turn their minds off. They are always thinking about something, and the constant stress on their mind is very draining.

There are also those who allow their emotions to get the best of them. They are emotional basket cases, and it leaves them lifeless. You have to find rest for your soul. A lot of people don't think about resting their souls because they don't know how to, or they don't know they're supposed to. But it's absolutely vital.

Jesus gives us the secret to resting our souls. We have to go with Him. **Psalm 62:1** – *My soul finds rest in God alone; my salvation comes from him* (NIV).

Maybe today your soul needs rest. Perhaps you've been searching, or maybe you didn't even know to look. The Bible says that rest for your soul is found in God alone. Be encouraged. The Lord has His hand extended to you today, and He's saying, "Come with Me."

He has the ability to heal your emotions and set your mind at ease. Perhaps you've lacked energy and have been unable to focus for a long time. I believe God is going to restore you today. Fall into His arms and find the rest you've been searching for.

> **Psalm 62:5** – *Find rest, O my soul, in God alone; my hope comes from him* (NIV).

a quiet, solitary place

Your soul needs rest and so does your physical body. The reason I talked about the importance of resting your soul first is because you will never be able to rest physically until your soul is at peace. If there's any uneasiness in your mind, will or emotions, your physical body cannot rest. It just won't happen for you.

Stress is one of the main causes of sickness, and even terminal illness. When your soul isn't rested, your body breaks down. So once we find rest for our souls in the presence of God, we can finally get some physical rest.

Jesus instructed the disciples to come with Him, but they didn't go just anywhere. Jesus told them to go to a quiet place by themselves. So they got in a boat and went to a solitary place. Another word for *solitary* is *private*. Jesus realized that He and the disciples had to get away from everything and everybody if they were going to be able to rest their minds and recoup physically.

You and I are no different. Many people never feel rested because they fail to separate themselves from the source of their mental or physical stress. Everyone needs a place to retreat to. Go be by yourself, or hang out with your family in the privacy of your home. Isolate yourself from unrest and chaos.

If work is wearing on you, turn your cell phone off and check messages later. If your family is driving you crazy, ask your spouse to watch the kids for a few hours and get away. It's okay. When you go on vacation, actually *go* on vacation.

Working, working, working at the expense of your mental and physical well-being doesn't make you responsible. It's actually very irresponsible. If you are physically drained today, I encourage you to escape to a quiet, solitary place.

you can't have one without the other

As I briefly mentioned yesterday, overworking is irresponsible. If you work, you need to rest. If you don't rest, you'll burn out. If you burn out, you won't be able to work. God set an example for us to follow from the very beginning. After He created the heavens and the earth, He rested.

My wife Heidi and I have been in full-time ministry for nearly eight years now, and we've learned that the words *ministry* and *work* are interchangeable. One of things we love to do the most is reach out to our surrounding community. We've planned, coordinated, worked and cleaned up outreaches to hundreds of people. A lot of time and effort goes into every event, but they are very rewarding.

There's no greater feeling than knowing you've made a positive impact in someone's life. Witnessing a person give his life to Christ, makes all the work worthwhile. You feel a great sense of achievement when you accomplish something you set out to do. Why? God rewards those who work.

Rest is one of those rewards. Resting is an opportunity to reflect on the work you've just finished, and it's preparation for the work yet to be done. This principle is the same no matter what your job is.

However, if you don't work, you will never feel rested. Work and rest go hand in hand. Laziness is not rewarded. Have you ever known a lazy person? Perhaps *you* are lazy. Lazy people are often tired and rarely feel like doing anything.

If you're not a worker, you need to become one. If you do work, God offers rest to you as a reward. Enter into it today. Take time to reflect on your achievements and prepare for what's next.

lazy people

God rewards and gives rest to those who work hard, but He does not reward laziness. You'd be surprised how many lazy people there are in the body of Christ (or maybe you wouldn't be). Many people have their own definition of laziness and their own way of identifying lazy people, but I want to talk about the lazy people mentioned in the above verse.

Most people typically label a person who doesn't do much of anything as being lazy. While this is true, laziness is not limited to this definition alone. **Proverbs 12:27** teaches that lazy people will hunt and catch a wild animal, but they won't cook it. They will actually put forth the effort to trap an animal, but they don't take the steps necessary to eat it.

Lazy people are often starters, but they are rarely finishers. Think about it. Many people are excited at the onset of certain projects. The thrill of a new challenge is intriguing, and they begin the process eager to reach the finish line. They have the greatest of intentions, and they may even meet some of their goals, but they always stop short of the end.

Proverbs 10:4 – *Lazy hands make a man poor, but diligent hands bring wealth* (NIV). The Bible teaches that laziness will make us poor. If you're lazy, you'll always have need of something, and what you do have will never be fully utilized. Nobody truly desires to constantly come up short of his potential.

The opposite of laziness is diligence. Diligence brings wealth, and the diligent make use of everything they have. They take nothing for granted, and they finish what they start. **Proverbs 21:5** teaches that diligence leads to profit. If you are an unmotivated person today, the only way to overcome your laziness is to become diligent in everything. Be a finisher!

> **Mark 16:15-16** – 15 *And He said to them, "Go into all the world and preach the gospel to every creature.* 16 *He who believes and is baptized will be saved; but he who does not believe will be condemned"* (NKJV).

Jesus ministered full-time on the earth for three and a half years. He went about preaching, teaching and healing the sick, but He saved arguably His most important lesson for last. His final teaching was direct and challenging. The disciples eagerly anticipated every word, and what they got was The Great Commission. I'm going to spend the next few days discussing Jesus' final words. May we never be the same!

The moment you accepted Jesus Christ as your Savior and Lord you were commissioned. Each of us has been given the task of taking the Gospel into the world. Nobody is exempt, and I believe it is sinful not to fulfill this command.

Jesus told the disciples to go. He did not suggest to them, "Oh yeah, if you guys get some free time, please preach the Gospel to the lost. But if not, it's all good." No, Jesus made His point very clear, and He expected them to do what He said. Imagine if Peter stood up and said, "I don't think so, Jesus. That's just not important to me. I've got better things to do." It probably would not have gone over too well.

Sadly, there are many Christians with this kind of a mindset. They verbally acknowledge the commission they've received, but they deny it by their actions. When Jesus brought this message to His disciples, they had a decision to make. Go, or sit around and wait for the lost to come. We must make the decision to go because the lost are not lining up outside the church.

You may not be able to physically travel the world and reach the globe for Jesus, but you can pray for the lost and affect the world around you. Humanity is literally dying to know Him.

> **Habakkuk 2:14** – *For the earth will be filled with the knowledge of the glory of the LORD, as the waters cover the sea* (NIV).

preach the Gospel

> **Mark 16:15-16** – 15 *And He said to them, "Go into all the world and preach the gospel to every creature.* 16 *He who believes and is baptized will be saved; but he who does not believe will be condemned"* (NKJV).

After you decide to go into all the world, you cannot afford to just float aimlessly. You have to be armed with a purpose, and that purpose is to preach the Gospel to everyone. There's three points I want to bring out from this portion of Scripture.

First of all, we are to preach. There are two different ways to preach: with your mouth and with your actions. A lot of people hear the word *preach*, and immediately withdraw themselves from the equation. You do not have to be an eloquent speaker to be an instrument of God. Just ask Moses.

Sometimes you won't even say a word. Your actions will either be your biggest ally or your biggest liability when sharing the good news. If your actions don't line up with your words, most people are not going to care what you have to say. Your actions should confirm your words and vice versa.

Secondly, the Gospel is what we should be preaching. Just so there's no confusion...the Gospel is the life of Jesus, His death and resurrection. That's it. There's no adding to it, or subtracting from it. We need to teach the lost about the redemptive work Jesus did on the cross in order to bring them salvation. Then we must show them how to live lives full of godly character.

Next, we must preach the Gospel to *everyone*. We cannot be selective. You must be willing to take the good news to every person who does not know Jesus. Don't limit yourself and reach out to only those you feel comfortable with. Every person is important to Him, so they should all be important to us as well. Ask Him to give you a heart for the lost today. May your words and actions reflect the life of Jesus Christ to those in need.

> **2 Corinthians 4:5** – *We do not preach ourselves, but Jesus Christ as Lord, and ourselves as your servants for Jesus' sake* (NIV).

believe it or not

> **Mark 16:15-16** – 15 *And He said to them, "Go into all the world and preach the gospel to every creature.* 16 *He who believes and is baptized will be saved; but he who does not believe will be condemned"* (NKJV).

Our duty is to preach the life, death and resurrection of Jesus Christ to all creation. Once you're obedient to God's commission, Jesus teaches that the lost will either believe it, or they won't. That's why it is so important that Christians share the whole truth and nothing but the truth.

We are responsible for how we portray the Gospel to the unsaved. The word of God is uncompromising. There is only one way to eternal life, and His name is Jesus Christ. **John 14:6** – *Jesus answered, "I am the way and the truth and the life. No one comes to the Father except through me"* (NIV). They will either believe Jesus is who He says He is, or they won't.

So we must teach people what it means to truly believe. Believing is more than verbal or mental assent. The word *believe* in **Mark 16:16** is translated the Greek word meaning to entrust your spiritual well-being to Christ.

To truly believe in Jesus means to devote your entire life to Him. It means laying down your way of life and patterning yourself after His. A mark of believing is obedience. A person who professes to know Jesus, but lives in disobedience to His word, will not be saved. Unfortunately, many new Christians are not taught this principle.

God created every person to one day spend eternity in fellowship with Him. Acknowledging that Jesus Christ is the Son of God is easy, but following in His footsteps is not. His grace has made it possible for each of us to inherit eternal life, but accessing this promise hinges on our obedience.

> **John 6:47** – *"I tell you the truth, he who believes has everlasting life"* (NIV).

those who believe

> **Mark 16:17-18** – 17 *"And these signs will accompany those who believe: In my name they will drive out demons; they will speak in new tongues; 18 they will pick up snakes with their hands; and when they drink deadly poison, it will not hurt them at all; they will place their hands on sick people, and they will get well"* (NIV).

A lot times this part of The Great Commission gets left out. When people get saved and come to know Jesus, they're often not taught what to do next. You may be one of those people. Perhaps you've been saved for a long time, or maybe just a short while, but no one has ever taken the time to explain to you the rest of Jesus' teaching here.

People who come into relationship with Jesus generally know they will inherit eternal life someday. Heaven is the most talked about perk of giving your heart to God, but there are many other benefits that accompany salvation.

I want to take the next few days to talk about the authority of the believer. The moment you asked Jesus to be the Lord of your life, you were endued with power from on high! There are many Christians who mope around defeated because they don't understand the authority God has invested in them.

The Bible promises that we will face trials and tribulations. Serving God is not for the faint of heart, but He has enabled us to be victorious. **Romans 8:37** – *In all these things we are more than conquerors through him who loved us* (NIV). You are not just a conqueror. You are *more* than a conqueror! What does this mean?

Imagine Nation 1 attacks and conquers Nation 2. Nation 2 is completely dismantled, but they begin to rebuild. Eventually, Nation 2 rises to power again and turns the tables on Nation 1, and the two go back and forth. Maybe this scenario mirrors your battle with the devil and the difficulties you face. You pray, fight and think you're victorious, but you eventually get overtaken again.

Here's where the authority of the believer comes in. When you realize that God has made you *more* than a conqueror, you will not only defeat your adversary, you will have dominion over him.

160

drive out demons

> **Mark 16:17** – *"And these signs will accompany those who believe: In my name they will drive out demons..."* (NIV)

The first thing Jesus teaches us about the authority of the believer is that we will drive out demons in His name. But we must understand how and when to walk in our authority. I want to share with you a story concerning this in Acts 19.

God had been doing some wonderful miracles through Paul, and certain Jews began trying to invoke the name of Jesus over the demon-possessed. The seven sons of Sceva were doing this. **Acts 19:13** – *They would say, "In the name of Jesus, whom Paul preaches, I command you to come out"* (NIV). The problem was these guys had no relationship with Jesus, and they were trying to bring attention to themselves.

Any authority we have is in the name of Jesus, so we must be careful not to misuse His name. The authority we walk in is not for self-promotion or to bring glory to ourselves. Unfortunately, there are many people who try to exploit the power of God. You and I cannot do anything supernatural in our own strength, but that does not give us the right to use *His* strength inappropriately.

Look at what happens to the seven sons of Sceva. They tried to cast a devil out of a certain man, and the evil spirit answered them, "Who are you?" *Then the man who had the evil spirit jumped on them and overpowered them all. He gave them such a beating that they ran out of the house naked and bleeding* (**Acts 19:16**).

Playing games with the supernatural is a recipe for disaster. We have to use discernment when driving out demons, and we must do so to bring glory to God. Walk in the authority God has given you, but do so wisely.

> **Ephesians 6:12** – *For our struggle is not against flesh and blood, but against the rulers, against the powers, against the world forces of this darkness, against the spiritual forces of wickedness in the heavenly places* (NASB).

speak in new tongues

Mark 16:17 – *"And these signs will accompany those who believe: In my name…they will speak in new tongues"* (NIV).

There's a lot of debate between the various religious establishments about whether or not speaking in tongues is relevant today. While speaking in a heavenly language is not required for salvation, I do believe that it is beneficial and available to every believer.

Jesus said that speaking in tongues is a sign that accompanies those who *believe*. If you don't believe that speaking in tongues is real, then you will never speak in tongues. It's that simple. People can debate all day long about its relevance, but it all comes down to whether you believe or not.

Speaking in a heavenly language is the second part of the authority of the believer. If you choose not to speak it tongues, it doesn't make you a sinner, but it will cause you to miss out on a valuable part of the authority He's given you.

Your prayers become more powerful when you receive the gift of speaking in tongues. When you pray in the Spirit (your heavenly language), you have great authority because you are praying the will of God. **Romans 8:27** – *And he who searches our hearts knows the mind of the Spirit, because the Spirit intercedes for the saints in accordance with God's will* (NIV).

Tongues is also valuable because it serves as a sign to the lost. **1 Corinthians 14:22** – *Tongues, then, are a sign, not for believers but for unbelievers* (NIV). Speaking in tongues is a wonder. It's a gift that only God can give, and unbelievers recognize it as such. There is power in your heavenly language!

If you don't believe in speaking in tongues, I encourage you to pursue this gift of the Spirit. What do you have to lose? Maybe you've believed for a while and are yet to receive this gift. Keep believing. Aim to walk in the fullness of His authority.

1 Corinthians 12:11 – *All these are the work of one and the same Spirit, and he gives them to each one, just as he determines* (NIV).

pick up snakes

A couple years ago, we had a teenager in our youth group who loved to handle snakes. He had no formal training; he was just fearless. He would be driving along, see a snake slithering across the road, pull over and go after it. He'd pick it up, and it didn't matter if it was poisonous or not.

This type of reckless behavior is not what Jesus is promoting here, and I'm not suggesting that you go around picking fights with snakes (though I have picked up a 4-foot mud snake before). Jesus is simply saying that if we walk in His authority, He will keep us from being harmed. There's actually an instance of this recorded in Acts.

In Acts 28, Paul arrived on the island of Malta. It was cold and rainy, and the natives welcomed him with open arms. They built a fire, and as Paul was adding more wood to it, a venomous snake fastened itself onto his hand. The natives were certain Paul was going to fall over dead, but he didn't. Read what happened. **Acts 28:5** – *But Paul shook the snake off into the fire and suffered no ill effects* (NIV).

Paul probably should have died, and the islanders obviously thought he was going to, but he was protected. Why? He had great faith, and he walked in divine authority. Protection is one of the greatest promises offered to those who believe.

You may not physically have a viper latched on to your hand, but maybe you are under attack today. The enemy of your soul is a snake, and sometimes it may seem like he's coming at you from all angles. Perhaps those you're in relationship with are slandering you, or maybe you're suffering physically. No matter what you are facing today, take authority in Jesus' name!

2 Thessalonians 3:3 – *But the Lord is faithful, and he will strengthen and protect you from the evil one* (NIV).

drink deadly poison

When Jesus was commissioning His disciples, this was no doubt something He knew they would face. I imagine they were faced with persecution of all sorts, and being poisoned was likely one of the tactics used by their enemies. He basically said to them, "No matter how your opposition tries to dispose of you, in My name they will not be able to hurt you at all." What an amazing promise!

I want to share with you something that I believe the Holy Spirit wants to say here to *you* about your authority as a believer. Your enemy, the devil, wants to kill you. His mission is to destroy mankind, and he will use any means possible to do so. One of the main devices he uses, especially against Christians, are the words of others. Words can bring life, but they can also be poisonous.

You may know exactly what I'm talking about today. Maybe you're someone who has had to drink your fair share of poison. Hurtful words have been spoken against you, and you've just had to choke them down.

Unfortunately, the most harmful words sometimes come from those closest to us. Maybe you've been hurt by the words of your parents, or maybe it's your children that have spoken against you. Perhaps your boss or coworkers have mistreated you. You may have even been the subject of your pastor's misguided words. I have no idea what forms of poison you've had to drink, but one thing is certain. If poison stays in your system long enough, it will eventually kill you.

But I have great news for you today. You have authority over the abusive things people have spoken over you and will speak over you in the future. You will still have to drink your fair share of poison, but Jesus promises that it will not hurt you at all!

sick people will get well

Everyone has been called by God to heal the sick. There are just not very many Christians who actually believe God can work through them in that way. For some reason, many people think God reserves healing ministries for an elite group of people. This couldn't be further from the truth.

The Spirit of God gives gifts of healing to people just as He determines (1 Corinthians 12). We don't decide who gets the gifts of healing. He does. And He gives them to those who desire them the most, those who are the most desperate. Anyone can lay hands on the sick and see them recover because Jesus is the one who does the work anyway.

I want to challenge your faith today. You may be the instrument God is waiting to work through to bring healing to someone. Don't allow your unbelief to rob you of such an awesome purpose.

I also want to encourage your faith today. If you will be obedient to step out and lay hands on someone, the Bible says they *will* get well. It's not a matter of if; it's a matter of when. Jesus cannot lie. If people are not being healed, it's not because Jesus is laying down on the job.

Allow your faith to be stretched as well! Not only will we lay hands on the physically sick and see them recover, but I believe we will lay hands on the emotionally and spiritually sick and see them recover! Don't allow your lack of faith to limit what God can do through you. We have great authority in Jesus' name.

You come across many people every day who are suffering from some type of sickness. Be bold. Step out. Lay hands on them, and believe that God can do what He says He can do.

Matthew 12:15 – *Many followed him, and he healed all their sick* (NIV).

even greater things

John 14:12 – *"I tell you the truth, anyone who has faith in me will do what I have been doing. He will do even greater things than these, because I am going to the Father"* (NIV).

I'm not sure it's possible for the human mind to grasp what Jesus said here, but I'm going to do my best to explain it. And I do know Jesus says what He means and means what He says.

I'd be floored if the greatest athlete of all-time walked up to me and said, "I am the most gifted athlete ever. I have accomplished and won more than anyone else ever to play any sport. Not only will you do what I've done, but you will surpass my greatness. And I will be there cheering you on and making sure you rise above me." Can you imagine how the disciples must have felt as Jesus promised they'd be greater than Him? Jaws must have been hitting the floor!

There are a few things we need to understand from this verse. First of all, Jesus did some pretty incredible things during His earthly ministry. He gave sight to the blind, opened deaf ears, enabled the mute to speak and He even raised the dead. Not to mention, He led countless people to salvation. He has given us the authority to do the same things, but that's not all.

He promises that if anyone has faith in Him, they will do even *greater* things. Wow! Jesus basically said, "What I did was great, but it's only the beginning compared to what God wants to do through you." Glory to God! I believe another part of this promise is that we will see greater multitudes of the lost impacted and changed by the power of God. Are you excited yet?

Lastly, Jesus proved His selfless nature. He was not threatened by the success of the disciples; He celebrated it. In fact, He has taken on the role of a cheerleader, constantly going to the Father on our behalf. Jesus is your biggest fan. I pray that your faith has increased. Walk in your God-given authority.

John 14:13 – *"And I will do whatever you ask in my name, so that the Son may bring glory to the Father"* (NIV).

out with the old

Ephesians 4:22 – *You were taught, with regard to your former way of life, to put off your old self, which is being corrupted by its deceitful desires* (NIV).

What does it mean to put off your old self, and why is it so important to do so? These are two questions I want to answer today. This a relatively familiar verse, but I pray for God to show you something new and fresh. Just because a passage of Scripture is familiar doesn't mean it's irrelevant.

To put off your old self means to do an about-face. When we come into relationship with Jesus, we are supposed to completely abandon our old lifestyle and walk in the opposite direction. It means cutting out sin and the things that cause us to sin. And you do so because you want to be more like Christ, not because someone tells you to.

You may be saying, "But I was a good person before I got saved. How would doing the exact opposite of good things be beneficial?" When you surrender yourself to Jesus, you don't quit doing what's right. You simply do what's right with different motives. Begin doing everything as unto the Lord. **1 Corinthians 10:31** – *So then, whether you eat or drink, or whatever you may do, do all for the honor and glory of God* (AMP).

It's important to put off your old self because your flesh is self-destructive. When you are not in right standing with God, your life is corrupted by its *own* deceitful desires. A life minus God will eventually kill itself off.

Please understand that we will never be perfect. Even after you put off your old lifestyle and purpose to do what's right, you will falter. As you mature in your faith, though, you will look more like Christ and less like your old self. You will no longer be a danger to yourself. I challenge you today to take a survey of your life. Declare over yourself, "Out with the old!"

Romans 6:6 – *For we know that our old self was crucified with him so that the body of sin might be done away with* (NIV).

in with the new

Ephesians 4:23-24 – 23 *To be made new in the attitude of your minds;* 24 *and to put on the new self, created to be like God in true righteousness and holiness* (NIV).

I believe countless Christians abandon their faith because they fail to put these verses into practice. Many people get saved and even put off their old selves, but they wind up returning to their former lifestyle. Maybe your life has followed a similar pattern. My prayer is for you to break that cycle today.

After we separate ourselves from our old lifestyle, Paul taught that we need to be made new in the attitude of our minds. This means that we have to renew our manner, feelings, position and outlook. Our perspective has to change, or there will be no lasting change in our lives.

How do we renew the attitude of our minds? Purpose to have the same attitude as Jesus. **Philippians 2:5** – *Your attitude should be the same as that of Christ Jesus* (NIV). Jesus was not in a competition with the Father, nor did He lobby for His own will to be done. The Bible says that Jesus made Himself nothing and took on the nature of a servant. He was humble and obedient, and our attitude should reflect His (see **Philippians 2:6-8**).

Once the attitude of your mind is renewed, you have to put on the new self. This truth is where so many people miss it. They take off their old selves, but they never put on the new. They walk around exposed and vulnerable, and eventually they cover themselves with what's familiar. The old self.

If you've been caught exposed today, I encourage you to put on the new self. You were created to be like God and to live in true righteousness and holiness. Allow your mindset to be altered. Humble yourself and become a servant to His kingdom. Make the declaration, "In with the new!" Glory to God!

Romans 13:14 – *Rather, clothe yourselves with the Lord Jesus Christ, and do not think about how to gratify the desires of the sinful nature* (NIV).

put off falsehood

Ephesians 4:25 – *Therefore each of you must put off falsehood and speak truthfully to his neighbor, for we are all members of one body* (NIV).

So you've put on the new self. Congratulations! Now comes everyday life. Even though we've declared, "Out with the old, in with the new," we still have to make the daily decision to live as Jesus did. Life does not get easier once we decide to surrender to Him. We still face the same set of choices and temptations, but now we have godly perspective and new purpose.

The Bible goes on to teach that we must put off falsehood and speak truthfully to our neighbor. The neighbors Paul refers to in this verse are our Christian brothers and sisters. Envy is far too prevalent in the church, and it causes many people to portray themselves as someone they're not. Why? It's usually for one of two reasons. They either want to be accepted, or they want to appear superior.

Many people, who have faced constant rejection, will try to fit in by masking who they really are. They blame themselves for being rejected, and so they attempt to cover up what they feel to be the source of that rejection by being someone they're not.

Maybe you find yourself doing this today. I want to encourage you to put off all falsehood, and be truthful with your church family. The church *should* accept you as you are, and if they don't, God will deal with them. But He does not expect you to reinvent yourself. He already approves of you.

Also, most people are not going to pretend to be someone less than who they actually are. They're going to portray themselves as being someone greater than who they really are. My boys always pretend to be superheroes; they never pretend to be losers. Don't be so competitive that you lose sight of who you are. Life is not about "one-upping" your brother or sister.

Galatians 6:3 – *If anyone thinks he is something when he is nothing, he deceives himself* (NIV).

in your anger

I know I've already devoted two whole weeks to anger, but I believe there is more to be said. The above verses offer three truths that are important for us to understand as we walk clothed in the new self.

First of all, anger is not a sin, and just because you've made the decision to be a new person doesn't mean you will never get angry again. Anger becomes sin because of a lack of self-control. We cannot allow our emotions to govern our lives, whether they're good or bad. When something or someone angers you, you need to step back, take a deep breath, and ask the Holy Spirit to help you produce the fruit of self-control. Don't just react.

Secondly, don't let the sun go down while you're angry. This is a point to be taken literally. If you are mad at somebody today, do not lay your head to pillow tonight until you make it right. Countless people have restless nights and go sleepless because of the ill feelings they hold toward others. If you don't discipline yourself and begin dealing immediately with your anger, bitterness and resentment is all you will ever know.

Lastly, do not give the devil a foothold. There are many ways we can give Satan a foothold in our lives, and one of them is through our anger. A *foothold* is a place or support for the feet; a place where a person may stand or walk securely. When you give into your anger and allow it to rule over you, the devil literally has free access to trample all over you.

Maybe today anger is getting the best of you. Perhaps you have broken relationships as a result of uncontrolled anger, and you recognize that the enemy has been given a platform in your life. Do not be discouraged. Today is the day to make it right.

do something useful

Ephesians 4:28 – *He who has been stealing must steal no longer, but must work, doing something useful with his own hands, that he may have something to share with those in need* (NIV).

Stealing means to take something that doesn't belong to you. It's in our human nature to want things we are not supposed to have. I knew a guy who would show absolutely no interest in a certain girl, but as soon as she started dating someone else, he would begin to pursue her.

Theft is more common among Christians than one might think. While most Christians don't rob convenience stores or swipe money out of the offering plate, many do struggle in less noticeable areas. Many believers misuse God's time and resources, which is a form of theft. Withholding your tithe is equivalent to robbing God (**Malachi 3:8**). A lot of Christians covet the positions and possessions of others. If you struggle in one of these areas, Paul gives a simple solution. Steal no longer!

I love the next part of this verse. We must work instead of stealing, and we must do something useful with our own hands. It's so important to pay careful attention to the way the Bible words certain phrases. We need to work and produce something with our *own* hands. We cannot afford to rely on other people to do the work.

If you are in leadership, you need to pay special attention to this. Don't ever allow yourself to come to a place where you feel certain tasks are beneath you. If you do, it won't take long for you to become idle and fruitless.

Make it a point in your life to be productive. If you purpose to be useful, then you will have something to share with those who are in need. Somebody is relying on your level of productivity. I want to challenge you today to work hard because idle people have nothing to offer.

Philemon 11 – *Formerly he was useless to you, but now he has become useful both to you and to me* (NIV).

unwholesome talk

Ephesians 4:29 – *Do not let any unwholesome talk come out of your mouths, but only what is helpful for building others up according to their needs, that it may benefit those who listen* (NIV).

I want to bring your attention to the first three words of this verse: *Do not let.* You are the only person that can control what comes out of your mouth. I understand that no man can tame the tongue, but the Holy Spirit *does* help us to think before we speak. But He does not press a mute button when we are about to say something stupid.

As I mentioned on a previous day, we must partner with the Holy Spirit in order to tame our tongues. His desire is for you to produce the fruit of the Spirit when you face adversity, but you still make the decision as to how you're going to react.

Even the godliest people will sometimes allow unwholesome talk to come out of their mouths. Why? Because they don't stop their unpleasant thoughts before they become words. We are all a part of the human race, and as long as we are still living on planet earth, there will be times that you and I think hurtful and derogatory thoughts about others.

The problem is we tend to meditate on those thoughts and allow them to spill out of our mouths. We must learn to take unhealthy thoughts captive immediately. The only person your thoughts can hurt is you, but unwholesome talk will bring down everyone who hears it.

I want to encourage you today to evaluate your speech. How would those closest to you describe their conversations with you? Would they say you're uplifting, or difficult to be around? Do you tear others down, or is your speech edifying? What comes out of your mouth when nobody is listening? Ask the Holy Spirit to help you, and choose not to engage in unwholesome talk.

Psalm 19:14 – *May the words of my mouth and the meditation of my heart be pleasing in your sight, O LORD* (NIV).

build others up

> **Ephesians 4:29** – *Do not let any unwholesome talk come out of your mouths, but only what is helpful for building others up according to their needs, that it may benefit those who listen* (NIV).

Okay, so you've made the decision not to let any unwholesome talk come out of your mouth. That's awesome! Now, since you will speak again at some point, I want to discuss what should come out of your mouth.

The Bible says we should say only what is helpful for building others up. There are some people who could make a pretty good living if tearing down others was a paying job. The vast majority of people can think of plenty of negative things to say, but it's often difficult for them to come up with anything nice. Ask yourself this question, "Is it hard for me to say something positive about certain people?" If you answered *yes*, ask the Holy Spirit to help you see people the way He sees them.

After you've purposed to speak positively about others, pay careful attention to how the rest of this verse reads. We are to build others up according to *their needs*. Notice it does not say we are to build others up according to *what we think they need*.

This is difficult for people who have the need to "fix" others. Many people are masters at pointing out what they think is wrong with someone else, and then they try to tell the person how to fix his problem. Doing so does not help build the person up. In fact, handling people this way can do quite the opposite.

Make it a point to be sensitive to the needs of those around you, and ask the Holy Spirit to help you raise them up. Your words should benefit those who listen, even if what you say doesn't bring you any benefit personally. I pray you will not take this challenge lightly. As you make an effort to change, I believe God will begin using your tongue to rebuild the lives of others.

> **1 Thessalonians 5:11** – *Therefore encourage one another and build each other up, just as in fact you are doing* (NIV).

grieving the Holy Spirit

The word *grieve* in this verse comes from the Greek word meaning to afflict with sorrow; to make sad. Have you ever made someone feel sad? Sure you have. I know I've done so more times than I'd care to admit, and it's a terrible feeling every time. In fact, there may be no worse feeling than letting someone down that you care about.

I hate the feeling that comes when I know I've let down one of my boys. It pains me to see Jack pooch his lip out, or to hear Noah cry because I didn't come through on a promise. I would never purposefully cause them to be sorrowful, but my good intentions don't make their grief any less real.

But as many times as I've caused my loved ones grief, it doesn't even begin to compare to how many times I've saddened the Holy Spirit. You, and many other Christians, have let Him down as well. My goal is by no means to make you feel bad about yourself; that wouldn't do anyone any good. I simply want you to be made aware and be empowered to change.

As I thought about the lifetimes of grief the Holy Spirit has endured, I asked myself, "What is the number one way in which we afflict the Holy Spirit with grief?" I believe the answer is inconsistency. Our character inconsistencies are the source of much heartache for those closest to us, including the Holy Spirit.

Sin, impure thoughts, neglect, ingratitude and resistance all cause Him sorrow. I challenge you today to become consistent in character. When you let someone down, or if you let the Holy Spirit down, repent and be willing to take the necessary steps to make sure it doesn't happen again. To God be the glory!

get rid of it

Ephesians 4:31 – *Get rid of all bitterness, rage and anger, brawling and slander, along with every form of malice* (NIV).

A couple times a year Heidi and I go through all the rooms in our house. We look through the closets, dressers and toy boxes searching for items that we no longer use but that are still in good enough shape to donate. We usually fill up four or five large trash bags with anything from clothes to books to toys. Then we give it all away.

In addition to the items worthy of donation, we also find plenty of weathered clothes, broken toys and books with missing or torn pages. These items find their way into a trash bag as well, but they are not given away. We get rid of them! The last thing we would want to do is give someone something that is useless or even harmful. They hold no value whatsoever to anyone, so we throw *all* of it away.

This is the point Paul was trying to get across to the church in this verse. He listed for us some of the "trash" that many Christians allow to clutter their lives. Perhaps your life is tainted by one or more of these qualities. If so, God is requiring you to get rid of all of it today.

These things are of no benefit to you or anyone else. Nobody wants your bitterness or wrath, and no one is interested in being insulted either. *You* have to rid yourself of these characteristics, and you cannot leave any trace of them. It's kind of like pulling weeds. You have to be careful to pull weeds up, root and all. If you don't, your flowerbed or garden may look clean initially, but after a short time the weeds will come back.

I encourage you to uproot all bitterness, rage, anger, brawling, slander and malice today. Leave no trace of any of it. Drop everything, and take out the trash that's in your life. You don't need it, and those closest to you certainly don't want it.

1 Peter 2:1 – *Therefore, rid yourselves of all malice and all deceit, hypocrisy, envy, and slander of every kind* (NIV).

175

kind and compassionate

Everyone wants to be forgiven unconditionally, but most people only forgive conditionally. This verse instructs us to be kind and compassionate to one another, but how do we do this? By forgiving others unconditionally as God forgave us.

God does not sit around and grade humanity based on an itemized list of everyone's sins, and then decide who He is and isn't going to forgive. I can't picture Him saying to Jesus, "Son, I'm sending you to die for the sins of mankind...except for this guy. He made fun of Me to some of his buddies, and they all laughed and called Me names. You won't be dying for this girl either. She used to love Me, but she rejected Me and caused much division in My church. I'll show her."

God is kind and compassionate, and He forgives everyone who repents and receives Jesus as their Lord. And He does so unconditionally. In fact, the Father loved us so much that He gave Jesus over to death for our salvation. Jesus was His most valued possession, yet He willing offered Him as a sacrifice for our sins.

Maybe there is someone in your life that you have been unable to forgive for whatever reason. Perhaps you've been stabbed in the back or even abused. I don't know how grossly you've been mistreated, but you must forgive as God forgave you. You cannot pick and choose who you forgive based on the level of hurt they've inflicted upon you.

Just like the Father gave up Jesus in order to forgive you, you may have to give up something valuable in order to forgive someone else. Ask God to help you forgive those who have wronged you. It's very liberating to let them off the hook.

a different type of jailbird

Philippians 1:2-5 – 2 *Grace and peace to you from God our Father and the Lord Jesus Christ.* 3 *I thank my God every time I remember you.* 4 *In all my prayers for all of you, I always pray with joy* 5 *because of your partnership in the gospel from the first day until now* (NIV).

I want to share four things with you that stand out to me in this passage. I pray that you are encouraged today as we learn together.

First of all, Paul wrote the book of Philippians while incarcerated in Rome. God had led Paul to a very uncomfortable place in his life, and he had every reason to be upset. But let's take a closer look at Paul's mindset. I believe you'll find his response to imprisonment to be a little different than most.

The second thing I want you to notice is how he begins his letter to the Philippians. He says, "Grace and peace to you." I don't know about you, but if I was writing a letter from jail, I would probably start by saying something more like this: "Get me out of here! I'm innocent. Get my lawyer in here!" From the loneliness of his cell, Paul did not curse God or beg for help. He spoke of God's grace and peace.

Then he thanked God. At that point in his life, what did Paul have to be thankful for? He was innocent of any crime, and he was imprisoned because of the God he served. Even so, he was thankful for his Philippian brothers and sisters.

Lastly, he said, "I always pray with joy." Though Paul was shackled, he was not bitter. What an awesome example he is to us as believers today. Paul was a different type of jailbird.

Perhaps today you feel imprisoned by your circumstances. I don't know what you're going through, but I pray you will pattern yourself after Paul's example. Only you can make the decision to handle adverse situations in a godly manner.

Psalm 146:7 – *He gives justice to the oppressed and food to the hungry. The LORD frees the prisoners* (NLT).

completion

Another version says that He will carry the good work He began in you on to completion (NIV). Have you ever been working on a project and felt like there was no end in sight? I was what you'd call a procrastinator in college. I would wait until the last possible minute to complete major assignments, so I'd stay up days on end writing papers and finishing projects. Many times I would finish just minutes before the deadlines.

I remember feeling overwhelmed by the avalanche of work I had created for myself. There were many times I wondered if I could endure to the end and get everything finished. And there were certainly times I'd question, "Why am I doing this to myself? Is it even worth it?"

I believe this is where a lot of Christians find themselves in their walks with the Lord. This is certainly true of someone who has a radical conversion. They receive Christ and are immediately thrust from a life of worldliness into one of holiness, and it can be overwhelming.

God begins a new work in us at salvation. From that day forward our aim is to be more like Him. It's an everyday process of renewing our minds and cultivating the fruits of the Spirit in our lives. We practice holiness and study His word. We surround ourselves with other believers and spend quality time in prayer.

Then one day we realize that we still have a long way to go. We become frustrated and begin to question whether finishing the race is worth it. Many people beat themselves up when they sin. If you find yourself in a similar position today, look back at how far you've already come. God is still working on you, and the process won't be complete until Jesus returns. Don't give up!

Colossians 4:17 – *See to it that you complete the work you have received in the Lord* (NIV).

love appropriately

Philippians 1:9-10 – 9 *And this is my prayer: that your love may abound more and more in knowledge and depth of insight,* 10 *so that you may be able to discern what is best and may be pure and blameless until the day of Christ* (NIV).

It's God's desire for our love to abound more and more. He wants our love to flourish and be plentiful, but it's our job to cultivate it. Many people want God to work in their lives, but they're unwilling to do any of the work themselves. These verses tell us how to grow our love.

Look at how another version translates these verses: *So this is my prayer: that your love will flourish and that you will not only love much but well. Learn to love appropriately. You need to use your head and test your feelings so that your love is sincere and intelligent, not sentimental gush* (MSG). Has your love for God or others grown stagnant? One of the major reasons love becomes ineffective is because people try to love, but they don't do so properly.

The Bible teaches that in order to love appropriately we have to use our heads and test our feelings. True love is not an emotion. Hearts are broken and relationships crumble everyday because people love based on how they feel. The character Marty in the movie *Dan in Real Life* said, "Love is not a feeling; it's an ability." God gives us the ability to love appropriately.

Loving someone is a decision you make, and you have to use discernment in order to love sincerely and intelligently. So much time and energy is wasted because people love from their hearts without using their heads.

Don't be misguided when it comes to who and how you love. God wants us to love purely and effectively. Ask Him for discernment today. Don't allow your emotions to lead you. I pray that your love will abound more and more. Hallelujah!

1 Thessalonians 3:12 – *May the Lord make your love increase and overflow for each other and for everyone else* (NIV).

179

why me?

As I studied Philippians 1, I marveled at Paul's attitude as he wrote from prison. He managed to keep his circumstance in perspective and focus on the big picture despite being in chains. What an awesome testimony! Maybe today you are facing a trial of some kind, and you've recently asked, "Why me?" If you are in a personal prison today, I pray your perspective changes. Be challenged by Paul's words.

First of all, Paul recognized that his imprisonment was an opportunity to spread the Good News. He understood that his response to incarceration would serve as a testimony to the lost prisoners and even the Roman soldiers. They all knew he was in prison for the cause of Christ, and Paul knew his reaction would either draw the lost to Him or push them away. He didn't whine and groan about being in jail; he took advantage of the opportunity.

So many Christians ruin their witness when faced with difficulty because they respond in a worldly manner. Nothing pushes the lost further from salvation than a Christian who acts just like them.

Paul also viewed his imprisonment as a chance to encourage the believers who were in jail. God will bring fellow Christians across your path who need a confidence boost. Don't be so consumed by your personal crisis that you miss out on an opportunity to help set someone free from his.

envy and rivalry

Philippians 1:15 – *It is true that some preach Christ out of envy and rivalry, but others out of goodwill* (NIV).

This verse indicates that there are two types of Christians. There are those who are in competition with one another, and there are those who live for Christ selflessly. I want to talk about the latter group of people first.

Many Christians have pure motives, and they live for Him out of goodwill. Their motivation is love, and they are in defense of the Gospel (**Philippians 1:16**). This is the manner in which God wants us to serve Him. He desires for us to set aside our personal agendas and conform ourselves to His.

On the other hand, listen to how Paul describes the second group of Christians. **Philippians 1:17** – *The former preach Christ out of selfish ambition, not sincerely, supposing that they can stir up trouble for me while I am in chains* (NIV). There are some who serve God for selfish gain. They promote their own agendas, and they abuse the gifts God has entrusted to them. They are in a constant power struggle with God and fellow believers. This kind of behavior hurts the heart of God, and it causes trouble for His kingdom.

Let this passage challenge you today. Are you engaged in a rivalry with someone else in the church? Do you envy the gifts or testimonies of other godly men and women? What's your motivation for serving God today? Don't get wrapped up in a competition with someone who is supposed to be on your team. Too many casualties take place in the church because of friendly fire.

Rid yourself of envy and selfish ambition, and promote Christ in everything you do. Learn to celebrate the victories of others and work together. Serve Him with pure motives.

Philippians 1:18 – *But what does it matter? The important thing is that in every way, whether from false motives or true, Christ is preached. And because of this I rejoice* (NIV).

help is on the way

I don't typically like to ask for help. Not because I'm macho or something caveman like that; I just don't like to be an inconvenience. I will help anyone, but I'd rather not have to be helped. However, I have learned that there are many things I cannot do on my own. It's for this reason that God has strategically placed certain individuals in my life to help me.

Perhaps as you're reading this today you are in desperate need of help. If so, I pray the message of this verse brings you great comfort. You need to understand that you are not alone in your circumstance. Paul was aware of this fact even though he was in prison, and he was confident that his help would ultimately bring him deliverance.

There were people praying for Paul, and there are people praying for you. Even if you are not mentioned specifically by name, I believe the Holy Spirit inspires people to pray for you. You may have pastors, friends or family members who stand in the gap for you. Someone is praying for you, and her prayers are powerful and effective. They sustain you when life is hard, and they fight for you when you're weak.

When people pray for us, it supplies us with the Spirit of Jesus Christ. What exactly does this mean? I'm glad you asked. I believe it means that we are able to endure our trials with the same attitude and strength Christ had as He faced similar trials.

His Spirit empowers you and gives you hope. When you persevere with the same peace and patience Jesus exemplified, you will be propelled to victory every time! Don't be afraid to ask others to partner with you in prayer, and don't forget the greatest promise of all: Jesus is interceding on your behalf as well!

no shame

> **Philippians 1:20** – *I eagerly expect and hope that I in no way will be ashamed, but will have sufficient courage so that now as always Christ will be exalted in my body, whether by life or by death* (NIV).

Paul, unlike so many Christians, was confident in his faith. His confidence could almost be mistaken for arrogance, but Paul was a model of humility & faith. Paul knew who he was in Christ, and he had no intention of ever being ashamed because of Him.

Another word for *ashamed* is *humiliated*. Paul was convinced that he would in no way be humiliated. Remember he was in prison as he wrote this letter to the Philippians. As I thought about what he was saying in this verse, I asked myself, "How could he *not* be humiliated?" I would think being imprisoned for your faith would be the ultimate slap in the face, but Paul was not ashamed while in chains.

I want to share with you the revelation I received regarding this verse. Being in prison was not humiliating for Paul; it was humbling. **Proverbs 16:18** – *Pride goes before destruction, and a haughty spirit before a fall* (NKJV). The opposite of humility is pride, and pride causes a person to fall. Since this is true, the opposite must also be true. A truly humble person will not fall or be humiliated. Hallelujah!

Paul realized that his life was not his own; he became a living sacrifice (**Romans 12:1**). He had nothing to hide and nothing to be ashamed of. His prayer was to have the strength and courage to forever magnify the name of Jesus, whether by life or by death. He exalted Christ without shame. Now that's humility.

I encourage you today to live a life of humility, presenting yourself as a living sacrifice to Him. True humility prevents humiliation. Ask God to reveal any arrogance there may be in your life. Repent, turn from it and be confident in your faith.

> **Luke 14:11** – *"For everyone who exalts himself will be humbled, and he who humbles himself will be exalted"* (NIV).

torn between two desires

I believe this is one of the most remarkable passages in all of Scripture. I hope I can properly depict to you the message Paul is conveying here. Paul was torn between two desires, but not the two most people would think of. The two desires most Christians struggle with are godliness and worldliness. They are torn between the lusts of their flesh and the longings of their spirit. They long to live for God with one foot in the world, but this is not even possible. It's either one or the other; there is no in between.

But this was not Paul's dilemma. Paul was so in love with Jesus that he no longer thought about the pursuit of fleshly gain. He was torn between living for Christ and dying for Him. On the one hand, life meant fruitful service for Christ. If he remained alive, it was for the benefit of those who would hear his message.

On the other hand, death meant eternity with Christ. Spending eternity in fellowship with our Lord and Savior is the ultimate reward for those who live for Him, but Paul understood that dying would only benefit him. Because of his selfless nature, he counted his mission to share the Gospel as being more valuable than his desire to go be with Jesus. Wow!

I challenge you today to change your mindset. If you're wrestling with worldly passions, crucify your sinful nature. I pray your dilemma becomes the same as Paul's, but don't get so caught up in daydreaming about eternity that you miss an opportunity to share the love of Jesus with someone.

don't be intimidated

Philippians 1:28-30 – 28 *Don't be intimidated by your enemies. This will be a sign to them that they are going to be destroyed, but that you are going to be saved, even by God himself.* 29 *For you have been given not only the privilege of trusting in Christ but also the privilege of suffering for him.* 30 *We are in this fight together* (NLT).

Do not be intimidated by your enemies! As long as you are still breathing, you will face opposition because of your faith. Unfortunately, you will be opposed by both Christians and non-Christians alike. The enemy of our souls uses people as tools of intimidation. His purpose is to cause us to become fearful and cower back, but we do not have to be timid.

In fact, if we resist the attacks of our enemies, Paul says it will serve as a sign to them that they are going to be destroyed and that we are going to be saved. The greatest way to respond to intimidation is to stand up to it. We are representatives of Jesus Christ. When we shrink back in the face of opposition, we portray Him as a wimp. But when we stand up and don't back down, it brings Him glory. What an awesome testimony for those attempting to intimidate you!

Each of us has been given the privilege of trusting in Christ and sharing in His blessings, but suffering for Him is also a privilege. Understanding this truth is key to breaking intimidation in your life.

Another word for *privilege* is *freedom*. Most everyone is willing to fight for their freedom. Our country fought for freedom and broke the intimidation of the nations threatening that freedom. If you count suffering for Christ as a privilege, you will be willing to do whatever it takes to protect that freedom.

Let me encourage you today. As Paul says, "We are in this fight together," and together we will win. Thank You, Lord!

Hebrews 10:39 – *But we are not of those who shrink back and are destroyed, but of those who believe and are saved* (NIV).

hate, not tolerate

We are to hate, not tolerate, our sin. It's easy enough to say, but it's a very difficult thing to do. When we make the decision to turn from our sin and follow Christ wholeheartedly, our worldly appetite doesn't vanish. In fact, it intensifies.

Many people decide to abstain from certain foods (usually sweets) in an effort to be healthier, but it doesn't take long for their bodies to start crying out for those foods once they're not being eaten anymore. They want what they're not supposed to have, and they often give in and eat.

The same is true spiritually. When we deprive our flesh of what it longs for, it begins to go through withdrawals. It's at this point that many people give up on holiness and begin satisfying their worldly appetite again. This lifestyle is not God's intention, nor is it pleasing to Him.

So why do so many people fall back into sin after giving their hearts to God? The answer is simple: They like their sin. Actually, they *love* their sin. Over the next few days, my goal is to use biblical principles to develop in you a holy hatred for *all* sin. No sin, no matter how big or small it may be in your eyes, should get a free pass.

Sin is sin, and God hates all of it. You and I are to hate the things He hates. To *hate* means to dislike intensely or passionately; to feel extreme hostility toward. My prayer is that you will passionately detest those things that have held you bound for so long. No more excuses! Prepare yourself today because you're about to go through some withdrawals. The process will be difficult, but I promise it will be worth it. Glory to God!

hats off

Proverbs 16:6 – *By mercy and love, truth and fidelity [to God and man—not by sacrificial offerings], iniquity is purged out of the heart, and by the reverent, worshipful fear of the Lord men depart from and avoid evil* (AMP).

If you are going to develop a hatred for sin, I believe you have to first fear God. This does not mean that you live your life afraid that God is going to strike you down if you mess up. God is not scary. To fear the Lord means to reverence Him and be in awe of Him. Those who fear God make Him their priority, and they adore Him because He is awesome.

When I was growing up, I always had some kind of hat on. I had a variety of hats ranging from my favorite sports teams to the coolest superheroes. I wore a hat everywhere I went. Before I started school, the only place I didn't wear a hat was church, and that was only because my parents told me I couldn't.

I would wear my hat in the car on the way to church, but I'd take it off as I was walking into the building. As soon as church was over and we stepped foot into the parking lot, the hat would appear back on top of my head.

It doesn't really matter what your feelings are on wearing hats in church. The point I'm trying to make is my parents taught me that wearing a hat in church was irreverent. Even at a young age, I loved and respected God so much that I obeyed my parents' wishes. I did not want to displease Him in any way because honoring Him was important to me.

When you fear the Lord, you will not want to do anything that might grieve Him. The reverent, worshipful fear of the Lord causes us to avoid evil. Nothing displeases God more than sin. If you have an unhealthy relationship with sin, there is no fear of God in you. Fearing God causes you to hate sin. You will never be perfect, but sin should never be condoned.

Psalm 2:11 – *Worship the LORD with reverence and rejoice with trembling* (NASB).

love God's commands

In order to hate sin, we have to love God's commands. This is a lot easier said than done. There are many people who profess a love for God's word, but they despise authority. A lot of people don't like to be told what to do, but the Bible is full of commands God expects His church to follow. And if we're going to develop hatred toward sin, we have to love His commands.

I'm not talking about an emotional, shallow love. The Bible says that those who love His commands more than pure gold will hate sin. Pure gold is one of the world's most valuable resources. It's a very precious metal and a symbol of wealth. I believe David refers to pure gold in this verse because it was something he held in high regard. Gold was obviously very important to him, but his love for God's commands outweighed his desire for financial gain.

Maybe accumulating great wealth is not of much value to you, and there's something else you hold dear. What do you value the most? Is it your family? Social status? Climbing the corporate ladder? It could be any number of things. But if you're going to truly hate every wrong path, you have to love His commands more than everything else that's important to you.

I'll be the first to admit that it's difficult to love all of God's commands. God requires a lot from His people, and often what He expects is very challenging or uncomfortable for us. If you're struggling with God's orders today, ask Him to develop a love in you for everything He commands you to do.

He's always right

Psalm 119:127-129 – 127 *Because I love your commands more than gold, more than pure gold,* 128 *and because I consider all your precepts right, I hate every wrong path.* 129 *Your statutes are wonderful; therefore I obey them* (NIV).

If you're going to hate every wrong path, you not only must love all of God's commands, you have to consider all His precepts right. Another word for *precept* is *law*. The Bible is God's law. It's full of godly guidelines and principles that are meant to help mold our character into Christ's. In order for us to develop a hatred for sin, we have to trust that the entire word of God is true.

Think about this for a minute. Would you willingly trust your life to someone who could possibly lead you astray or harm you? Of course not. Most people are not going to put their lives into someone else's hands without doing a thorough character evaluation.

I encourage you to begin a daily investigation of the character of Jesus Christ. Get into the Word, search God's promises, and discover His faithfulness. **Psalm 33:4** – *For the word of the LORD is right and true; he is faithful in all he does* (NIV). You must trust that all of God's ways are right, or you will never completely turn away from sin.

Trusting God completely is tough. It means relinquishing our rights as the "play caller" of our lives giving ourselves to Him. It's not enough to believe all of God's precepts are right; we have to obey them as well. Acknowledging God's word is true is far different than doing what it says. A lot of Christians give God's law mental assent, but they live in disobedience.

If you trust His word entirely, it will become the blueprint you use to build your life. God cannot lie, and His character has been proven trustworthy time and time again. Allow Him to develop hatred in you for any path that is contrary to His will.

Psalm 119:160 – *All your words are true; all your righteous laws are eternal* (NIV).

don't flatter yourself

Psalm 36:1-2 – 1 *Sin whispers to the wicked, deep within their hearts. They have no fear of God at all.* 2 *In their blind conceit, they cannot see how wicked they really are* (NLT).

The Message puts it this way: *He has smooth-talked himself into believing that his evil will never be noticed.* Another version says: *For in his own eyes he flatters himself too much to detect or hate his sin* (NIV). This passage describes a person who is in a very dangerous position.

Many people have tricked themselves into thinking they are holy, and it's caused them to be unaware of the sin that has taken up residence in their lives. They've flattered themselves so much so that they unwittingly condone sin. Please understand this passage is not referring to someone who openly sins on purpose. David is writing about people who are self-deceived and oblivious to their grave condition.

There are many Christians who are so high on themselves that they've lost all sense of reality. They're masters of pointing out the flaws of others, but their self-righteousness veils their eyes from their own transgressions. The idea of this kind of condition may seem far-fetched, but this is the sad state of many believers.

Holy Spirit, give us a reality check today! Search our hearts. Make this your prayer today. **Psalm 139:23-24** – 23 *Search me, O God, and know my heart; test me and know my anxious thoughts.* 24 *See if there is any offensive way in me, and lead me in the way everlasting* (NIV).

Ask God to light up the dark places of your heart. If you're going to hate your sin, you have to be aware of it. The enemy will flatter you and puff you up, but you must have an attitude of humility and repentance. Perfection is not humanly possible, so constantly ask the Lord to search your heart.

Ephesians 5:13-14 – 13 *But everything exposed by the light becomes visible,* 14 *for it is the light that makes everything visible* (NIV).

like a palm

One of the oddest sights I've ever seen are palm trees growing in Louisiana. I typically think of palm trees growing in tropical areas near beaches, not in the middle of swamp country. What's amazing is these trees were flourishing despite the unfavorable climate. And when I came across the above passage of Scripture, it prompted me to research palm trees further.

The psalmist writes that the righteous will flourish like a palm tree, but what exactly does this mean? Palm trees grow slowly but steadily, and they are not influenced by the alternation of the seasons. They are unmoved by heavy rain, and they remain strong under intense sunlight. Violent winds blow, but the palm tree remains perfectly upright. Palm trees consistently produce fruit year in and year out.

Who are these righteous people who will flourish like the palm tree? They are the ones planted in the house of the Lord. Every Christian needs to be planted in a local church body. It is unhealthy for a tree to be uprooted and replanted multiple times, and the same can be said for believers.

There are many people who jump around from church to church, and they are largely unfruitful because of it. Their lives are marked by inconsistency, and they are tossed to and fro by the storms of life. Many of them do not flourish in favorable conditions, let alone unstable ones.

If you're not already, I encourage you to plant yourself in a local church as soon as possible. Ask God to direct you to a church that rightly divides His word and allows the Holy Spirit to move. Surround yourself with people of faith.

like a cedar

Psalm 92:12-14 – 12 *The righteous will flourish like a palm tree, they will grow like a cedar of Lebanon;* 13 *planted in the house of the LORD, they will flourish in the courts of our God.* 14 *They will still bear fruit in old age, they will stay fresh and green* (NIV).

If you live righteously and are planted in the house of God, not only will you flourish like a palm tree, you will grow like a cedar of Lebanon. This is very significant, so please allow me to explain.

The Lebanon cedar is an evergreen tree with a strong root system. Its trunk measures at up to eight feet in diameter, and it can grow up to 130 feet tall. It helps to form forests at various altitudes between 3,300 and 7,200 feet. The cedar of Lebanon is a majestic tree, and its wood was used in building King Solomon's temple, as well as his and King David's palaces. They are sturdy, and they flourish alongside different types of trees.

Now let's apply these characteristics to the life of a believer who is established in a local church. These Christians will have a deep root system founded in the word of God. They are strong, firm and steadfast. They stand tall and grow in adverse conditions. They are a vital part in building the kingdom of God, and they serve His body in various capacities. Not to mention, they are able to flourish alongside all different types of people.

Do you understand where I'm going with this? Many Christians are models of inconsistency. Their relationship with God is here, there and everywhere, and it filters down through every area of their lives.

I ask you today: Are you a cedar of Lebanon? Are you fulfilling a purpose in a local church, or do you just appear in a pew on Sunday morning? Perhaps you jump from church to church. I encourage you to get established and involved in *one* church, and begin to grow like a cedar of Lebanon.

Psalm 104:16 – *The trees of the LORD are well watered, the cedars of Lebanon that he planted* (NIV).

immeasurably more

Ephesians 3:20 – *Now to him who is able to do immeasurably more than all we ask or imagine, according to his power that is at work within us* (NIV).

I don't know about you, but I have big dreams for me and my family. I have a creative imagination, and I can come up with some pretty awesome ideas. Even so, God is able to do an immeasurable amount more than anything I could ever dream up.

The problem is that too many Christians put God in a box, and they limit His ability to work within them. What's happened to the dreamers? Where are the people who believe God is omnipotent and capable of blowing their wildest expectations out of the water? Many people's dreams have been stifled, but why?

I believe there are multiples reasons as to why people place limits on God Almighty. Some lose their ability to dream after childhood; they simply "grow out of it." Others stop dreaming because they've been disappointed, and the list goes on. It's time for the church to dream again and believe God can do what He says He can do. He is an infinite God, and He has no deficiencies.

If you're a dreamer, continue to dream. Never stop. Our two boys have great imaginations, and Heidi and I celebrate their creativity. Don't allow naysayers to rob you of your God-given aspirations. There a lot of "wet blankets" out there who have made it their mission to put out the fire of passionate believers.

If you've lost your ability to dream, I dare you to dream again! Don't put limitations on God; He is too awesome to put inside a box. And don't be discouraged when disappointment comes. Keep things in perspective. Just because He is *able* to do more than all we ask or imagine, doesn't mean He's going to. He works in His timing and according to His will, not ours. Dare to dream today; there is supernatural power at work within you!

Ephesians 3:20 – *God can do anything, you know—far more than you could ever imagine or guess or request in your wildest dreams!* (MSG)

blameless and pure

Philippians 2:14-15 – 14 *Do everything without complaining or arguing,* 15 *so that you may become blameless and pure* (NIV).

I tend to tie being blameless and pure to avoiding immorality, and there are likely many others who share in my way of thinking. While this is true, purity is so much more. That's why, when I came across this passage, it was a new revelation for me. Paul teaches that in order to become blameless and pure, we have to do everything without complaining or arguing.

After I read this, I almost laughed out loud. It's really not funny, but I thought to myself, "Man, there must not be very many pure people in the world. Myself included." Complaining and arguing begin at a very young age. It's human nature to grumble and quarrel over certain tasks or commands we find undesirable.

When I was in elementary school, I spent a lot of time playing outside with my friends. My house was the place to be after school let out for the day. Once the bell rang, we would scurry down the road from the school to my house, and we'd play baseball, basketball or football out in the yard.

At dinnertime, my mom would come outside and call for me to come in. I rarely went inside without mumbling under my breath, or voicing my displeasure in some other way. I remember there was one day in particular that I was very belligerent. She asked me to come in for dinner, and I told her I wasn't ready. We had a tree in our front yard that produced some kind of berries, and I decided to use them as ammo. My friends and I began pegging my mom with the berries, and she went inside. I thought I was victorious, but I just wound up sorry and in a lot of trouble.

I ask you today, "What have you been whining about?" Stop grumbling, and discipline yourself. Do everything as unto the Lord. Then you will be on your way to purity.

1 Timothy 4:12 – *Be an example to all believers in what you say, in the way you live, in your love, your faith, and your purity* (NLT).

a trustworthy saying

> **2 Timothy 2:11-13** – 11 *Here is a trustworthy saying: If we died with him, we will also live with him;* 12 *if we endure, we will also reign with him. If we disown him, he will also disown us;* 13 *if we are faithless, he will remain faithful, for he cannot disown himself* (NIV).

There are four truths listed in this passage, and I want to briefly discuss them. Three of them will bring you great encouragement, but one of them may serve as a reality check. I pray that you are encouraged today as you read.

First of all, if we died with Him, we will also live with Him. The *Him* referred to in this passage is Jesus. So that there's no confusion, let me say that Jesus has already died and rose again, and He's not going to do so a second time. **Romans 6:10-11** – 10 *The death he died, he died to sin once for all; but the life he lives, he lives to God.* 11 *In the same way, count yourselves dead to sin but alive to God in Christ Jesus* (NIV). When we die to sin, as Christ did, it's then that we become alive. Hallelujah!

Secondly, if we endure, we will also reign with Him. Unfortunately, there are many Christians who give up before they reach the finish line, and they forfeit the right to sit with Jesus on His throne. **Revelation 3:21** – *"To him who overcomes, I will give the right to sit with me on my throne, just as I overcame and sat down with my Father on his throne"* (NIV).

Next is the reality check. If we disown Him, He will also disown us. This truth almost appears to go against Christ's nature, but He does not reject anyone. He will not disown you unless you disown Him. Jesus will not let go of you, but He will never force anyone to accept Him. Do you belong to Him today?

Lastly, Jesus is always faithful. When your faith is lacking, or even non-existent, He remains constant. I hope that you have found comfort in His word today. God will never let you down.

> **Psalm 145:13** – *The LORD is faithful to all his promises and loving toward all he has made* (NIV).

He knows, but do you?

> **Jeremiah 29:11** – *"For I know the plans I have for you," declares the LORD* (NIV).

God knows the plans He has for you, but do *you* know the plans He has for you? If you were to sit and write down all of the reasons as to why people don't know God's plan for their lives, the list would be extensive. And if you were to survey people to find the number one reason as to why people don't know God's plan, the answers would no doubt vary from person to person.

So I asked God this very question, "Why don't people know the plans You have for them?" He answered me with two reasons, and it's those reasons I want to share with you today. Perhaps you're struggling with what God's plan is for your life. My prayer is that this message will help bring clarity and give you direction.

The first reason people don't know God's plan for their lives is they don't ask. It's true! I'm not trying to insult your intelligence here. If I wanted to know what my wife's favorite kind of food is, I'd have to ask her in order to find out. Unless the subject came up in casual conversation, I'd likely never know.

The same is true when it comes to knowing God's plan for your life. If you never ask Him what it is, you'll never know. Many people don't ask because they're so busy living their lives however they want to, and they could care less about what God's plan is. Others don't even know to ask Him.

The second reason people don't know God's plan for their lives is they ask, but they don't listen. If I asked my wife what her favorite food is and then walked away as she answered, I still wouldn't know what it is. Many Christians will pray and ask God to give them direction, but they don't wait around long enough to listen to what He has to say. I encourage you today to ask God to show you the plans He has for you. Then wait on Him to answer.

> **Proverbs 3:6** – *In all your ways acknowledge Him, and He shall direct your paths* (NKJV).

plans to prosper

Jeremiah 29:11 – *"For I know the plans I have for you," declares the LORD, "plans to prosper you and not to harm you"* (NIV).

God has specifically designed a plan that is unique to you. He never has, and never will, author two identical stories. Even so, there are two common threads running through the plans He has for every person He's ever created. I'm going to discuss the first one today and the second one tomorrow.

First of all, He has plans to prosper you and not to harm you. Another word for *prosper* is *thrive*. God's desire is for us to thrive in every area of life, including spiritually, physically, relationally, financially, emotionally, etc. His intention is for us to experience success in everything we purpose in Him to do.

Proverbs 28:25 – *He who trusts in the LORD will prosper* (NIV). Those who trust in God wholeheartedly will be prosperous. The problem is many people put their trust in themselves, and they follow plans that are contrary to God's will. Some allow themselves to be led astray by the plans others have for them. This is why it's so important for us to discover God's plans for our lives. If you don't, you're going to cause yourself more harm than good. Plus, He measures success on a different scale than we do.

Not following God's plans for our lives leaves us vulnerable. Many people live for themselves and then blame God when they are harmed by life's circumstances. Listen to me carefully. God does not harm you, nor does He lead you into a place of insecurity. His plans are to prosper you!

Perhaps today you find yourself in a precarious position. You're not prosperous in every area of your life, and you are ready to get back on track. Surrender yourself to the plans He has for your life, and He will cause you to thrive no matter how unfavorable the conditions surrounding you may be.

Luke 10:19 – *"I have given you authority to trample on snakes and scorpions and to overcome all the powers of the enemy; nothing will harm you"* (NIV).

hope and a future

Jeremiah 29:11 – *"For I know the plans I have for you," declares the LORD, "plans to prosper you and not to harm you, plans to give you hope and a future"* (NIV).

If God has plans to prosper you and not to harm you, then He certainly has plans to give you hope and a future. Unfortunately, there are countless individuals who are blinded by hopelessness, and they can't see the bright future God has for them. You may find yourself in this same position today. If so, I pray that hope is restored to you through this message.

As I was thinking about why so many people have lost hope, I received this revelation from the Lord: Everyone puts their hope in something. If you lose hope, it's because you put it in the wrong thing. Hope is invaluable. You can't put a price on how much it is worth, so it's important to invest your hope wisely.

Compare it to investing in the stock market. When you put your money into a certain stock, your assets are at the mercy of the market. There will be times that your stock rises or falls because the market can be very unpredictable. And as the market fluctuates, so does the mood of the investor. When your stock is hot, you're on top of the world, but when it cools off, worry sets in.

The same is true when it comes to investing our hope. If we put our hope into a temporary, worldly stock, our measure of faith will vary depending on the present circumstances surrounding our lives. So many people, Christians included, lose sight of the plans God has for them because they have invested their hope poorly.

I encourage you today to invest your hope into an eternal stock. God's market does not fluctuate because He does not change and neither does His word. In Psalm 119, David says five times, "I have put my hope in Your word." I encourage you to do the same. Your future has never looked so bright!

Psalm 119:114 – *You are my refuge and my shield; I have put my hope in your word* (NIV).

He listens to you

Have you ever tried to speak to someone, and you knew they weren't listening to you? Sure you have, and I'm sure you're as annoyed by it as I am. It's even more aggravating when you are conveying important information or trying to give someone specific instructions.

My wife and I have two little boys. I'm almost positive they have a built-in mechanism that blocks out the sound of our voices, especially when we ask them to clean up or get ready for bed. Sometimes it's like talking to a couple of brick walls. Other times we know they hear us, but our words go in one ear and out the other. If you have, or have had, small children, you know exactly what I'm talking about.

We don't ever have to worry about this issue when it comes to speaking to God. If there is a communication gap between us and God, He is never the one at fault. He is always listening, but we have to speak to Him in order to be heard. And often times it seems like He's not paying attention because we pray things that are contrary to His will.

Another thing I've found annoying in conversation is when I'm talking and the other person stares a hole through my head with his mouth hanging open. Nobody wants to talk to a robot. Most people want to be engaged in conversation; they're not interested in giving a monologue to a person who could care less. When somebody actually participates and listens to you, it reinforces that they care about you. What you have to say is important to him or her.

Be sure of this: When you pray according to God's will, He actively listens. He may not always act or respond the way you want Him to, but I guarantee He hears you.

manhunt

Jeremiah 29:13-14 – 13 *"You will seek me and find me when you seek me with all your heart.* 14 *I will be found by you,"* declares the LORD, *"and will bring you back from captivity"* (NIV).

Growing up, I was an avid fan of all the different versions of hide and seek. My personal favorite was Kick the Can, and my youth group always seemed to find a way to incorporate an intense game of hide and seek into any event we did at our church. When I became a youth pastor, I planned many events that included some form of hiding and seeking.

One particular game that became a big hit was Manhunt. It was especially fun in large groups. In Manhunt, one person is allotted a certain amount of time to go and hide. Once the time limit expires, everyone else is released to go find (or hunt down) the person hiding. The "man" being hunted then remains hidden until found, or he shows himself after a ten-minute time restraint.

There were always one or two people who the group could never find (I wasn't one of them). They excelled at Manhunt, and it was extremely frustrating to those seeking them out. In fact, it was so wearisome that many people would just quit searching for them altogether.

This is the dilemma many Christians find themselves facing today. They are seemingly lost searching for God in a never-ending game of Manhunt, and they eventually give up. But God is not playing hide and seek. He said Himself that He will be found by you, *if* you seek Him with all of your heart. He does not elude you as you draw closer to Him. God wants you to find Him!

Have you ever played hide and seek with a child? Normally, our boys hide and start giggling as I get closer to where they're at. Why? Because they love it when I find them. I can picture God responding in much the same way. He longs for us to come near to Him, and as we do, it puts a huge smile on His face.

Proverbs 8:35 – *For whoever finds me finds life and receives favor from the LORD* (NLT).

submit yourself

1 Peter 2:13-14 – 13 *Submit yourselves for the Lord's sake to every authority instituted among men: whether to the king, as the supreme authority,* 14 *or to governors, who are sent by him to punish those who do wrong and to commend those who do right* (NIV).

The passages we're going to look at over the next few days can be some of the most frustrating in all of Scripture to understand. God is a God of order, and sometimes His order seems disorderly to us. God requires us to submit ourselves to the authorities instituted among us. Many times this can be frustrating and seem unfair.

First of all, Peter states above to submit *yourself* to every authority established over you. It's not the duty of those who are in authority over us to coerce us into submission. Trust me; they have better things to do. In fact, you will likely come across a leader that will do absolutely nothing to merit your submission.

Nobody can cause us to submit to anyone. It's a decision that only you and I can make. We have to purpose in our hearts to honor the position of those who are in authority, whether they deserve it or not. I warned you this might be frustrating.

Another word for *submit* is *surrender*. When we choose to submit ourselves to authority, we are in many ways surrendering our rights. Submission to authority equals trust in God. Since God has established all the governing authorities (see Romans 13), we demonstrate total trust in Him by submitting to the leadership He's set up over us.

I want to encourage you today to submit yourself to the pastors, teachers, bosses, parents, government officials, law enforcement, etc. that God has placed in your life. You may need to ask Him to give you an extra dose of grace in order to do so.

Romans 13:5 – *Therefore, it is necessary to submit to the authorities, not only because of possible punishment but also because of conscience* (NIV).

they keep watch

Hebrews 13:17 – *Obey your leaders and submit to their authority. They keep watch over you as men who must give an account. Obey them so that their work will be a joy, not a burden, for that would be of no advantage to you* (NIV).

God reiterates here that we are to obey our leaders and submit to their authority, but I want to point out a couple other things from this verse. I pray that this message brings you understanding today.

The Bible says our leaders keep watch over us. Keep in mind, though, this doesn't mean they always do a good job of it. As I mentioned yesterday, there will be times in your life that those in authority over you don't deserve honor. Unfortunately, there are many leaders who have self-seeking motives and have little regard for those God has entrusted to them to watch over.

This problem exists in government, as well as in the church and everyday life. Many government officials forget about the people who elected them. Some bosses overlook the needs of their employees, and too often, pastors neglect their congregations. This is not God's intention.

God desires for those He's placed in leadership to pay careful attention and protect those that are under their guidance. Take for example the parable of the lost sheep (see Matthew 18). Jesus tells the story of a shepherd who was the overseer of one hundred sheep. The shepherd paid such close attention that he realized when one sheep had wandered away, and then he dropped everything to bring that one back to safety.

Perhaps there is a leader in your life that is neglecting you. If so, it is not for you to judge or condemn. Pray for all of your leaders on every level. Each one of them will give an account for how well they did, or didn't, keep watch. And the one they'll give an account to won't be you.

Hebrews 4:13 – *Everything is uncovered and laid bare before the eyes of him to whom we must give account* (NIV).

no advantage to you

There are many employees who have made it their mission to cause their bosses headaches. Church staff members undermine their senior pastors, children rebel against their parents and nations attempt to overthrow their government officials. This kind of behavior is the exact opposite of what God requires.

The Bible says to obey our leaders so that their work will be a joy, not a burden. It's unfortunate, but most people don't view authority in this manner. This is especially true of those who don't agree with the one in charge. They try to make life as difficult as possible for the very people God has put in their lives to watch over them.

Leadership will inevitably fail time and time again, but that doesn't give us the right to cause them misery when they do. A lot of people dishonor authority because they believe they are justified in doing so. You may have a great argument built against a certain authority in your life, but if you handle the matter in an ungodly manner, you will lose the case every time.

Others cause trouble for their leaders in order to gain some sort of personal advantage. Their mindset is, "If I can make my boss look incompetent, he'll get fired. Then I'll be hired as his replacement because I exposed his incompetence."

Please hear me today. Your goal should be to make the work of your leaders less burdensome for them. When asked about you, the authority in your life should describe you as being a joy to work alongside of. How are you treating the leadership in your life? Be reliable, not a liability.

no lip service

Isaiah 29:13 – *The Lord says: "These people come near to me with their mouth and honor me with their lips, but their hearts are far from me. Their worship of me is made up only of rules taught by men"* (NIV).

God wants us to honor Him with our words, but He's most concerned about where our hearts are. Many people give God lip service, but He is not their priority. Submission to authority starts with the condition of your heart.

Our words mean nothing to God if they don't come from a heart full of love for Him. Let me take this a step further. The worship of many believers has become ritualistic. They profess their love and devotion, and they even appear to act as if they love God, but their hearts are far from Him. Some people do so out of ignorance, while others do so intentionally. It's wrong either way.

Honoring God with our lips, but not with our hearts, is called flattery. David had some pretty harsh words for those who might try to "butter God up." **Psalm 12:3-4** – *3 May the LORD cut off all flattering lips and every boastful tongue 4 that says, "We will triumph with our tongues; we own our lips—who is our master?"* (NIV)

When you sweet talk God, but don't honor Him with your lifestyle, you mock Him. It's as if you're boasting, "God, I love You. You are awesome, but You are not the Lord of my life. Who *is* my master? I am." What a tragedy!

I know this has been a difficult word today, but I hope you understand the urgency of its message. My prayer is that you will allow the Holy Spirit to investigate your heart. Are you going through the motions today, or have you given Him your entire heart? Submit your heart to Him; He wants all of you. May your words and actions confirm what's in your heart, not cover it up.

Job 32:21-22 – *21 I will show partiality to no one, nor will I flatter any man; 22 for if I were skilled in flattery, my Maker would soon take me away* (NIV).

unity

Psalm 133:1 – *How good and pleasant it is when brothers live together in unity!* (NIV)

Have you found this verse to be true? I know I have. In fact, I've found out how bad and unpleasant it is when brothers live together in disunity! It's a sad truth, but many Christians can't stand the sight of one another, let alone live together in unity. I'm left asking the age old question, "Why can't we all just get along?"

I believe the answer is simple. Church unity is detrimental to the kingdom of darkness, so Satan has made it his mission to sow discord among believers. In **John 17:23**, Jesus prayed the following regarding the body of Christ, *"May they be brought to complete unity to let the world know that you sent me and have loved them even as you have loved me"* (NIV).

Complete unity in the church serves as a testimony to the lost that Jesus is the Son of God and that the Father loves them as much as He loves His own son. Wow! It's no wonder Satan is trying so hard to cause the church to implode. Just look at how many different religious establishments there are. The devil must fall out of his chair laughing every time a new religion is founded.

Local churches are divided and falling apart, and many are competing with one another rather than partnering together. Christians are at odds with one another, and the image of Christ we portray is often times unattractive. Please hear me on this: The kingdom of God will make its greatest impact on the earth when the church unites.

Unity starts with us. Is there someone you're offended with in your local church today? Perhaps someone is offended with you. Maybe there is division between you and multiple people. I challenge you to make amends today. Swallow your pride, and bring yourself to complete unity.

Romans 15:5 – *May the God who gives endurance and encouragement give you a spirit of unity among yourselves as you follow Christ Jesus* (NIV).

drop and give me ten...percent

Tithing is probably not a topic generally found in a daily devotion, but I felt compelled to include it. One of the purposes I have in writing this devotional is to challenge you to become more like Christ on a daily basis. My desire is to help make His word come alive in you. I want you to experience God's blessings to the fullest, and you have to be in covenant with Him in order to do so.

A tithe is ten percent of any increase you receive; it is your payment owed to God. If you want to be in covenant with Him, tithing is a requirement. In **Malachi 3:10**, the Lord says, *"Bring the whole tithe into the storehouse, that there may be food in my house"* (NIV).

Many people withhold their tithe, though, because they are more concerned about food being in *their* house. But when you give God what is His, He pays careful attention to your needs. The Lord goes on to say in **Malachi 3:10**, *"Test me in this, and see if I will not throw open the floodgates of heaven and pour out so much blessing that you will not have room enough for it."* Now that's the kind of blessing I'm talking about!

However, on the flipside, look at what God says to those who do not tithe. **Malachi 3:9** – *"You are under a curse—the whole nation of you—because you are robbing me"* (NIV). I absolutely do not want to be under a curse, and I certainly don't want to get caught stealing from God.

If you faithfully give your tithe to your local church, I want to encourage you to remain doing so. Even if money gets tight, stay in covenant with God. If you give sporadically, discipline yourself to be consistent. If you're not giving at all, I challenge you to test God in this. After all, He gives you permission to do so, and I guarantee He will make good on His promise. Glory!

Matthew 22:21 – *Then he said to them, "Give to Caesar what is Caesar's, and to God what is God's"* (NIV).

sowing and reaping

I want to take the next few days to share with you some of the basic principles of giving. Your tithe is the ten percent payment you owe God, but there are other forms of giving that are not required of you. They're very beneficial, but they're not requirements. Today I want to discuss the principles of sowing and reaping. I pray you are enlightened as you read.

To *sow* means to plant seed for; to scatter seed over for the purpose of growth. The purpose of sowing is to produce growth, and you're going to produce whatever you plant. You can't plant corn and produce watermelons. It just doesn't work that way.

This same principle is true when it comes to sowing and reaping in the kingdom of God. If your family is believing God for a new house, sow a seed into someone else's home. If you need new clothes, try donating your old ones. Ask the Holy Spirit to direct you where and how to sow, but do *not* sow your tithe.

The Bible says you will reap generously if you sow generously, but you don't want to be a misguided giver. Whoever sows stupidly will likely regret doing so. If you don't plant any seed at all, it's foolish to expect a harvest of any kind.

Let's say a farmer has a 20-acre field. His desire is to produce a harvest of corn. He dreams of a thriving crop, and he waits anxiously for it to come. He goes out religiously and tends to the field, watering it and working long hours, but nothing ever grows. Why? He never planted any seeds.

I encourage you today to begin sowing seeds as the Lord leads you, and I believe with you for a mighty harvest in your life. May God bless you abundantly as you sow into good soil.

decide in your heart

2 Corinthians 9:7 – *Each man should give what he has decided in his heart to give, not reluctantly or under compulsion, for God loves a cheerful giver* (NIV).

Another way to give is in offerings. Your tithe is what you owe to God, and God directs you how to sow and where, but you decide how much offering to give. An offering is a contribution you make over and above your tithe.

Paul taught that each man should give what *he* has decided in *his* heart to give. A person doesn't decide how much tithe he should give; a tithe is always ten percent. God doesn't decide how much offering you should give; you decide in your heart what to give above your tithe. Offerings are an act of worship. You give an offering to honor and thank Him. Nobody else can decide how much you love God, nor can they tell you what your offering should be.

The Bible goes on to teach that we should not give reluctantly or under compulsion. Let me give you an example of each. A reluctant giver says, "Why should I give above my tithe? I'm already giving ten percent; that's plenty. Nevertheless, my wife wants me to add a little extra to the check this week, so I'll go ahead and do it."

A person who gives under compulsion doesn't put any thought or prayer behind his offering. Many people give at random, and they'll sometimes give when they shouldn't. God doesn't want you to give foolishly; He wants you to give cheerfully.

Being a cheerful giver is not human nature. In fact, our flesh is penny-pinching. I believe cheerful giving is a quality developed over time. I want to encourage you today to be a giver, but don't give frivolously. If you are in love with God, you will want to praise Him with offerings.

Revelation 11:17 – *"We give thanks to you, Lord God Almighty, the one who is and who was"* (NIV).

some cool promises

2 Corinthians 9:8 – *And God is able to make all grace abound to you, so that in all things at all times, having all that you need, you will abound in every good work* (NIV).

God makes some cool promises to those who give faithfully. My hope is that you will be encouraged today as you read this. God is reliable, and He will make good on His word.

First of all, God is able to make all grace abound to you. How much grace? *All* grace. What an awesome promise! The word *grace* in this verse comes from the Greek word meaning divine favors, benefits, blessings and gifts. I don't know about you, but sign me up for all the divine benefits I can get please!

Paul goes on to say that in all things at all times you will have all that you need. It's important for us to understand this. If we are faithful to give, we will have everything that we *need*, no matter the circumstance. When times get tough and we're strapped for cash, God assures that all of our needs will be met. There will no doubt be times that we are left *wanting* certain things, but He will provide all that we *need*, not what we think we need.

He also promises that we will abound in every good work. This means that He will cause us to flourish as we work according to His purpose. You will thrive, but not if you are out doing your own thing. God does not prosper works done selfishly or outside of His will, no matter how much money we give. God's favor cannot be bought.

I pray that you have been enlightened as you've read about giving. Now that you have the information, though, you will be held responsible for it. I've heard it said, "Ignorance is bliss," but you're not ignorant any more. Become the faithful giver that God desires you to be, and begin experiencing His divine favor.

Luke 6:38 – *"Give, and it will be given to you. A good measure, pressed down, shaken together and running over, will be poured into your lap. For with the measure you use, it will be measured to you"* (NIV).

209

for life

> **2 Peter 1:3** – *His divine power has given us everything we need for life and godliness through our knowledge of him who called us by his own glory and goodness* (NIV).

Security. That's what most people are looking for, both physically and emotionally. Whether it's through slaving at work, or trying to work over the government, many individuals and families are fighting to provide the basic needs of life. Some even turn to a life of crime in an effort to meet their physical needs.

There are others who are emotionally bankrupt. They wander from relationship to relationship searching for someone who can meet their emotional needs. Many walk away from their marriages, willingly leaving their spouses and children because their needs are not being met. This kind of behavior is prevalent in both secular and Christian circles. It's very disheartening.

What is the underlying cause? The vast majority of people are trying to get everything they need for life in their *own* power. They try one thing, and if it doesn't work, they try something else. If that doesn't work, then they might make a drastic move. But instead of finding what they need, their lives become more unstable and unpredictable.

You may find yourself in a similar position today. You are desperately trying to make things happen in your own strength, and your life is in shambles. Please listen to me. You cannot provide for yourself everything you need for life in your own power. You might come close, but you will never be completely satisfied. You will remain in a constant struggle that you can never win.

It's by *His* divine power that we have everything we need for life. You might say, "Surely you don't mean *everything* I need, right?" Yes, *everything* you need. I want to encourage you today to rely on His power. Maybe you've been self-absorbed for a long time. I pray that today you will begin to trust Him. Glory to God!

> **Matthew 6:8** – *"Do not be like them, for your Father knows what you need before you ask him"* (NIV).

210

for godliness

2 Peter 1:3 – *His divine power has given us everything we need for life and godliness through our knowledge of him who called us by his own glory and goodness* (NIV).

It's by His divine power that we have everything we need for life and for godliness. Another word for *godliness* is *holiness*. If you are ever going to live a holy life, you have to understand this verse. I pray you are enlightened today.

Holiness is not humanly possible. You can be the most disciplined person on the face of the earth and still fall short of godliness. You can spend your lifetime doing good, but a lifetime of good deeds does not make you holy. In fact, a lifetime of good deeds doesn't even guarantee salvation. Why? Your flesh cannot be holy, and there is nothing you can do in your own strength to merit salvation.

It's by His divine power that you are made holy; it is a gift from God. **Romans 3:22-24** – 22 *This righteousness is given through faith in Jesus Christ to all who believe. There is no difference between Jew and Gentile,* 23 *for all have sinned and fall short of the glory of God,* 24 *and all are justified freely by his grace through the redemption that came by Christ Jesus* (NIV).

Are you grasping this? So many Christians constantly beat themselves up because of their sin. They see godliness as a lost cause because they've failed in their pursuit of it. Our righteous acts are like filthy rags (**Isaiah 64:6**).

I want to encourage you today. Perhaps you've been overcome with guilt and shame because you have tried to attain holiness by your own means. Jesus Christ already paid the price for your shortcomings. His divine power has given you everything you need for godliness. All you have to do is believe He's done His job, and allow His word to mold your character on a daily basis. Renounce your sinful nature, and be led by the Spirit.

Romans 9:30 – *The Gentiles, who did not pursue righteousness, have obtained it, a righteousness that is by faith* (NIV).

that's Mine

Humans are possessive by nature. We don't want anyone to take what belongs to us, especially if it's something of value. Most people are willing to fight to protect what is rightfully theirs, and this is even true of young children.

After learning to say *daddy, mommy* and *no*, the next word out of a child's mouth is often times, *"Mine!"* If we had a dime for every time we hear the word *mine* on a daily basis from our two boys, Heidi and I would be receiving preferential treatment from our bank by now. It never fails. Jack will be playing with something, Noah takes it away, there's a scream and then the words, "Hey, that's *mine*! Give it back to me!" Then five minutes later there's a role reversal, and the same scene plays out. It's quite painful to listen to.

When it comes to mankind, God the Father is very possessive. Heidi and I are constantly teaching our boys to share, but God will not share you with anyone or anything. He makes His feelings about each one of us very clear. He says, "You are Mine!" I pray that you find comfort in this truth today.

Sometimes you may feel unnoticed or unwanted, especially when you are in great distress or under attack. The enemy is out to destroy you. He wants to steal you away and cause you to feel inferior. Be confident of this: God has redeemed you, and He knows you by name. He has not lost or misplaced you. You are special to Him, and He protects and fights for you.

Maybe today you don't feel like you belong. Perhaps you are having a difficult time fitting in or finding purpose in the kingdom of God. It's in those moments that Satan will come and attempt to lure you away. Find peace in God's word today. You belong to Him! Hallelujah!

Song of Solomon 7:10 – *I belong to my beloved, and his desire if for me* (NIV).

you've got a friend in Me

Isaiah 43:2 – *"When you pass through the waters, I will be with you; and when you pass through the rivers, they will not sweep over you. When you walk through the fire, you will not be burned; the flames will not set you ablaze"* (NIV).

Our son Jack loves the character Woody from the Toy Story movies. A couple of years ago, when he first watched Toy Story, he became obsessed with everything Woody. One day we made the mistake of walking down the toy aisle of a certain store. Jack caught a glimpse of a Woody doll, and he just had to have it.

We bought the doll, and the two of them were inseparable. Jack wouldn't allow anyone to play with his new toy, and if someone tried, he'd do his best to defend Woody. He tried to take the doll everywhere we went. Jack loved Woody, and Woody loved Jack. They were a match made in heaven.

However, after a few weeks, Woody found himself buried at the bottom of the toy box. The excitement had worn off. Woody still belonged to Jack, but Jack lost his passion to play with him. Video games, books and other toys became more important. Recently, though, the newest Toy Story movie was released, and Jack's passion for Woody returned (he now has a full costume).

I want to share with you something that I've learned. God doesn't say you are His, and then sit you on the top shelf to collect dust. He doesn't change the way He feels about you from week to week. You are precious to Him, and He is with you everywhere you go. He will never bury you in the toy box.

When you pass through the waters, He doesn't say, "Oh wait, I can't swim. You got this." When you pass through the rivers, He doesn't toss you a life jacket and wish you luck. He doesn't abandon you when you walk through the fire either. God is always interested in you, and His interest doesn't vary from day to day. His passion for you never wears off.

Matthew 28:20 – *"And surely I am with you always, to the very end of the age"* (NIV).

precious and honored

> **Isaiah 43:4** – *Since you are precious and honored in my sight, and because I love you, I will give men in exchange for you, and people in exchange for your life* (NIV).

There is no good reason why a Christian should have poor self-esteem, and those who do have a low self-worth, have chosen to view themselves in that way. Pity parties are not godly. Beating yourself up repeatedly for mistakes and walking around guilt-ridden does not equate holiness. It's foolishness, and it gives the devil glory.

This is not to say that you won't feel remorse when you make mistakes. You *should* feel bad when you mess up, but there's a problem when you repeatedly swim in a pool of regret. Those who wallow in self-pity will eventually identify themselves according to their failures. This kind of behavior grieves the heart of God.

Low self-esteem results from a lack of understanding how God views us. If you struggle with your self-worth, look to the word of God. He makes His feelings about you very clear. He actually says in the above verse that you are precious and honored in His sight. In other words, you are dear to Him, and He has great respect for you. If you were truly worthless, God would not place such a high value on your life.

David writes that the Lord takes delight in His people (**Psalm 149:4**). You are a source of joy to Him; He finds pleasure in thinking about you. When He looks at you, He does not say, "Oh, here we go again. This guy can't get anything right. I knew I shouldn't have created a person like him."

You may be struggling with your self-worth today. I want to encourage you not to feel sorry for yourself. If you do, you're going to live a miserable life, and nobody is going to want to be around you. Search His word, and see yourself the way He does.

> **Psalm 147:11** – *The LORD delights in those who fear him, who put their hope in his unfailing love* (NIV).

follow the Leader

Ephesians 5:1 – *Imitate God, therefore, in everything you do, because you are his dear children* (NLT).

As parents of small children, it's important for my wife and me to be acutely aware of every move we make and every word we speak. Why? Our boys are paying careful attention to every detail of our lives. This time of their lives is crucial to their development. Their personalities, character and beliefs are being shaped on a daily basis, and they are taking their cues from us.

It's our responsibility as parents to show our children how to live godly lives. I welcome this responsibility because I want our children to learn from Heidi and me. I know there will be other people who positively (and negatively) influence our kids, but we are the ones who primarily shape their lives. It's a great responsibility, but I don't want someone else to raise our boys.

I also understand that our children, especially as they get older, will make their own decisions as to whether or not they will follow the example Heidi and I have set for them. I had to make the same decision as I was growing up. My parents are God-fearing people, and they taught me to work hard and to value others. They set a great example for my sister and me, but I ultimately decided whether I would follow their lead or not.

The same is true in your walk with the Lord. Jesus has set the ultimate example for His children to follow. He lived a flawless life, and He's even given us a written record to draw from. If you are His child, His desire is for you to imitate Him, but you make the final decision as to how you are going to live your life.

Unlike Heidi and me, our heavenly Father is perfect. He doesn't wish He could take back anything He has said, thought or done. Others no doubt have, and will continue to influence your life, but God should be the standard example you hold yourself to.

1 Peter 2:21 – *To this you were called, because Christ suffered for you, leaving you an example, that you should follow in his steps* (NIV).

215

eww...gross

Ephesians 5:2 – *Live a life filled with love, following the example of Christ. He loved us and offered himself as a sacrifice for us, a pleasing aroma to God* (NLT).

What's the nastiest odor you've ever smelled? When was the last time you smelled it? Where were you? What caused the odor? Got it yet? Have you ever smelled something so bad you could taste it? I know I have. I'm not going to go into details (you can thank me later), but I've smelled some dreadful odors before.

Jesus loves us, and He offered Himself as a sacrifice for us. Paul called His sacrifice a pleasing aroma to God. Now ask yourself this question, "What must I smell like to God?" I can't answer that question for you, but I will tell you this. If you don't live a life filled with love, following the example of Jesus Christ, you don't smell very good. In fact, you probably cause Him to turn His nose up.

Maybe you've come to the conclusion today that you're not putting off a pleasing aroma to God. I want to encourage you to live a life full of love. Many Christians live their lives with the love tank half empty. Their love for others is partial when it should be impartial. When we purpose to imitate Christ's character, He will give us the ability to love unconditionally. Once we are full of His love, we will start to smell a little better. Our aroma will almost be bearable.

Paul urges that we should offer ourselves as holy, living sacrifices to God. Why? Doing so pleases Him (**Romans 12:1**). What does it mean to offer yourself as a sacrifice to God? It means forfeiting your rights as the "shot-caller" of your life and surrendering it to Him. Nobody wants to stink, but so many Christians do. If you're one of them, learn to love and offer yourself as a living sacrifice to Him.

2 Corinthians 2:15 – *For we are a fragrance of Christ to God among those who are being saved and among those who are perishing* (NASB).

no sexual immorality

Ephesians 5:3 – *Let there be no sexual immorality, impurity, or greed among you. Such sins have no place among God's people* (NLT).

I realize that today's message may not be a very popular one, but I'm not interested in winning a popularity contest. My heart is for your life to be changed by the word of God, and if your *entire* life is going to be changed, then the *entire* word of God must be applied to it. That includes the less than desirable truths found in Scripture. So here we go.

Sexual immorality has no place among God's people. Most people hear the words *sexual immorality*, and they immediately think of infidelity or adultery. While being unfaithful is definitely sexually immoral, it is important for us to understand that sexual immorality includes more than cheating on a spouse.

Pay careful attention to these words spoken by Jesus: *"You have heard that it was said, 'Do not commit adultery.' But I tell you that anyone who looks at a woman lustfully has already committed adultery with her in his heart"* (**Matthew 5:27-28**). First of all, these verses are relevant to both men and women. If a woman looks at a man lustfully, she has already committed adultery with him in her heart.

Also, Jesus is talking about a *look* being immoral. When we look at a man or woman and desire to be with that person sexually, God considers it adultery and immoral. In His book, a lustful look is equivalent to the physical act.

Jesus is talking about *every* woman (or man) that you may look at lustfully, not just a married person. If you fantasize over a movie scene or a person in a magazine, you are sexually immoral. If you gawk at billboards or television ads, you need to learn to turn your head. **1 Corinthians 6:18** says to flee sexual immorality. Purify your mind; don't condone immorality at all.

1 Thessalonians 4:3 – *It is God's will that you should be sanctified: that you should avoid sexual immorality* (NIV).

no impurity

> **Ephesians 5:3** – *Let there be no sexual immorality, impurity, or greed among you. Such sins have no place among God's people* (NLT).

The Bible says there should be no impurity among God's people. Impurities are anything that contaminates your body, mind or spirit. It's important for us not to have any impurity in our lives because all it takes is one drop of impurity to compromise innocence.

Sergio Scataglini gives a great illustration of this in his teaching on holiness. He says that ninety-eight percent holiness is not enough. He uses the example of drinking water. Would you drink water from a bottle labeled ninety-eight percent purified and two percent sewage? No way! You'd put it back on the shelf. Just a small percentage of impurity contaminates the whole bottle and causes it to be undrinkable.

God looks at us in much the same way. Let me ask you a question: How much impurity do you think God is going to allow into heaven? Two percent? One? No! God expects His church to be holy, washed in the Word, without stain or wrinkle (**Ephesians 5:27**). Any measure of impurity you allow in your life pollutes your whole being.

I want to encourage you today to guard yourself. If you don't, your heart will eventually harden, and you will become desensitized to sin. **Ephesians 4:19** – *Having lost all sensitivity, they have given themselves over to sensuality so as to indulge in every kind of impurity, with a continual lust for more* (NIV).

Many people start out "small." They allow a little impurity at a time to seep in. They dabble here and there, but then they find themselves indulging here, there and everywhere. Eventually they can't get enough, and they constantly desire more. If you are bound by impurity today, ask Jesus to cleanse you now.

> **1 Thessalonians 4:7** – *For God did not call us to uncleanness, but in holiness* (NKJV).

no greed

Ephesians 5:3 – *Let there be no sexual immorality, impurity, or greed among you. Such sins have no place among God's people* (NLT).

Judging by the way many people act, you would think they don't believe that greed is a sin. Show me a greedy person, and I'll show you someone who is self-centered. A person overcome by greed has an insatiable hunger for power or possessions that gratify the sinful nature.

Greed causes a person to never be content with what he has, whether it's assets, status or relationships. He or she is always left wanting more. I'm not talking about a casual, "Oh, it sure would be nice to have a little more of that." No, greed is a bottomless pit. It is a ravenous desire to be on top. Such people are never satisfied or thankful for what they *do* have.

Another word for *greed* is *gluttony*. Listen to what the Bible has to say about those given to gluttony. **Proverbs 23:2** – *Put a knife to your throat if you are given to gluttony* (NIV). Wow, those are some pretty strong words, but what do they mean? A person who allows greed to rule over him is killing himself.

Greed is a heart condition. Many Christians masquerade as righteous, but their hearts are far from Him. They are self-serving people who have given themselves to gluttony. Jesus likened such individuals to a cup and dish that were clean on the outside, but full of greed and self-indulgence on the inside. He commanded them to clean the inside first, and then the outside would become clean (see **Matthew 23:25-26**).

My hope is for you to be set free from greed today. I pray that your insatiable desire for worldly possessions would be replaced with a relentless pursuit of His character. Do not pretend to be someone you're not; become the person God sees you as.

Luke 12:15 – *"Watch out! Be on your guard against all kinds of greed; a man's life does not consist in the abundance of his possessions"* (NIV).

devoted to prayer

Colossians 4:2 – *Devote yourselves to prayer, being watchful and thankful* (NIV).

Another version of this verse says to *continue earnestly in prayer* (NKJV). If you are going to have a successful prayer life, you have to commit yourself wholeheartedly. The problem is many Christians have become casual with their prayers. Perhaps you're one of them. If so, today is your day to start afresh.

The best way I know to show you the importance of a devoted prayer life is to compare it to marriage. Communication is one of the most significant aspects of the relationship between a husband and wife. Ask someone who has a successful marriage, and they'll tell you their success relies heavily on their level of communication. Ask someone whose marriage has crumbled, and they'll tell you the same thing. Communication is key.

My wife and I work very hard everyday to maintain a successful marriage. We constantly communicate. Sometimes the conversation is pleasant, and other times it's not so much. There are times one of us wants to talk, and the other one doesn't feel like it (usually me). We both work full-time, and we're full-time parents, and we often have to make time at the end of a long day to talk and listen to each other. We have to separate ourselves from everything else that's going on and just be together.

The same is true in your relationship with God. You have to be disciplined and separate yourself unto God. Life is going to be very difficult at times, and the last thing you're going to want to do is offer a prayer of thanks. Do it anyway. It's inevitable that you're going to get tired; don't sacrifice a few minutes of quality communication with God to hit the sheets a little early.

Consecrate yourself to prayer. Make prayer a priority. Don't plan your prayer time around your life; plan your life around your prayer time.

Acts 2:42 – *They devoted themselves to the apostles' teaching and to the fellowship, to the breaking of bread and to prayer* (NIV).

licensed to offend

> **Luke 17:1** – *Then He said to the disciples, "It is impossible that no offenses should come, but woe to him through whom they do come!"* (NKJV)

There is a one hundred percent chance that you will have multiple opportunities to become offended. You can try to avoid it, but offense will find you. I guarantee it. And many people use their offense as a license to offend. This is not God's will. I want to share with you a story that demonstrates how we should respond when offended. I pray you are encouraged today.

In Acts 6-7, you can read the brief account of a man by the name of Stephen. Stephen was one of seven men chosen for a leadership role in the first church. He was described as being full of faith and of the Holy Spirit (**Acts 6:5**). He was also full of God's grace and power, and he did great miracles among the people (**6:8**). Stephen was highly favored, and it didn't take long for opposition to rise up against him.

Some members of a local synagogue began arguing with Stephen, but they were no match for his wisdom. So they started a rumor that Stephen had blasphemed against Moses and God. These men caused such a stir that Stephen was seized and taken before the Sanhedrin. False witnesses were produced to testify against him, but Stephen did not back down. Instead he rebuked their unbelief. The angry mob rioted and dragged Stephen out into the street and began to stone him.

Talk about a bad day. Perhaps you can relate on some level to what Stephen went through. Stephen had every opportunity to become offended with his accusers. They humiliated him, lied about him and sentenced him to death, but look at how Stephen responded to their offensive behavior. **Acts 7:59-60** – *While they were stoning him, Stephen prayed...Then he fell on his knees and cried out, "Lord, do not hold this sin against them"* (NIV).

I challenge you today to respond to your offenders in the same way. Do not be overtaken by self-pity or revenge. Forgive those who persecute you, and learn to hold them up in prayer.

to all the husbands

> **Ephesians 5:25** – *Husbands, love your wives, just as Christ loved the church and gave himself up for her* (NIV).

This message is specifically for all the husbands out there, but I believe it's beneficial for everyone. Ladies, if you're married, it's important for you to understand what God expects of your husband. Unrealistic expectations ruin marriages. Knowing what God requires of your spouse will help you set sensible goals for your relationship.

If you're not married yet, but intend on getting married at some point, you'll want to pay attention as well. One day you'll be a spouse *and* have one, so you need to know what a godly marriage looks like. I pray your marriage (or future marriage) is made stronger as we look at what God has to say.

There are many men who are more interested in being manly than they are in being the loving spouse God desires them to be. Perhaps you're one of them. Being a godly husband is more than being a provider. Husbands, you are to love your wife just as Christ loved the church and gave Himself up for her. But what does this mean?

You should love your wife unconditionally. Your love for her is to be without restraint. This means you withhold nothing, and you commit to giving her your very best, always and in every area. To give yourself up for her means that sometimes you will set aside your personal wants and comfort for what's in the best interest of your relationship.

The Bible also says that husbands ought to love their wives as their own bodies (**Ephesians 5:28**) and be considerate of them (**1 Peter 3:7**). Do the laundry without being begged, and learn to be sensitive to her needs. Clean up after yourself, and communicate effectively. You're not a caveman, so don't grunt at her. Pray for your wife, support and provide security for her.

> **Colossians 3:19** – *Husbands, love your wives and do not be harsh with them* (NIV).

to all the wives

Please notice this passage does not mean that women are inferior or weaker than men. It doesn't mean God prefers men to women either. It simply means that God has established the husband as the authority over the household, and it's his job as the head to lead, provide for and protect his family.

Ladies, you must submit to your husband in order to remain under God's covering, but submission doesn't mean you sign off on every harebrained idea he has. What it does mean, however, is that the two of you should be in agreement in every area. Sometimes you will agree to disagree, but when a decision is made regarding your family, the two of you should be united.

Also, when you submit to your husband, it doesn't mean you're not allowed to give input. Maybe your husband says things like, "I'm the man, and this is what we're going to do," and then he doesn't allow you to contribute your thoughts on the matter. This is not right, and he will answer for it. Your opinion *does* matter.

When a man and woman are married, the Bible says they become one flesh (**Genesis 2:24**). It doesn't say the two enter into a relationship in which one person lords over the other. God created man with no ability to reason, so He gave man a wife to reason for him. I'm kidding, but I want to encourage you to be the helpmate your husband needs. He needs to know your feelings and opinions, and he should honor them.

Ultimately, the husband has the responsibility of leading his household, and he will be judged accordingly. God is a God of order, and you are to submit to your husband's authority. Don't allow your husband to act foolishly. Help him. He needs it.

to all the parents

Proverbs 22:6 – *Train a child in the way he should go, and when he is old he will not turn from it* (NIV).

Have you ever trained for anything before? Maybe you went through some training courses at a new job, or perhaps you trained for a marathon or for some other sport. If you've ever been in the military, then you certainly know what it means to train.

Normally a person goes through training in order to learn something they didn't know before, or to be able to do something they couldn't do before. However, if the trainee does not receive proper instruction from the trainer, he won't be any better off than he was to begin with.

I once had a basketball coach who was not very good at preparing us for games. Our practices were generally unproductive. And when game time came around, we usually had not received proper instruction from our coach. The final score reflected our team's incompetence, and we were frequently left frustrated. You may know exactly what I'm talking about.

It's important for you to understand this. I believe there are a lot of frustrated children in the world today because so many parents are sending mixed signals. God expects parents to train their children to live godly lives. This process starts at birth and goes until they move out on their own. You must begin to instill godly values into your children when they are young, and then you need to remain consistent as long as they live under your roof.

Heidi and I try to be firm, fair and consistent in every area of our lives, especially when it comes to raising our boys. Training someone is hard work, and being trained is often hard as well. Don't make an already difficult task even harder by being inconsistent. Set boundaries and stick to them. Spend time reading the Bible and praying with your kids. Train them to be godly because they may not figure it out on their own.

Ephesians 6:4 – *Do not provoke your children to anger; but bring them up in the discipline and instruction of the Lord* (NASB).

a blameless home

Psalm 101:2 – *I will be careful to lead a blameless life—when will you come to me? I will conduct the affairs of my house with a blameless heart* (NIV).

I want to focus on the second part of this verse today. Say this with me: "I will conduct the affairs of my house with a blameless heart." Now say it again. Say it as many times as you need to until it sinks in. If it hasn't already, I pray this becomes the motto by which you conduct the affairs of your home.

God desires your home to be a place of integrity, not a place of compromise. Many people live double lives. They appear one way in public while practicing a different lifestyle at home. They are loved by coworkers and teach Sunday school at their local church, but their families are afraid of them. They seem to be upstanding citizens, but their character defects hide just barely beneath the surface.

Every area of our homes should be governed by holiness. There should be no gray areas. I have often heard people say, "Would you do that *if* Jesus was there with you?" The fact of the matter is He *is* there with us always. Our finances should be managed with integrity. Our families should be treated with respect. The way we entertain ourselves should be pure. What television shows and movies do you promote? What's being looked at on the Internet? The list goes on.

If you are struggling to live blamelessly at home, there is hope for you! You need accountability, and boundaries need to be established and adhered to. If the Internet is a problem for you or your children, put firewalls on your computers and only set them up in rooms accessible to everyone. Bedrooms are not a good place. If mistreating others is an issue, hold the guilty parties responsible for their actions. Invite the Holy Spirit into your home right now. Live righteously without compromise.

Joshua 24:15 – *"But as for me and my household, we will serve the LORD"* (NIV).

225

in the dark

John 12:46 – *"I have come as a light to shine in this dark world, so that all who put their trust in me will no longer remain in the dark"* (NLT).

Have you ever walked around blindfolded or in a room that is pitch black? If not, I encourage you to stop and try it before you continue reading. Just be careful.

I've done both on multiple occasions. Walking around unable to see where I am going is an awkward experience, especially at first. It's very uncomfortable not knowing what obstacles are around me. I've walked into walls, knocked things over and even hurt myself before. Perhaps you can relate.

After carefully walking around for an extended period of time, though, I eventually become more and more accustomed to my surroundings. By putting my hands out in front of me, I can feel where I'm going and protect myself from potential hazards. Even though I still can't see anything, I become more comfortable with being in the dark.

The same is true spiritually. I believe there are two types of people who are spiritually "in the dark." There are those who are in the awkward stage. They're wandering around aimlessly bumping into things, trying this way and trying that. They have no direction, and they are searching for the light switch.

Then there are others who have grown accustomed to living in the dark. They have accepted darkness as their way of life because it's familiar to them. They've lost hope, and because they can't see a way out, they don't care to keep looking. Constant darkness leads to low self-esteem, depression and even suicide.

I want to encourage you today if you find yourself in the dark. Jesus is the light of the world. The more you trust Him, the closer you get to Him. The closer you are to Him, the clearer the path before you becomes. Glory to God!

1 John 1:5 – *God is light, pure light; there's not a trace of darkness in him* (MSG).

you may have peace

I can't stress enough how important it is for you to pay careful attention to how Scripture is worded. Many Christians will jump and shout for joy when they read verses like the one above, but they fail to grasp the full meaning. Jesus says some very interesting things in **John 16:33**. Some of His message is encouraging, and some of it is very sobering. My purpose for writing today is for you to fully understand everything He's saying. I pray you are blessed.

We live in a world that is suffering from a widespread shortage of peace. It's an epidemic that is affecting both Christians and the unsaved. Families are in turmoil, as marriages split and children rebel. Many people are experiencing financial ruin due to the economic crunch. Suicide is on the rise, and substance abuse is rampant. Maybe today peace seems like a figment of your imagination. If so, please don't misunderstand what I'm about to tell you. If your life lacks peace, it's because Jesus isn't the center of it.

It's understandable that those who don't know Christ live in a constant state of chaos, but it's inexplicable to me as to why Christians live their lives absent of peace. The only explanation I can offer is that there are far too many believers who don't know who they are in Christ. If your identity is found in Him, Jesus Himself promises peace. There is no peace outside of Jesus Christ.

My goal today is not to frustrate you or cause you to feel guilty. I want you to live the life God has purposed for you, and His desire is for your family to know overwhelming peace. If something or someone has taken priority over Jesus in your life, establish Him as number one again right now. Peace is yours.

Philemon 1:3 – *Grace and peace to you from God our Father and the Lord Jesus Christ* (NIV).

He has overcome

John 16:33 – *"These things I have spoken to you, so that in Me you may have peace. In the world you have tribulation, but take courage; I have overcome the world"* (NASB).

Notice how the second part of this verse begins. Jesus says, *"In the world you have tribulation."* Another version reads, *"In this world you will have trouble"* (NIV). This is not the kind of promise many Christians want to believe, and they certainly don't shout about it. Jesus *has* overcome the world, but in order for Him to overcome, you and I have to face trials we can't conquer in our own strength. What a sobering truth.

How do you handle yourself when you walk through difficulties? Many people quote this verse as they experience tribulation, but they are not victorious. Why? It could be that they skip the part that says *but take courage*.

We all know we're going to have trouble in this lifetime, and we also know Jesus has overcome the world. But God's promises are all conditional. He's not just going to deliver you out of your circumstance; He expects you to step up and face your trials with courage. Jesus cannot overcome on your behalf if you allow your faith to roll over and die in the midst of tribulation.

When faced with the fiery furnace in Daniel 3, what would have happened to Shadrach, Meshach and Abednego if they had tried to flee from their accusers? They likely would have been captured and killed. But because they took heart and trusted God, He delivered them from certain death.

No matter how rough the circumstances may be surrounding your life today, I want to encourage you to go toe-to-toe with your trial. Take courage and trust God. Look at tribulations as an opportunity to build your faith. Perhaps you've been engaged in a lengthy battle. Don't raise the white flag. Stand your ground. Give Jesus a reason to overcome on your behalf.

1 John 5:4 – *For every child of God defeats this evil world, and we achieve this victory through our faith* (NLT).

think before you speak

James 5:12 – *But above all, my brethren, do not swear, either by heaven or by earth or with any other oath; but your yes is to be yes, and your no, no, so that you may not fall under judgment* (NASB).

In order for us to fully grasp the importance of this verse, we must first understand the five verses preceding it (**James 5:7-11**). This passage was written as an exhortation to all believers, which hopefully includes you.

In verses 7-11, James urged us to be patient and to strengthen our hearts as we wait for Him to come. There are many Christians who are overly anxious and remain a step ahead of God's timing. Don't rush Him. Contrary to what you may think, He knows better than you do.

He also instructs the church not to complain against one another, and He warns of impending judgment for those who do. I tremble at the thought of how many Christians quarrel with one another, including myself. Bickering amongst believers would cease if all parties involved would become more concerned about God's desires than their own.

You'd probably agree that these commands are all equally important, and they should be practiced by everyone. Even so, the most significant command was saved for last. James begins verse 12 by saying, *"But above all."* He's basically saying, "Everything I just encouraged you to do is important, but the next thing I'm about to tell you is even *more* important."

Do not swear. Let your yes be yes and your no be no. In other words, God expects us to be patient, strong of heart and not to complain, but more than that, He desires for us to be a people of our word. I exhort you today: Don't make promises you don't intend to keep, and back up your words with your actions. Be reliable and credible. Think before you speak.

Psalm 34:13 – *Guard your tongue from profanity, and no more lying through your teeth* (MSG).

the very last

> **Mark 9:35** – *Sitting down, Jesus called the twelve and said, "If anyone wants to be first, he must be the very last, and the servant of all"* (NIV).

Finishing last doesn't set well with very many people I know, including myself. There's nothing more humiliating than being picked last on the playground. It's always embarrassing when your team comes in last place, and it's a rare person that volunteers to get in the lunch line last.

Last place is not celebrated in our society. In fact, those who finish last frequently become punch lines and are widely regarded as inferior. And since last place is looked upon as unacceptable, many people are in a relentless pursuit to get to the top. Nobody wants to be a loser, so many are bent on proving how valuable they are. And they're willing to do whatever it takes to prove their worth.

If you ask a professional football player at the beginning of the season what his goal is for the upcoming year, he will likely tell you it's to win the Super Bowl. No truthful player is going to say, "Well, we're gunning for last this season." No! Last place is intolerable to most athletes. The President doesn't invite the last place team to visit The White House. He invites the champs.

Businessmen and women want to climb the corporate ladder, not fall off of it. They want to be successful, and the world measures success by a person's bottom line. Unfortunately, many people in the church have adopted the world's distaste for finishing last. But Jesus said the person who is very last, and the servant of all, shall be first in the kingdom of God.

I realize this teaching goes directly against what society is trying to engrave into your mind, but I want to challenge you. Become a servant. I'm going to take the next few days to share with you a biblical perspective of servanthood.

> **Mark 10:43** – *"Instead, whoever wants to become great among you must be your servant"* (NIV).

great leaders serve

Ephesians 4:11-12 – 11 *It was he who gave some to be apostles, some to be prophets, some to be evangelists, and some to be pastors and teachers,* 12 *to prepare God's people for works of service* (NIV).

Great leaders are servants. If you don't serve, you're not a good leader; it doesn't matter what your title is. Effective leaders lead by example. In the above passage, Paul listed five different types of church leaders: apostles, prophets, evangelists, pastors and teachers. They have different functions in the body of Christ, but they all have the responsibility of preparing God's people for works of service. In other words, if you are a person in authority, it is your duty to teach those under you how to serve.

It's important for us to understand that we cannot teach something we have not learned ourselves. Before we try to teach someone how to serve we need to first become servants.

One of the biggest frustrations facing leaders in general is the inability to find good help. I've heard it said that most people only do what is inspected, not what is expected. Others just want to be celebrated or be in the spotlight. There are very few people who are content with serving where needed, whether it be behind the scenes or out in front.

Why are such people a rarity? It's largely because their leaders forgot, or never learned, how to serve. Many leaders develop a "rock star" mentality, expecting everything to be done for them when and how they want it to be done. They do very little for themselves. A leader who expects to be served is teaching those under him to expect the same thing.

If you are in leadership, become a servant. Don't expect those who are under your authority to be someone you're not. Take your cues from Jesus, and be willing to make sacrifices in order to better serve others.

Matthew 20:28 – *"The Son of Man did not come to be served, but to serve, and to give his life as a ransom for many"* (NIV).

serve to build up

Ephesians 4:12-13 – 12 ...*to prepare God's people for works of service, so that the body of Christ may be built up* 13 *until we all reach unity in the faith and in the knowledge of the Son of God and become mature, attaining to the whole measure of the fullness of Christ* (NIV).

Teaching others to serve should be one of the top priorities of any leader, especially in the church. But why? Paul answered this question in **Ephesians 4:12**: so that the body of Christ may be built up. In order for the church to become the fortified body God desires it to be, servanthood is mandatory.

Many churches are on life support because a lot of Christians have become "me first." Show me a church full of people who know how to serve, and I'll show you a church that is unified. Show me a church full of selfish people, and I'll show you a church that's in disarray. Paul said that works of service lead to *unity* in the faith.

Selfish people don't serve, and they're not concerned about uniting with anyone. They are only interested in doing what benefits them. This pandemic is tearing down the body of Christ at an accelerated pace. New believers are not looking to join a church that could care less about them.

Servanthood also helps the church reach unity in the knowledge of the Son of God. Jesus came to serve, and those who truly know Him will serve as well. I challenge you to study the life of Jesus, and there you will find the heart of a servant.

Being able to serve someone else is a mark of maturity. It takes a very stable and confident individual to faithfully serve another person. A servant is typically viewed as a lowly position, and many people cannot serve because they simply refuse to swallow their pride. My prayer is that you will begin to humbly serve. Let's do our part in building up the body of Christ.

Matthew 11:29 – *"Take My yoke upon you and learn from Me, for I am gentle and humble in heart"* (NASB).

as you would obey Christ

Ephesians 6:5 – *Slaves, obey your earthly masters with respect and fear, and with sincerity of heart, just as you would obey Christ* (NIV).

Imagine you're at home, and there's a knock at the door. You walk over and open it to greet your guest, and there stands Jesus Christ in the flesh. You reverently bow before Him and begin to worship with fear and trembling. After a few moments, He looks at you and says, "I need you to do something for Me."

How would you respond? You would probably drop whatever it was you were doing, no matter how important, and begin serving Jesus immediately. You likely wouldn't say, "Oh, not right now. I don't really see the point, Jesus. Why are You asking me? Don't You have someone else who can take care of that for You?"

Most God-fearing people would try to fulfill Jesus' every wish because they have great respect for Him. They'd even be willing to do things that are less desirable and that don't benefit them personally. If this is how you would serve Christ, you should serve those you are subject to in the same way.

Paul wrote that servants are to obey their earthly masters with respect, fear and sincerity of heart. God expects us to serve those who are in authority over us just as we would serve Him. **Colossians 3:23** – *Whatever you do, work at it with all your heart, as working for the Lord, not for men* (NIV).

Unfortunately, those who follow this command are few in number. You should be giving your employer, pastor, parents and government honor, not a hard time. Unless you're asked to do something illegal or unbiblical, your heart's delight should be to get it done. Be quick to accomplish even the mundane and menial. You may need to ask the Holy Spirit to help you. I pray that your attitude becomes the same as that of Christ Jesus.

Philippians 2:7 – *When the time came, he set aside the privileges of deity and took on the status of a slave* (MSG).

serve with your gift

Another version says that each one of us has been given a *special* gift (NASB). You've probably received numerous gifts in your lifetime, but have you ever been given a present that was very dear to you? Maybe it was a piece of jewelry from your spouse, or perhaps one of your children made you something. Got it yet?

This past Christmas I received a brand new laptop from my wife for Christmas. Needless to say, it's very special to me for multiple reasons. First of all, I needed it. My old one had various problems from missing keys to a broken disk drive. Also, writing is one of my passions, and the new laptop allows me to do so more efficiently. I love it!

It's also an expensive piece of equipment, so I'm very protective of it. Truth be told, I really don't want anyone (other than my wife of course) to touch it or be anywhere near it. I guess you could say I'm selfish when it comes to my new laptop because it's valuable and very special to me. I keep it hidden in a secure place, and I only take it out when I want to use it. Surely you can relate to what I'm saying on some level.

This is how many people are in the body of Christ when it comes to the gifts and talents that God has graciously given them. They keep their special gift safely stowed away until an opportunity presents itself that profits them personally. This is not how God wants us to act.

His desire is for you to serve others with the abilities He's blessed you with. If you excel in a particular trade, offer your services to your local church or even your neighbors. If you are good with a mop and vacuum, help clean after a special event. Whatever your gift, use it to serve those around you.

are you desperate yet?

Mark 10:17 – *As Jesus started on his way, a man ran up to him and fell on his knees before him. "Good teacher," he asked, "what must I do to inherit eternal life?"* (NIV).

I want you to put yourself at the scene of this story as it unfolds, or imagine that you're watching it on a movie screen. This is one of the most important passages of Scripture you will ever read. I pray that you are challenged over the next few days as we take a look at the rich young ruler.

As this story begins, Jesus had just finished ministering to a multitude of people. A group of Pharisees had challenged Him with questions about divorce. Jesus took the opportunity to rebuke the religious leaders and teach the crowd that had gathered. He also blessed the children that were there, and He was just about to leave when a certain man ran up to Him.

This gentleman was very rich and well known throughout the region. He was likely a polished, attractive man, and he wore the finest clothes. He was a man of authority. The people were used to seeing him carry himself with dignity, yet here he ran and threw himself down at the feet of Jesus. He cried out, "Good teacher, what must I do to inherit eternal life?"

This man was desperate. He had fame, fortune and power, but here he is knelt in the dirt at the feet of Jesus. Even though he had the finer things in life, there was an inescapable void he'd been unable to fill. His question was genuine, and he was willing to look foolish in front of the crowd.

I ask you: Are you desperate for Him yet? Have you come to the realization that your life is empty without Him? Earthly riches cannot replace a relationship with Jesus Christ. I challenge you today to declare your total dependence on Him. When was the last time you ran and fell at His feet? Forsake what others might think about you, and pursue Christ at all costs.

Psalm 79:8 – *May your mercy come quickly to meet us, for we are in desperate need* (NIV).

who you callin' good?

Mark 10:17-18 – 17 *As Jesus started on his way, a man ran up to him and fell on his knees before him. "Good teacher," he asked, "what must I do to inherit eternal life?" 18 "Why do you call me good?" Jesus answered. "No one is good—except God alone"* (NIV).

Here we have a desperate, rich man genuinely seeking salvation. He appeared to be in the right place, at the right time, with the right attitude, but today I want to take a careful look at the opening exchange between him and Jesus. There is a very valuable lesson to be learned.

The rich young ruler knelt in the dirt at Jesus' feet. He looked longingly into the eyes of the Son of God and called Him *good teacher*; then he asked how to inherit eternal life. Before the words "big deal" run through your mind, notice Jesus' response. He answered the man's question by asking one of His own: "Why do you call Me good? No one is good—except God alone."

What did Jesus mean by this? He could have only meant one of two things. He was either saying, "I am not good," or "I am God." You likely know that Jesus *is* God the Son, but this young ruler had no idea. Jesus was trying to reveal Himself to him.

This distinguished gentleman had likely heard many testimonies of the miracles Jesus had performed. Jesus' teaching was widely popular and full of wisdom, and news traveled fast. The rich young ruler was fascinated by the things Jesus did and taught, and he wanted a piece of the action. He knew all about Jesus, but he did not *know* Jesus. And he had no interest in getting to know Him; he just wanted something.

Are you like the rich young ruler today? Are you in awe of what God does, or are you in awe of who He is? So many people use God, but God wants to reveal Himself to you.

John 14:7 – *"If you had really known me, you would know who my Father is. From now on, you do know him and have seen him!"* (NLT)

236

past righteousness

> **Mark 10:19-20** – 19 *"You know the commandments: 'Do not murder, do not commit adultery, do not steal, do not give false testimony, do not defraud, honor your father and mother.'"* 20 *"Teacher,"* he declared, *"all these I have kept since I was a little boy"* (NIV).

Jesus tried to show the young ruler who He was, but he wasn't getting it. So Jesus rattled off a handful of commandments, and the young man quickly replied that he had followed all of them since he was a little boy. He likely thought to himself, "Jesus will be impressed with all of my good deeds. I'm sure He will tell me that my righteous acts make me worthy of heaven."

Many times Christians do this very thing. They try to impress God with their righteousness, but He is not concerned with how good of a person you are. Isaiah equates our righteous acts to filthy rags (**Isaiah 64:6**). Notice how Jesus responded to the young man's boasts. Jesus looked at him and loved him.

Aren't you glad Jesus doesn't knock you upside the head when you are lost and confused? He loves you too much to condemn you and give you what you deserve, but He will not force you to know Him. He gives the rich young ruler yet another chance. **Mark 10:21** – *"One thing you lack,"* he said. *"Go sell everything you have and give to the poor, and you will have treasure in heaven. Then come, follow me"* (NIV).

Here Jesus taught one of the most valuable lessons a Christian can learn. Past righteousness does not equate present obedience. The young ruler bragged about the good deeds he'd done, but Jesus was more interested in his obedience right then.

Listen to me. A lifetime of righteous acts will not save you, but a lifetime of obedience will. The young man walked away from Jesus unwilling to do what was asked of him. What is God asking you to do today? Will you do it?

> **Ezekiel 33:12** – *The righteousness of the righteous man will not save him when he disobeys* (NIV).

idolatry

> **Mark 10:22** – *At this the man's face fell. He went away sad, because he had great wealth* (NIV).

Jesus presented the rich young ruler with the opportunity of a lifetime—the chance to be one of His disciples. Instead of accepting the invitation, the man walked away downcast. How could he pass up a chance like that? Imagine how cool it would have been to follow Jesus around. So what was the problem? Idolatry.

Jesus told the young man to go sell all of his possessions and give to the poor. He promised him treasure in heaven and the opportunity to follow Him, but the man turned it down. The Bible makes it clear that the young ruler was very wealthy, and he was unwilling to part with his fortune. His wealth had become an idol.

An idol is anything, or anyone, we value more than our relationship with the Lord. Prosperity was more precious to the rich young ruler than devoting his life to Christ. Where does your treasure lie? Idolatry is a heart condition. Jesus encouraged us to store up our treasures in heaven, not on earth. **Matthew 6:21** – *"For where your treasure is, there your heart will be also"* (NIV).

Maybe material possessions are your downfall. You are more concerned about keeping up with the Joneses than following God's will. You may enjoy a certain sin and are unwilling to lay it down. Even your family can become an idol (please understand that this is a rare condition). Some people abandon God's will to cater to their family's needs. Doing so is idolatry.

Why do you think God told Abraham to sacrifice his son Isaac in Genesis 22? He wanted to know where Abraham's treasure was—in his family or in Him. Is there something, or someone, in your life that has taken priority over your relationship with Christ? If so, repent! Make Jesus the Lord of your life.

> **Exodus 20:4** – *"You shall not make for yourself an idol in the form of anything in heaven above or on the earth beneath or in the waters below"* (NIV).

thieves and robbers

Imagine someone is planning to rob a particular home. On the night he decides to go through with the robbery, the family is at home asleep. It's not likely he's going to waltz up the sidewalk, ring the doorbell and ask for permission to steal all their stuff. No, he is more cunning than that. He looks to enter the home undetected, so he checks the windows and the doggie door.

To his delight he finds an unlocked window. He slides it up, and no alarm sounds. If the house had been equipped with a security system, the intruder would have retreated, but now he's inside. He plunders the family while they're safely sleeping.

Satan works in much the same way. He's crafty and very intelligent. Even so, he has no authority over you unless you give it to him. Unfortunately, there are many Christians who have not installed an alarm system. When you have a relationship with the Holy Spirit, a siren will sound in your spirit when your well-being is compromised. If you have no such warning system, the enemy has direct access to your life.

Jesus encouraged believers to be aware of wolves in sheep's clothing. They are agents of the devil. They look and smell like sheep. They can "baa" with the best of them, but He says we will recognize them by their fruit (**Matthew 7:15-16**). They will have the appearance of someone in love with Jesus, but their mission is to destroy us.

Be on the lookout for people who promote themselves. Is there someone who is subtly trying to turn you against an authority figure in your life? Pay careful attention to the character of those you allow to be close to you. Do their attitudes and actions line up with the fruit of God's word? If not, look out!

Matthew 7:18 – *"A good tree cannot bear bad fruit, and a bad tree cannot bear good fruit"* (NIV).

the gate and watchman

> **John 10:2-3** – 2 *"The man who enters by the gate is the shepherd of his sheep.* 3 *The watchman opens the gate for him, and the sheep listen to his voice. He calls his own sheep by name and leads them out"* (NIV).

There are both godly men and women *and* thieves who have integrated into the church. Unfortunately, it is sometimes very difficult to distinguish between the two. As I mentioned yesterday, the wolves look like sheep. So how do we really know who is of God and who isn't?

Jesus taught that the shepherd of the sheep enters through the gate. Jesus Christ is that gate (**John 10:7**). Shepherds are the pastors or leaders that God has established to care for the body of Christ. They are His true servants. They are not self-indulged, and they point the people to Jesus. They do not teach others to rely on them, but rather to depend on Christ.

There are others who approach the gate and desire to gain access to the sheep. They are not godly men and women. These people cannot enter through the gate. Why? The watchman, or the Holy Spirit, will not open the gate for them because He does not recognize them. The watchman only opens the gate for the shepherd, and He warns the sheep not to listen to impostors.

So if they can't get through Jesus, and the Holy Spirit doesn't allow them in, then how do wolves gain access to the sheep? Certain sheep are swayed by the cunning words of wolves. These individuals are many times disgruntled, or they don't have an intimate relationship with the Holy Spirit. They ignore, or are unaware of, the warning signs. So they go open up a window and let the wolf inside the church.

Please understand I'm not trying to scare you. I want to encourage you to be aware of those influencing your life. Ask the Holy Spirit to help you, and discipline yourself to listen.

> **Acts 20:29** – *I know that after I leave, savage wolves will come in among you and will not spare the flock* (NIV).

know His voice

John 10:4-5 – 4 *"When he has brought out all his own, he goes on ahead of them, and his sheep follow him because they know his voice.* 5 *But they will never follow a stranger; in fact, they will run away from him because they do not recognize a stranger's voice"* (NIV).

A true shepherd tends to the needs of his sheep. He leads them down paths of righteousness, and he possesses the character of Christ. He never sacrifices the well-being of his sheep to protect himself. The good shepherd always goes ahead of his sheep, and they follow him because they know his voice.

It is absolutely vital that you know God's voice, because if you don't, you *will* be led astray. You will not be able to distinguish between His voice and the voice of a stranger. It's for this reason that so many Christians are living outside of God's will.

So why do people have a hard time recognizing God's voice? I'm glad you asked. More times than not it is because they don't spend quality time listening to Him on a daily basis. When my wife calls me on the phone, I immediately recognize her voice when she begins to talk. Why? We've spent countless hours talking and listening to each other. I don't have to ask who she is, and she doesn't have to announce, "Hey Michael, this is your wife Heidi," every time she calls.

Prayer should be a daily, two-way conversation between you and God. A lot of people, though, have turned prayer into a monologue of complaining or asking God for things. I want to encourage you to listen during your prayer time. This means you're going to have to sit still and be quiet.

Once you know His voice, you will never forget it. He doesn't ever disguise His voice or try to fool you, and He will never say anything contrary to the Bible. Get to know God's voice for yourself because even godly, well-meaning leaders will miss His voice from time to time. Have you listened yet today?

Psalm 46:10 – *"Be still, and know that I am God"* (NIV).

life to the full

John 10:10 – *"The thief comes only to steal and kill and destroy; I have come that they may have life, and have it to the full"* (NIV).

I'd imagine it is very rare that a person knowingly breaks into an empty house or a vacant store. Most thieves are looking to steal things of value, so they usually plot to rob places that are known to have valuables in them. This is why the enemy relentlessly pursues some Christians. If he's not constantly trying to pry his way into your life, it's likely because you don't have anything he wants.

Jesus said He came so that you may have life, and have it to the full. A lot of people think of the "life" Jesus refers to here as being eternal life. While this is true, He's also talking about our lives here on earth. Another version says: *"My purpose is to give them a rich and satisfying life"* (NLT). God's desire is for us to experience abundance in every area of our lives, while we are still in the flesh.

I've heard it said before, "Earth is the only hell that a Christian will ever experience." I can kind of understand where people are coming from when they say something like this, but I just can't bring myself to agree with it. Jesus wasn't crucified so that we could experience hell on earth. No! He wants us to enjoy our lives.

Don't get me wrong. There will be multiple times of suffering as we follow Christ, but we do not have to be overcome by life's obstacles. And the thief has no right to come in and steal the abundance Jesus has given us.

Be encouraged today. You have a gift, and it's called "life to the full." If you've already opened the gift and are living the blessed life God intended you to, then safeguard your heart. Do not give the thief access to it. But if you are living a defeated life, void of God's promises, then receive His fullness now. Glory!

James 1:17 – *Every good gift and every perfect (free, large, full) gift is from above; it comes down from the Father* (AMP).

thanksgiving

Do you want to know the secret to experiencing more of God's presence on a daily basis?   Thanksgiving!   Giving God thanks opens up the gates and gives you access to where He is.   If you are grumpy and ungrateful most of the time, then it's probably safe to say you haven't felt God's presence in a while.

Think of it like this.   You probably know someone who is very difficult to be around.   Maybe he or she is mostly negative, and they suck the life out of you with constant criticism.   His glass is always half empty, and the grass is always greener in someone else's yard.   You know who I'm talking about; you're picturing *that* person right now.

Let's say this certain individual calls you up one day and says he's coming to your house to visit.   After you run out of excuses as to why this day and that day would be bad for you, you reluctantly agree to a date.   The day eventually arrives, and he shows up at your door.   Normally you're excited to greet your guests, but today you do your best to appear as if you're gone.

Why?   You don't want to subject yourself to the nagging and complaining.   I know it's hard for me to be around an ungrateful person for an extended period of time.   Sometimes I think God must feel the same way.   He doesn't dodge people or push them away, but many Christians live their lives absent of His presence because they do not appreciate Him.

Perhaps today you are having a difficult time finding something to be thankful for.   I challenge you to offer up praise to Him right now.   When you face trials, thank Him for the coming victory.   When you're sick, thank Him for the blood of Jesus. When people lie about you, praise Him because His word is true.

He's testing you

> **John 6:5-6** – 5 *When Jesus looked up and saw a great crowd coming toward him, he said to Philip, "Where shall we buy bread for these people to eat?"* 6 *He asked this only to test him, for he already had in mind what he was going to do* (NIV).

I believe one of the most dangerous prayers a person can pray is: "Dear Lord, increase my faith." Our faith only grows when it is stretched. Faith is not required for things we can do in our own strength. So if you desire more faith, then ready yourself for trials and impossibilities. Be prepared to face situations and have needs that will require total trust in God.

Times of testing are inevitable for believers. In John 6, Jesus had recently finished ministering, and He and the disciples retreated to a mountainside to rest. They were sitting together when Jesus noticed a large crowd had followed them and was drawing closer. In fact, the Bible says it was a crowd of about five thousand, and they were hungry.

Jesus decided to take this opportunity to test Philip's faith. He asked him, "Philip, where are we going to buy food for all these people?" All of a sudden, Philip went from relaxing with Jesus on the side of a mountain to being faced with an impossibility. Philip likely thought to himself, "Are you serious, Jesus? We're on the side of a mountain, and you're asking *me* where we can buy bread for thousands of people!"

The Bible says that Jesus already knew what He was going to do, but faith isn't about what Jesus can do. It's about *you* believing in what He can do. Your faith, or lack thereof, doesn't determine whether or not Jesus *can* do something. But your measure of faith often determines whether or not He *will* do something.

How do you respond to life's impossibilities? Do you get angry or give up? Tomorrow we'll look at Philip's response.

> **Luke 18:27** – *But He said, "The things that are impossible with people are possible with God"* (NASB).

logic and the supernatural

John 6:7 – *Philip answered him, "Eight months wages would not buy enough bread for each one to have a bite!"* (NIV)

Philip was facing an impossible situation. There were over five thousand hungry people, and Jesus asked *him* where they could buy food to feed them all. Philip's response is not uncommon. He reasoned, "We could work for almost a year and still not have enough money to buy everyone even a bite of bread!"

Philip was presented with an opportunity for his faith to grow, but he failed miserably. He'd already witnessed Jesus turn water into wine, and he was there when Jesus healed the invalid at the pool of Bethesda. Even so, he questioned whether Jesus could somehow feed five thousand people, but why?

He allowed his logical reasoning to override Jesus' supernatural ability. I imagine Philip's thought process went a lot like this: "Okay, bread for five thousand costs this much. There are twelve of us, and we can find jobs earning this amount per hour. We'll be able to work eight to ten hours a day, so that means it will take over eight months for us to earn enough wages to feed everyone!" Philip didn't leave room in his thought process for Jesus to intervene. Jesus was left out of the equation.

Many people reason themselves out of receiving a miracle. Don't get me wrong. God gave you a brain, and He expects you to use it. You have to find a balance between the two. Some people are so heavenly minded that they're no earthly good, but others are so earthly minded that they put God in a box.

How do you view the circumstances you are facing today? Like Philip, does your human reasoning leave no room for the supernatural? Perhaps you have swung way over to the other side, and you have become idle while you wait on God to intervene. Ask the Holy Spirit to help you balance your logic and faith.

Luke 12:30 – *"These things dominate the thoughts of unbelievers all over the world, but your Father already knows your needs"* (NLT).

more than enough

Philip was not the only disciple whose faith was stretched that day. Andrew was tested, too. The condition of Andrew's faith was far different from Philip's. Philip allowed logic to totally override God's supernatural ability, but Andrew actually introduces us to the eventual solution. He brought a boy to Jesus who had five small barley loaves and two small fish.

Andrew's faith represents that of many Christians today. They know what God can do, and they may even know how He wants to do it, but they still reason that He is not enough. Andrew basically said, "Jesus, this boy has five loaves of bread and two fish, but not even *You* can use them to feed all these people."

A lot of people have witnessed God's miracle working power. They know the Scripture inside and out, yet they still place limits on Him. Listen to me very carefully: God is more than enough! Period. Don't talk yourself out of a miracle. Know what God's word says regarding your impossibilities, and allow the Holy Spirit to work on your inadequacies.

Ephesians 3:20 – *God can do anything, you know—far more than you could ever imagine or guess or request in your wildest dreams! He does it not by pushing us around but by working within us, his Spirit deeply and gently within us* (MSG). There are many passages in the Bible that are taken out of context, but the message of this verse is very clear. God can do anything.

He will meet you at the point of your expectation and then blow it out of the water! Unbelief will cause you to lower your expectations. How can you have faith for God to do anything if you don't believe He's enough for everything?

cool, calm and collected

John 6:10-11 – 10 *Jesus said, "Have the people sit down." There was plenty of grass in that place, and the men sat down, about five thousand of them. 11 Jesus then took the loaves, gave thanks, and distributed to those who were seated as much as they wanted. He did the same with the fish* (NIV).

Imagine you are one of the five thousand plus standing on the mountainside. You're tired and hungry. Jesus asks where they're going to buy food for everyone. You listen as Philip and Andrew rule out any possibility of feeding the large crowd. Everyone turns to Jesus and waits anxiously to see His reaction.

You marvel as He calmly instructs for everyone to be seated. Then He gives thanks for the five loaves and two fish. You're awestruck as the disciples distribute food to everyone in attendance. But even as this unbelievable miracle unfolds before you, you can't seem to take your eyes off of Jesus. You're captivated by how cool He is under pressure.

Jesus demonstrated perfectly how we should respond to the impossibilities we face. He was confident and at peace, and He gave thanks to God in the middle of the crisis. Many people wear themselves out worrying about the situations surrounding their lives. If that's you, I encourage you to learn from Jesus' example.

Be confident and trust the One you serve. Don't allow anything to rob you of your peace. Learn to give God thanks no matter what you may be facing. It's easy to thank Him when all is well, but train yourself to praise Him always. When you do, sometimes He'll even surprise you.

As I mentioned yesterday, God will meet you at the point of your expectation and then blow it out of the water. Notice that Jesus gave thanks for something that was not enough to meet the need. Give God thanks today for what you *do* have.

John 6:13 – *So they gathered them and filled twelve baskets with the pieces of the five barley loaves left over by those who had eaten* (NIV).

be teachable

Acts 2:42 – *All the believers devoted themselves to the apostles' teaching, and to fellowship, and to sharing in meals (including the Lord's Supper), and to prayer* (NLT).

I once worked with a guy who not only knew everything, but he knew *how* to do everything. He could tell you all there was to know about *this*, and he was highly skilled at doing t*hat*. It was quite annoying. Even if he had absolutely no experience in a certain field, he would argue against someone who was highly experienced in that same field (I'm sure you're thinking of that person in your life right now).

He had a tendency to put his foot in his mouth, as know-it-alls often do, and he eventually lost all credibility with our coworkers and me. The sad thing about it was that he was actually gifted and knowledgeable in some areas, but nobody paid him any attention because he'd proven he wasn't trustworthy.

Know-it-alls are unteachable, and few people want to be around them, let alone listen to them. Their egos are bigger than their ability. Perhaps you have become one yourself. If so, please pay very careful attention to what I'm about to say: You don't know everything, and you can learn something from everyone.

The Bible says in the above verse that the believers devoted themselves to the apostles' teaching. In other words, they purposed to learn everything they could from the apostles. They were not puffed up in their minds, and they were hungry for truth. They didn't pretend to have it all figured out.

I want to encourage you today to become a life-long learner. I've learned many valuable lessons by watching and listening to those who are in leadership over me, and I've learned from the examples of small children as well. I've been taught what to do and what not to do. Don't become so religious that you miss out on opportunities to gain wisdom.

1 Corinthians 8:2 – *Anyone who claims to know all the answers doesn't really know very much* (NLT).

fellowship with believers

Acts 2:42 – *All the believers devoted themselves to the apostles' teaching, and to fellowship, and to sharing in meals (including the Lord's Supper), and to prayer* (NLT).

Not only should believers become life-long learners, but they need to spend quality time with each other as well. Going to church should be a priority, but we should also surround ourselves with fellow believers outside of the church walls. Living a life of holiness is next to impossible if the only Christians you see are in a church service.

Godly relationships bring accountability. You need to surround yourself with people who challenge you to be a better person, not who stroke your ego or condone your sin. The believers in the first church were devoted to each other. The Bible says they shared meals together. When was the last time you opened your home and invited someone to dinner? Do you avoid church fellowships? Nothing good comes from isolating yourself.

A vital, and often overlooked, part of fellowship is prayer. Believers need to spend time together in prayer on a consistent basis. **Acts 4:31** – *After they prayed, the place where they were meeting was shaken. And they were all filled with the Holy Spirit and spoke the word of God boldly* (NIV).

Something significant happens every time men and women of God come together in agreement. Prayer sends shockwaves through the kingdom of darkness, and it also helps build the confidence of those involved. Pray for each other's needs and for boldness to preach the Gospel. Ask for the gifts of the Spirit to be in operation in your church. Pray for your city and for souls.

I want to encourage you today to build godly relationships. If you've avoided spending time with other believers, make an effort to change. We need each other.

Acts 2:46 – *They worshiped together at the Temple each day, met in homes for the Lord's Supper, and shared their meals with great joy and generosity* (NLT).

the awe factor

Heidi and I have been married going on ten years now, and I remember our wedding day like it was yesterday. But there's one moment in particular that I'll never forget.

The families were seated, and the groomsmen and bridesmaids were in position. I remember standing at the front of the chapel waiting in anticipation. The music changed, and everyone stood up and turned their attention to the back doors. The doors opened, and there she was.

I remember being awestruck as Heidi began to walk down the middle aisle. I couldn't take my eyes off of her; she took my breath away. In fact, everyone's eyes were on her. She was the center of attention, and we were all captivated by her. It was her moment. Everyone stopped what they were doing, and focused on her. I was so excited to spend the rest of my life with Heidi, and you know what? She was just as excited to share her life with me!

I imagine the first church reverenced the presence of God in much the same way. The Bible says that a deep sense of awe came over all the people. They held Him in high esteem. Unfortunately, many believers have lost, or never had, a deep respect for Him.

It's a shame, but a lot of people treat God's house with contempt. They throw trash all over the floor and talk over the preacher. Many are irreverent and spoiled. Some churches have become so self-absorbed that God doesn't even show up anymore.

I challenge you to take a look at your life today. Perhaps this has been a difficult message for you to swallow because you realize you have lost that "awe factor." Do not take Him for granted. Change your way of thinking, and honor God now. Once that reverence returns to our churches, the miraculous will follow.

the greatest miracle ever?

Acts 2:44-45 – 44 *And all the believers met together in one place and shared everything they had.* 45 *They sold their property and possessions and shared the money with those in need* (NLT).

There are many miracles recorded throughout Scripture. Blind eyes were opened, the mute spoke, bodies of water were dried up, and even the dead were raised. Lame people walked, food fell from heaven, and the demonized were set free. God's power was on display on a regular basis, and it still is today.

But perhaps the greatest miracle of all time is recorded in the above passage. *All* the believers shared *everything* they had. And not only that, they sold their property and possessions to give to those in need!

You may be thinking, "This isn't a miracle. The supernatural has nothing to do with people sharing their stuff." I beg to differ. It's actually unnatural for any *one* person to want to share all of his possessions, let alone *hundreds* of people. If this wasn't miraculous, I don't know what is! The fact that the entire church shared everything they owned is truly an act of God.

God did a supernatural work on the inside of the first church because human beings are selfish by nature. Most people are very protective of their belongings, but these believers were more concerned about the welfare of others than their own earthly comfort. Their generosity was an investment into the kingdom of God, and as a result, they had everything they needed and a multitude of souls were saved. Glory to God!

The majority of churches don't look like this anymore, yet this is the example Christ desires us to follow. Many Christians hoard God's blessings and judge those who are less fortunate. I encourage you to resist your selfish nature. Ask God to do a supernatural work on the inside of you, but also use discernment as you invest into the lives of others. Be a good steward.

Hebrews 13:16 – *And do not forget to do good and to share with others, for with such sacrifices God is pleased* (NIV).

251

wrong place, wrong time

2 Samuel 11:1 – *In the spring, at the time when kings go off to war, David sent Joab out with the king's men and the whole Israelite army. They destroyed the Ammonites and besieged Rabbah. But David remained in Jerusalem* (NIV).

For the next several days we're going to take an in depth look at temptation. In 2 Samuel 11, we find the account of David's temptation and subsequent sin with Bathsheba. I want to take the time to point out to you the events leading up to David's infidelity. My prayer is that you will learn from his mistakes and make the proper adjustments in your life to avoid falling into sin.

David was the king of Israel and one of the most successful warriors of all time. He was generous, full of integrity and loved by the people. David was a man after God's own heart, but he was still just a man. He was an imperfect human being just like you and me, and I believe one of the biggest struggles David faced was "getting the big head." At times he allowed his ego to cloud his better judgment. Let's look at one such occurrence.

At the time when kings normally go off to war, David decided he'd hang back at the palace and send someone in his stead. So Joab went to war, and David remained in Jerusalem. David didn't realize it then, but he was setting himself up for failure. Maybe he was tired, or perhaps he just didn't want to go. But I doubt very seriously his intent was to scope out a bathing woman and commit adultery with her. Nevertheless, it happened.

He was in the wrong place at the wrong time. Some temptations are unavoidable, but as in David's case, temptation is often the product of a foolish choice. If David had gone to war like he was supposed to, he likely would not have fallen into sin.

Ask God today to help you avoid temptation. He's given you the ability to make wise decisions. Don't allow your ego to override sound judgment. No one is untouchable.

Matthew 26:41 – *"Watch and pray so that you will not fall into temptation. The spirit is willing, but the body is weak"* (NIV).

the *second* second

> **2 Samuel 11:2-3** – 2 *One evening David got up from his bed and walked around on the roof of the palace. From the roof he saw a woman bathing. The woman was very beautiful,* 3 *and David sent someone to find out about her* (NIV).

Today I want to share with you a principle that will change your life forever. I was first introduced to this concept by Sergio Scataglini. It's called the principle of the *second* second.

As I mentioned yesterday, some temptation is unavoidable. For instance, if you've ever driven on the interstate, odds are you've passed by billboards with sensual images on them (It's really unfortunate how liberal advertising has become). It's not uncommon, especially in larger cities, to be driving along, look up and see a half-dressed person draped across a billboard. Here's where the principle of the *second* second comes into play.

You didn't put the advertisement there, and it's not your fault that you drove by it. The first second you look at the billboard is temptation. Now you have a decision to make. Whether you realize it or not, you ask yourself and answer the following question: "Am I going to continue staring at the ad, or am I going to look away?"

If you choose to look away, you avoid the temptation to sin. But the *second* second you look at that billboard sin is virtually inevitable. Your mind begins to entertain fantasies, and the longer you look, the more difficult it is to get the image out of your mind once the sign is out of sight.

David was walking around on the roof of his palace when he happened to catch a glimpse of a woman bathing (the first second). He did not mean to see her, but rather than look away, he stood watching her. In fact, the Bible says he studied her long enough to see she was *very* beautiful, and he desired to have her.

If you struggle with a certain vice in your life, don't fall victim to the *second* second. When temptation comes, look away. Run from it if you have to. Don't allow your mind to lead you into sin. Remember: The first second is temptation; the second is sin.

253

snap out of it!

---

2 Samuel 11:3-4 – 3 *The man said, "Isn't this Bathsheba, the daughter of Eliam and the wife of Uriah the Hittite?"* 4 *Then David sent messengers to get her. She came to him, and he slept with her* (NIV).

One of my favorite animated movies of all time is Pinocchio. There are many valuable lessons to be learned throughout the movie, but I want to focus on one of them in particular today. Pinocchio was a wooden puppet that eventually came to life. He was given the opportunity to become a real boy, but he had to prove himself by following the instruction of his conscience. His conscience was a cricket named Jiminy.

At one point in the film, Jiminy and Pinocchio sing a duet. The main line of the song is, "Always let your conscience be your guide." Throughout the movie Pinocchio faced various temptations, and Jiminy constantly tried to steer him away from trouble.

This may sound funny, but for Christians, I believe the Holy Spirit performs the same function as Jiminy Cricket. He is that still, small voice behind us saying, *"This is the way; walk in it"* (**Isaiah 30:21**). When we begin to venture off track, He gently reminds us to stay on course. When we are faced with temptation, He provides us with a way out (**1 Corinthians 10:13**). God also places people in our path to be His voice to us, but we have to listen to the Holy Spirit's instruction.

David sent someone to find out about Bathsheba because he was interested in her, but God attempted to use the messenger as a voice of reasoning. The man said to David, "Isn't this Bathsheba, the daughter of Eliam and the wife of Uriah the Hittite?" In other words, "You do realize you're asking about a married woman, right? Snap out of it!"

Unfortunately, David ignored God's final attempt at steering him away from sin. He committed adultery. When you face temptation, the Holy Spirit will try to talk sense into you. I encourage you to listen because He won't make you do anything.

dragged away by desire

James 1:13-14 – 13 *When tempted, no one should say, "God is tempting me." For God cannot be tempted by evil, nor does he tempt anyone; 14 but each one is tempted when, by his own evil desire, he is dragged away and enticed* (NIV).

God does not tempt anyone, nor would He ever want to. He does not desire to see His children stumble and fall. I would never set one of my sons up for failure, and our heavenly Father is no different. So where does temptation birth from?

Temptation is a product of our own evil desires; it is a craving of our fleshly nature. We can only be tempted by something we desire. For instance, I have never had any urge to consume drugs or alcohol. If someone were to come to me and offer me a drink or a joint, I would not hesitate to turn it down. On the other hand, someone who has a history of drug or alcohol abuse would have a more difficult time refusing such an offer.

King David apparently had a problem with attractive women; he had a roaming eye. The Bible says that Bathsheba was a beautiful woman. Something about her caught his attention and perked his interest because he became consumed by a desire to be with her. That desire conceived and eventually gave birth to adultery (see **James 1:15**).

If Bathsheba had been ugly, David probably would not have given her a second glance. The same is true for you. Satan does not waste his time tempting you with things you have no interest in. No, he carefully studies you and strategically sets sin traps for you.

Declare war on your sinful nature today! Ask God to give you a holy hatred for the sins that your flesh desperately wants to commit. Live your life governed by righteousness, not by your evil desires. Fix your mind on the Spirit, and His desires will become yours.

Romans 8:5 –*But those who live in accordance with the Spirit have their minds set on what the Spirit desires* (NIV).

be at peace

Paul wrote that we need to be at peace with all men *if possible*. This means that if there is unrest between two people, one of three scenarios will play out. The sides will either reach a peaceable agreement, nothing will change, or one person will have peace and the other one won't. If peace cannot be restored to both parties, God expects *you* to be the one at peace.

Hebrews 12:14 says to pursue peace with all men. If there is a conflict between you and someone else, and the other person is unwilling to compromise, God's desire is for you to do everything you can to make it right. Then if there is still no resolution, you are to live at peace.

I once had a relationship with a certain coworker turn sour. For two years I could not understand why this person had it in for me. He would openly criticize me, and he was always competing against me. I met with him numerous times to try and settle our differences, and I even spent time with him away from work to try and build our relationship. Many times I would get angry because it seemed I was the only one willing to compromise.

When I later left that particular position, we had merely learned to tolerate one another in order to get the job done. Our relationship was no better, and it was constantly on my mind. I had no peace. Some time later, I called him up and asked him to forgive me for holding our broken relationship against him. I was finally at peace, but he was not. I have since tried to contact him, but he has refused to respond. He is obviously not at peace with everything, but I'm thankful I am.

So far as it depends on you, I encourage you today to make peace in all your relationships. If peace cannot be restored to both sides, then *you* live at peace knowing you have done all you can.

spiritual flabbiness

1 Timothy 4:7 – *Do not waste time arguing over godless ideas and old wives' tales. Instead, train yourself to be godly* (NLT).

If you've ever spent any time in the gym, you know that the majority of the people you see there can be grouped into one of two categories. There are those who take nothing for granted. They are focused on accomplishing their goals, and they make the most of every minute in the gym. Then there is another group of people who are wasting their time and resources. They are in the gym, but they are lazy. They want others to think they are in shape. They show up to the workout, but their effort is lacking. Going to the gym is a social engagement.

The same two groups can be found in the church today. There are those who are focused on becoming more like Christ. They are mature, and they don't misuse their time. They are good stewards of their resources, and they are constantly spending time in prayer and study. They take nothing for granted, and they don't waste anything.

Then there are those in the church who have no interest in becoming godly. They show up, but for the wrong reasons. They know the right things to do, but they refuse to do them. Their lives are governed by unbelief, and they are like a wave of the sea tossed to and fro by the wind (**James 1:6**). They are spiritually flabby.

The difference between the two groups is self-discipline. To *train* means to form the behavior of by discipline and instruction. For godliness to be formed in your life, you are going to have to be disciplined. Spend time with Him daily.

Another part of training is listening to helpful instruction. Many athletes have personal trainers to help them train. Listen carefully to the instruction of the pastors and teachers in your life. Take advantage of every opportunity you have to learn.

1 Timothy 4:8 – *Workouts in the gymnasium are useful, but a disciplined life in God is far more so, making you fit both today and forever* (MSG).

257

have pity on me!

> **Luke 17:12-13** – 12 *As he was going into a village, ten men who had leprosy met him. They stood at a distance* 13 *and called out in a loud voice, "Jesus, Master, have pity on us!"* (NIV)

Ten men with a chronic skin disease came to Jesus. They knew He was capable of healing them, so they cried out for pity. Maybe today you are facing some kind of a chronic condition as well. You're desperate for relief, and you find yourself calling out, "Master, have pity on me!" If so, please pay careful attention.

First of all, there are two types of pity. There is self-pity, which says, "Woe is me. Feel sorry for me and share in my misery." Another word for self-pity is *depression*. Many people become depressed because they make the decision to wallow in their difficulties. They accept, and live in, their woeful condition. This kind of an attitude isolates us from God. Jesus does not plan on attending our pity parties. He has better things to do.

In 1 Samuel 30, David and his men returned from battle to find their homes burned and their families captured. On top of losing his possessions and family, the other men began to talk about stoning David. David likely thought, "Do I accept this situation and become depressed, or do I ask God to intervene?"

The second type of pity says, "Jesus, I acknowledge that I cannot overcome this on my own, but I also know that you are more than able. I give you permission to intervene. Have mercy on me!" In fact, another word for pity is *mercy*. When we ask for God's mercy, we are not asking Him to feel sorry for us. We are admitting our need for Him and declaring that He is the answer.

David chose not to throw a pity party. Instead he found strength in God, and God instructed him on how to get out of his dilemma (see **1 Samuel 30:6-8**). Likewise, the ten lepers knew Jesus could cure them, and He did. How will you choose to respond to your present difficulty?

> **Luke 17:14** – *When he saw them, he said, "Go, show yourselves to the priests." And as they went, they were cleansed* (NIV).

ungratefulness

Luke 17:15-16 – 15 *One of them, when he saw he was healed, came back, praising God in a loud voice.* 16 *He threw himself at Jesus' feet and thanked him—and he was a Samaritan* (NIV).

Ten lepers cried out for Jesus to have pity on them, and He did. He commanded them to go show themselves to the priest, and all of them were cleansed as they went. The Bible says one of them realized he had been healed and returned to thank Jesus. This Samaritan gentleman praised God *loudly*. He was no longer ashamed of himself, and he bowed at Jesus' feet in worship.

Jesus asks the Samaritan, "Where are the other guys? I'm pretty sure I cleansed all of you. Why are you the only one that came back to thank Me?" Then Jesus commended the Samaritan for his great faith and then sent him on his way.

So what *did* happen to the other nine? Allow me to offer two possibilities. Number one, maybe they didn't realize they'd been cleansed. Yeah right. I doubt very seriously these guys didn't notice that they had been cured of an incurable disease. I'm sure they were just as happy as the Samaritan. With that said, the prospect of them not realizing they were healed can be ruled out.

The fact of the matter is they were in desperate need of a different kind of cure—one for ungratefulness. Jesus healed their disease, but He could not force them to give thanks. Being thankful is a decision you and I must make. Heidi and I have had the opportunity to bless many families in need. Some were very grateful and showered us with thanks. Others took what we gave them without even acknowledging we'd given them anything. They acted as if it were owed to them. Though I would have liked to, I did not say, "Hey, you ingrates! Tell us thank you!"

God will never manipulate you into thanking Him, but I believe His heart breaks every time you don't. I want to encourage you to be grateful in the good times and the bad. He is worthy!

Psalm 107:8 – *Let them give thanks to the LORD for his unfailing love and his wonderful deeds for mankind* (NIV).

God listens, but...

2 Chronicles 7:14 – *"If my people, who are called by my name, will humble themselves and pray and seek my face and turn from their wicked ways, then will I hear from heaven and will forgive their sin and will heal their land"* (NIV).

I recently heard a good friend teach on how to persuade God. His message was so enlightening that it caused me to dig deeper. Then I came across this very familiar verse of Scripture found in 2 Chronicles 14. I pray you receive fresh revelation today. God never ceases to amaze me.

The number one reason people pray is to be heard. We want God to hear our praises and complaints. We pray to thank Him and ask Him for things. Nobody goes into a time of prayer thinking, "God, I really don't care if you hear what I'm saying or not." No! When I take time to pray, I want God's full attention.

Now, it's important for us to understand that there is a major difference between listening and *actively* listening. Many times I'll be in conversation with my wife, and she will ask me to do something. I'll admit that I sometimes hear what she says, but it goes in one ear and out the other. I forget about her request, and she's left wondering why I didn't do what she asked me to do.

Other times I'll be fully engaged in our conversation. I'm involved in the dialogue, and if she asks me to do anything, I'll usually follow through. I'm sure my inconsistency is frustrating to her at times, but rather than holding a grudge against me, she works at trying to better engage me.

Your attitude should be the same as hers in your conversation with God. Many people become frustrated in prayer because they don't realize that while God *does* listen to everything they say, prayer has to align with His will in order for Him to act. Over the next two days I'm going to teach you how to cause God to actively listen.

2 Chronicles 7:15 – *"Now my eyes will be open and my ears attentive to the prayers offered in this place"* (NIV).

then will I

In the second part of this verse, God said, *"Then will I* hear from heaven, forgive their sin and heal their land." The words "then will I" imply that He is waiting for certain criteria to be met before He hears, forgives and heals. Once His conditions are met, He acts. Until then, it's as if He doesn't hear us at all. So what do we have to do to get God's attention and persuade Him to move?

I believe the first thing we must do is come to understand who we are in Christ. God said you are called by *His* name. He has given you His name, the name that is above every name. You are His mouthpiece and a representative of Jesus Christ (**2 Corinthians 5:20**). Be confident and unashamed, and praise Him because you bear His name (**1 Peter 4:16**). Hallelujah!

You are His child, and He has granted you an audience with Himself. Many Christians don't realize they have direct access to the Father, and their insecurities cause their prayers and petitions to be ineffective.

The second thing you need to do is humble yourself. **James 4:6** – *God opposes the proud but gives grace to the humble* (NIV). **Proverbs 3:34** says, *"He gives proud skeptics the cold shoulder"* (MSG). Are you beginning to understand why God doesn't always listen actively? When you approach Him with a haughty spirit, He may hear what you say, but He is not inclined to answer.

I want to encourage you today. You are God's child; He chose you! You have the right to approach Him and command His attention. Be confident, yet humble. May you experience God's unmerited favor today!

seek and turn

2 Chronicles 7:14 – *"If my people, who are called by my name, will humble themselves and pray and seek my face and turn from their wicked ways, then will I hear from heaven and will forgive their sin and will heal their land"* (NIV).

In order for God to actively listen, we must pray and seek His face (Notice we should take care of the first two steps *before* we pray). It's important for us to understand the difference between seeking God's hand and seeking His face. If you want God's attention, make your prayer about Him, not what He can do for you. Don't get me wrong. God is most definitely interested in doing things for you, but He wants you to show interest in Him.

I try to spend quality time with my wife everyday. We take turns talking and listening to each other. During our conversation, my focus is on her. We make eye contact because we're interested in getting to know one another better. We're committed to building our relationship.

Our marriage would quickly crumble if the main objective of our communication were to see what we could get from one another. The same is true in our relationship with God. If you get the "gimmies" every time you go to prayer, God is not impressed. He will not be used by anyone. Honor Him, study His character, worship Him, and then move on to step four.

The next step is to turn from your wicked ways. Repentance is key if you want God to move on your behalf. **Ephesians 5:11** – *Have nothing to do with the fruitless deeds of darkness, but rather expose them* (NIV). It's no wonder so many people's prayers don't produce any fruit. They are committed to the fruitless deeds of darkness.

If you are in need today, seek His face. Turn your back on things that are not pleasing to Him. He longs to bring forgiveness and healing to our land. Do your part to untie His hands today.

Psalm 105:4 – *Seek the LORD and His strength; seek His face continually* (NASB).

have a seat

Luke 5:2 – *He saw at the water's edge two boats, left there by the fishermen, who were washing their nets* (NIV).

Picture this scene with me. Jesus was standing by the Sea of Galilee teaching the word of God to a group of people. As the crowd grew, He looked over and saw two boats at the edge of the water. The boats belonged to some fishermen who were busy washing their nets.

One of those men was Simon Peter, and little did he know, his life was about to be completely transformed. Over the next several days, we are going to take a look at his transformation. My prayer is that you too will take the steps necessary to change from a fisherman into a disciple.

Peter had been fishing all day and was probably exhausted. I imagine he was hungry and looked forward to going home for some much needed rest. He was busy washing his nets, and Jesus came and got in his boat. But not only that, Jesus asked him to put out a little from shore. Peter obliged, and Jesus sat down and continued to teach the people (**Luke 5:3**).

I'm amazed by Peter's response here. He could have very easily said, "Hey! What are you doing? Can't you see I'm cleaning my nets? It's late, I'm tired, and I'm ready to go home. I don't have time to give you a ride, so please get out of my boat." Instead he made room for Jesus to sit down.

Peter put aside his personal comfort to accommodate Jesus. This was a divine appointment that Peter chose not to miss. Unfortunately, there are many people who miss God's will because it's not convenient for them. I want to encourage you to allow Jesus to sit down in your boat. Fishing was Peter's livelihood, and he gave Jesus a front row seat. My prayer is that you will do the same. Make Him a priority today. Invite Him to take His place as the Lord of your life, family, job, finances, etc. Hallelujah!

2 Corinthians 3:18 – *And we...are being transformed into his likeness with ever-increasing glory* (NIV).

263

because I said so

Luke 5:4 – *When he had finished speaking, he said to Simon, "Put out into deep water, and let down the nets for a catch"* (NIV).

The Bible isn't clear as to how long Jesus spoke to the people from Peter's boat, but we do know that He didn't start teaching until after the fishermen had worked all night. They were tired, and I imagine the subtle rocking of the boat by the waves made it difficult for Peter to stay awake. I wonder how many times he nodded off as Jesus taught.

Though he was exhausted, Peter had been very accommodating up to this point. But as Jesus closed the service, Peter's mind probably wondered to his bed. And I'm sure his excitement grew as Jesus dismissed the crowd. "This is it!" he must have thought, "I can finally go get some sleep."

Instead Jesus told Peter to go out into deep water and let down the nets. Briefly look back at **Luke 5:3**, and you will notice that Jesus initially *asked* Peter to take Him out on the boat to teach the people. This time He didn't ask; He gave Peter a command.

If there was ever a moment for Peter to get upset, this was it. "First he asks to sit in *my* boat and teach. I let that slide, but now he's telling *me* what to do with *my* boat! The nerve of that guy. Doesn't he know I worked all night and I'm tired?!" This is the kind of response you would expect from most people, but Peter did not react this way. He was being tested. Peter answered, *"Master, we've worked hard all night and haven't caught anything. But because you say so, I will let down the nets"* (**5:5**).

Jesus will never force us to follow Him. But once you allow Him aboard your boat, you give Him the authority to direct your life. Sometimes He will ask you to do things you don't want to do or that don't make sense, but He does not owe you an explanation. It's during those times that you need to trust and do what He wants simply because He says so.

James 1:22 – *But don't just listen to God's word. You must do what it says. Otherwise, you are only fooling yourselves* (NLT).

264

the breaking point

Luke 5:6 – *When they had done so, they caught such a large number of fish that their nets began to break* (NIV).

Without questioning Jesus, Peter and his partners followed His instruction. They let down their nets and made the catch of a lifetime, but they still didn't have the fish in the boat yet. In fact, the number of fish was so great that their nets began to break. They were on the verge of losing their catch!

Many people come to this point in their walk with God and miss out on His blessing. They are weary, yet faithful. They persevere when others give up, and it looks like they have it all together. Then all of a sudden, just before they receive their reward, they hit a breaking point.

Peter and his buddies had faithfully followed Jesus' command, but now they were faced with one final test. They had to figure out a way to haul in the catch of fish, or their nets would break and God's blessing would swim away.

The final step to receiving God's blessing is usually the toughest one to take. Peter could have easily decided the catch wasn't worth the effort and cut the ropes. He could have reasoned, "This is too much for one day. I'm completely overwhelmed. Maybe Jesus is available to come out on the boat again tomorrow after I get some rest." Rather than throwing in the towel, Peter called for backup.

May this be a lesson we all learn. When you become overwhelmed, don't give up or try to be superhuman. Ask for help. God places people in your life to encourage you and propel you to victory. Learn to work together, and don't fight over God's blessings. If Peter had tried to hoard his catch, he would have lost it. I encourage you to share God's blessings with those around you. We are blessed to be a blessing.

Luke 5:7 – *So they signaled their partners in the other boat to come and help them, and they came and filled both boats so full that they began to sink* (NIV).

go away from me

Luke 5:8 – *When Simon Peter saw this, he fell at Jesus' knees and said, "Go away from me, Lord; I am a sinful man!"* (NIV)

After making the catch of a lifetime, you'd think Peter would fall at Jesus' feet and worship Him. Instead he told Jesus to go away! But why? Peter was scared.

Then Jesus said to Simon, "Don't be afraid" (**Luke 5:10**). What was he afraid of? In the holy presence of Jesus Christ, Peter suddenly realized what a wretch he was. He became very aware of his sin, and he cried out, "I am a sinful man!" Peter felt unworthy and uncomfortable.

Let me ask you a question: Don't you think Jesus already knew Peter was a sinful man? Sure He did. He was very aware of Peter's spiritual condition, yet He chose to bless him and use him in the ministry anyway.

This is the kind of person Jesus is looking for—someone who is broken and repentant. God cannot effectively use someone who is comfortable in his or her sin. Many people stand calloused in the presence of God. Their hearts have been hardened; there is no fear in them. They're not concerned with how God views them.

I've sometimes wondered how an unrepentant believer can be in the presence of God, yet not be moved to change. It's because he or she has chosen sin over Jesus. God will not break a person's will, but man can break his own will.

Peter was broken in the presence of Jesus. He was filled with awe, and the holiness of Jesus caused Peter to fear for his safety. His sin-stained life quivered in the presence of such purity, but Jesus told him not to be afraid.

My prayer for you today is that you would have a holy fear of God. Search yourself. God is looking to use someone who is broken in His presence. Guard yourself against becoming numb to sin. Separation from God should never be comfortable for you.

Psalm 51:9-10 – 9 *Hide your face from my sins and blot out all my iniquity.* 10 *Create in me a pure heart, O God* (NIV).

leave everything

Luke 5:11 – *So they pulled their boats up on shore, left everything and followed him* (NIV).

Jesus told Peter, Andrew, James and John that they were no longer going to catch fish. Instead they were to catch men. He commanded them to follow Him, so the fishermen pulled their boats up on shore and went with Him. These four gentlemen became Christ's first disciples.

The Bible says that Peter and his partners left *everything* to follow Jesus. This included the massive catch of fish they had just made. Scripture doesn't mention any deliberation on the part of the fishermen. They didn't have a pow-wow to discuss whether or not they should go; they just went.

Even so, I imagine at least one of them thought to himself, "Wait a minute. Shouldn't we do something about all the fish we just caught? There's a lot of money on those two boats. Hey, I need to call my family. Hold on a second! Let's think this over!"

There's an important lesson to be learned here. When we choose to follow Christ wholeheartedly, it will many times cost us things, or even relationships, that are very valuable to us. These men left their jobs, families and possessions. It would be easy to leave everything and follow Christ if we had nothing to lose.

The fact of the matter is it's very difficult to let go of things that are dear to us. In his letter to the Philippians, Paul wrote about forgetting what is behind and straining toward what is ahead (**Philippians 3:13-14**). Forgetting what is behind includes past defeats, as well as victories—the bad things and the blessings.

Jesus wants all of you. I encourage you today to lay your entire life down to follow Christ. God has great plans for you, but you cannot move on to your future while dragging your feet in the past. Past blessings are a great source of encouragement during hard times, but don't allow them to rob you of the blessings ahead.

Luke 5:27-28 – 27 *"Follow me,"* Jesus said to him, 28 *and Levi got up, left everything and followed him* (NIV).

the nature of a servant

Philippians 2:7 – *He made himself nothing by taking the very nature of a servant, being made in human likeness* (NIV).

We make numerous decisions on a daily basis, and they range in variety. We decide what to eat for breakfast, lunch and dinner, and whether we're going to dress casually, business-like or stay in our pajamas all day. We choose whether to lose our tempers or stay cool under pressure. We make decisions concerning our families, our jobs and our free time. Though the choices we make are many and diverse, they all share one thing in common. *We* make them.

Nobody else can make your decisions for you, not even God. He has given every person a free will, and you ultimately decide how you're going to live your life. Every choice you make affects your life one way or another. Some are vital to your survival, while others are inconsequential. I want to talk to you today about one of the most important decisions you will ever make—the decision whether or not you will become a servant.

Jesus made Himself nothing and took on the nature of a servant. In other words, He was something (or someone) before and decided to become nothing. He was God by nature before, and then He chose to become a servant.

A person's nature is a mixture of his or her personality and character. Some of these qualities are present at birth, and others are formed over time. And contrary to popular belief, you have the ability to change your very nature. With God's help, you can choose for your personality and character to become more like His.

Many people excuse the possibility of becoming a servant because it's not their personality. Others don't have the character it takes to effectively serve. If you're one of them today, don't accept the way you are. Over the next few days, we're going to look at the qualities of a true servant. May you never be the same!

Ephesians 3:7 – *I became a servant of this gospel by the gift of God's grace given me through the working of his power* (NIV).

be a team player

Philippians 2:2 – *Then make me truly happy by agreeing wholeheartedly with each other, loving one another, and working together with one mind and purpose* (NLT).

Servants are team players. Jesus prayed in **John 17:21** that all believers would be one as He and the Father are one. If Jesus prayed this for you and me, then working together must be pretty important to Him.

Philippians 2:2 lists three characteristics of a team player. As we go through them today, I challenge you to do a self-evaluation. Be honest, and ask yourself, "Do I lack in any of these areas?" If you're going to effectively serve the body of Christ, these three characteristics must become a part of your nature.

First of all, a team player is like-minded with all the other players on the team. Everyone must be in agreement, and the first thing you need to agree on is submission to authority. You cannot serve in any capacity if you are in rebellion. If a time comes when you don't understand or agree with the person in charge, don't slander or try to gang up on him. Humbly go to the person you are serving under and try to resolve your issues. Don't poison someone else on your team.

Secondly, we will only be able to effectively serve as a team if we love one another. Notice you don't have to *like* everyone, but God can give you the ability to love people the way He does. It's very difficult to work alongside someone you despise. Ask God to give you unconditional love for His body.

Lastly, we must serve together with one purpose. Everyone has their own idea of how things should be done, but you must discipline yourself to work toward a common goal. Do your part to fulfill the vision of your pastoral staff and encourage others to do so as well. If you are not currently serving your local church, find a team to join. Be the team player God has called you to be.

John 13:35 – *"By this all men will know that you are My disciples, if you have love for one another"* (NASB).

269

the recipe for selflessness

Philippians 2:3 – *Don't be selfish; don't try to impress others. Be humble, thinking of others as better than yourselves* (NLT).

True servants are team players, and they are selfless. In fact, there is no room on a team for selfishness. In the above verse, Paul gave three qualities of a selfless person. I pray today that you would lay down any self-centeredness there may be in your life.

The first quality of a selfless person is he or she does not try to impress others. Another version of **Philippians 2:3** says not to sweet-talk your way to the top (MSG). Many people spend countless hours pretending to be someone they're not in order to impress people who don't care. Don't use servanthood as a means to self-promotion. God is the one who promotes.

Selfless people are also humble. It's very important for us to guard ourselves against false humility. A person who delights in false humility is a danger to himself and others. Such a person becomes puffed up in his mind. He is rogue and has lost connection with the Head (which is Jesus Christ). False humility stunts the growth of the entire body (see **Colossians 2:18-19**). We must clothe ourselves in humility in order to serve effectively.

The third quality of a selfless person is he thinks of others as better than himself. You cannot serve anyone if you think you're better than they are. A selfish person looks down his nose at others, but a selfless person values everyone (including those he serves alongside of).

Evaluate yourself today. Are you pretending to be someone you're not in order to impress others? Maybe you are trying to gain the approval of someone you work with or for. If so, be yourself. Also, don't try to disguise selfishness with false humility. God knows what's beneath the surface. Lastly, celebrate others; don't climb over them in order to get to the top.

Philippians 2:3 – *Don't push your way to the front; don't sweet-talk your way to the top. Put yourself aside, and help others get ahead* (MSG).

take an interest

Philippians 2:4 – *Don't look out only for your own interests, but take an interest in others, too* (NLT).

There are a couple key points in this verse that I want to bring to your attention today. My prayer is for you to take them to heart, and allow God to mold you more into His image.

Paul said not to look out *only* for our own interests. Though it's a rare condition, some people serve to a fault. They become so consumed with the needs of others that they neglect their own needs. Over-serving does not please God; it causes burnout.

Burnout is actually the point at which a rocket engine stops because it runs out of fuel. In other words, the engine stops producing and the rocket comes to a standstill. Burnout affects people in much the same way. Working yourself until you're overwhelmed by fatigue and frustration will cause you to run out of gas. Then you will stop producing. In fact, when you don't take care of yourself, it puts a strain on everyone around you.

On the flipside, you cannot serve people that you have no interest in. The point of serving is to meet a need. You cannot effectively meet someone's need if you only look at it from your perspective. You have to put yourself in the shoes of the people you are serving. Ask yourself this question, "How would I want to be treated if the roles were reversed?"

You also need to take an interest in the person who is in authority over you. When you serve in a certain area, you should do so with the same excellence and attitude your leader serves with. Ask yourself, "Is this how my pastor or boss would do this?"

I pray you have been enlightened and challenged by this word today. Don't neglect yourself. Don't give your best to others and save the leftovers for your family. Serve others with excellence but not at the expense of good stewardship.

Mark 10:45 – *"The Son of Man did not come to be served, but to serve, and to give his life as a ransom for many"* (NIV).

attitude is everything

> **Philippians 2:5-6** – 5 *You must have the same attitude that Christ Jesus had.* 6 *Though he was God, he did not think of equality with God as something to cling to* (NLT).

Now read these verses again from The Message: *Think of yourselves the way Christ Jesus thought of himself. He had equal status with God but didn't think so much of himself that he had to cling to the advantages of that status no matter what. Not at all.*

This is mind-boggling to me. Jesus was the prototypical servant. No human being ever has, or ever will, reach equality with Jesus Christ. He is God the Son, yet He did not consider His godly status as something to hold on to. He relinquished the privileges of deity to become a servant to all of mankind.

After reading something like this, I can't help but be challenged personally. What I have achieved does not even begin to compare to deity status, yet I struggle at times to cling to myself. My human nature wants to hold on to what's comfortable, and becoming a servant means letting go of what comes natural.

I want to encourage you today with what Jesus said in **John 12:26**, *"Whoever serves me must follow me; and where I am, my servant also will be. My Father will honor the one who serves me"* (NIV). Taking on the nature of a servant may cost you a lot, but look at the promises Jesus makes to those who serve Him.

First, His servants will be wherever He is, and He will be wherever His servants are. Jesus will not give you an assignment and then throw you to the wolves. You are not a hired hand; you're very valuable to Him. He is with those who serve.

Secondly, the Father honors His servants. In other words, the God of the universe will hold you in high regard if you serve Him wholeheartedly. He rewards you. There is no earthly treasure or fame worth clinging to if it means sacrificing the respect of the Father. Lord, I will serve you faithfully today. Amen.

> **Romans 12:11** – *Never be lazy, but work hard and serve the Lord enthusiastically* (NLT).

272

do what it says

The church is full of people who know what to do, but they don't do it. James tells us it's as if they look at themselves in the mirror and then walk away immediately forgetting what they look like (**1:23**). They're ever hearing, but rarely doing. Just because you hear something doesn't mean you practice it. People who *only* listen to, read or memorize, the word are deceived.

Knowledge alone does not produce results. Many people know how to become physically fit. They are aware that they need to exercise and change their diet, but they don't discipline themselves to put their knowledge to action. They know they should take care of themselves, but they don't.

Reading <u>Shape</u> magazine and attending health classes will not make a person physically fit. Quoting calories and memorizing workout regimens will do nothing for your figure. Studying the fat grams in certain food items will not cause you to lose inches off your waistline. In fact, a person who thinks he is in shape because of their knowledge of fitness is ignorant.

The same is true in the realm of the Spirit. Reading and memorizing the Scripture *alone* does not make a person more like Jesus. You have to apply biblical principles to your everyday life in order to become like Him. God is not impressed if you memorize the entire Bible, but refuse to give Him your heart. Knowledge does not equal relationship.

I want to encourage you today to practice what you preach. Are you a person with integrity or someone who refuses to do what you know is right? Do you quote the Bible at others, but live however you want to? If so, you are self-deceived. Begin doing things that please God. Otherwise, you're going to fall into a pit.

nothing but trouble

Titus 3:10-11 – 10 *Warn troublemakers once or twice. Then don't have anything else to do with them.* 11 *You know that their minds are twisted, and their own sins show how guilty they are* (CEV).

"That person is nothing but trouble!" I've heard this phrase countless times, and I've even said it before myself. Maybe *you* have been called a troublemaker. Troublemakers come in all shapes and sizes, and causing strife is not age or gender sensitive. Many people cause more problems than they solve, but *nobody* is nothing but trouble. Everyone has the ability to change with God's help. If you are someone who stirs up trouble, or knows of someone who causes a lot of it, please pay careful attention today.

If you are reading this and you are a troublemaker, let this serve as a warning to you. The Bible says that God is just, and he will pay back trouble to those who cause trouble (**2 Thessalonians 1:6**). I don't know about you, but I get myself into enough trouble as it is. I certainly don't need to set myself up for more difficulty.

Also, if you are known for causing problems, don't be surprised when people start distancing themselves from you. Most people have enough to deal with. They're not going to add to their troubles if they can help it. Troublemakers are expendable.

The Bible also says to warn those who cause trouble no more than twice. If you know people who frequently create problems for others, don't constantly harass them or point out their errors. Ask God whether to warn the person once or twice. Then if the person continues to cause strife, cut off the relationship.

God does not want you to bring judgment to troublemakers. Do not drag their names through the mud, or try to expose them to others. Have nothing to do with them! Causing trouble for a troublemaker will only cause you more trouble. Their minds are unstable, and they are self-condemned. Leave it in God's hands because He alone is just.

Proverbs **12:21** – *Good people never have trouble, but troublemakers have more than enough* (CEV).

give God a chance

Jeremiah 1:12 – *The LORD said to me, "You have seen correctly, for I am watching to see that my word is fulfilled"* (NIV).

I recently learned a very valuable lesson, and I want to share it with you today. My wife Heidi is a children's pastor, and we have the wonderful opportunity to share the love of God with kids on a weekly basis. It's one of the most rewarding things we've ever done.

Heidi was sharing with me not long ago that God had challenged her to begin exercising her faith more in children's church. Now, every week she asks the kids if there is anyone who needs a physical healing. She explains to them the price Jesus paid on the cross for their health (see **Isaiah 53:5**), and then she lays hands on them in agreement with His word.

The results have been miraculous! Children are being healed on a weekly basis, and they are sharing their testimonies. Upset stomachs have been healed, headaches have gone instantaneously, congestion and coughs have left, and the list goes on. It's amazing what God can do when He's given a chance.

The lesson I've learned is that many times we miss out on miracles because we don't give God a chance to move. The truth is God is always ready to work a miracle, but He needs someone to believe and agree with Him. The miracle-working power of Jesus Christ is not reserved for an elite group that God has handpicked to have a healing or deliverance ministry. The miracle-working power of Jesus is reserved for all who believe and understand that all authority is in the name of Jesus!

I want to encourage you to exercise your faith today. Give God a chance to work a miracle in your life. Don't turn to Him as a last resort. Believe His word concerning your situation, and remind Him of the promises He has made. God is watching over His word to fulfill it, but you must believe and agree with Him.

Matthew 24:35 – *"Heaven and earth will pass away, but my words will never pass away"* (NIV).

275

intimacy with the Spirit

There is a vital truth that we must understand today. The Holy Spirit lives on the inside of *every* believer, period. When a person is "born again," or accepts Jesus Christ as Lord and Savior, the Holy Spirit makes His dwelling in that person. Need proof? We could argue about it for hours on end, but I'll let the Scripture prove it to you. **Romans 8:9** – *But if anyone does not possess the [Holy] Spirit of Christ, he is none of His [he does not belong to Christ, is not truly a child of God]* (AMP).

It's also important for us to understand that the Holy Spirit is a person. He is not some mystical being or a figment of our imaginations. If you are a believer, He is a person who lives on the inside of you. How amazing!

Now, let me ask you a question. How well do you know Him? Like with any other person in your life, you have to spend time with the Holy Spirit to get to know Him. This may be groundbreaking information for you, but it is absolute truth. There are great benefits to having an intimate relationship with the Holy Spirit, but most people are oblivious as to what they are. They know Christ as Lord, but their relationship with His Spirit is surface level at best.

I want to challenge you today to begin developing intimacy with the Holy Spirit. If you're not sure where to start, ask Him to reveal Himself to you through the word of God. Listen and learn His voice. Open yourself up to the enormity of who He is.

teaching, leading and reminding

> **1 John 2:20, 27** – 20 *But you are not like that, for the Holy One has given you his Spirit, and all of you know the truth…*27 *But you have received the Holy Spirit, and he lives within you, so you don't need anyone to teach you what is true. For the Spirit teaches you everything you need to know, and what he teaches is true—it is not a lie. So just as he has taught you, remain in fellowship with Christ* (NLT).

Today I want to share with you one of the benefits to having an intimate relationship with the Holy Spirit. In **John 14:17**, Jesus called the Comforter (the Holy Spirit) the Spirit of truth. He goes on to say in **John 15:26**, *"When the Helper comes, whom I will send to you from the Father, that is the Spirit of truth who proceeds from the Father, He will testify about Me"* (NASB).

Since Jesus is no longer here in the natural, the Holy Spirit serves as His mouthpiece to believers. That still, small voice you hear Christians refer to is the voice of the Spirit speaking to you on behalf of Jesus. If you don't learn the voice of the Spirit, you cannot hear when Jesus speaks to you. Are you grasping this?

When Jesus was teaching the disciples about the Holy Spirit, He was doing so because He knew He would soon leave them. Jesus did not expect them to recollect everything He had taught them for three plus years, so He promised them the Holy Spirit would come and guide them into all truth (**John 16:13**). This promise is for all believers, including *you*. Plus, if He guides us into all truth, He will also steer us away from all fallacy.

Look at what else He says in **John 14:26**, *"But the Counselor, the Holy Spirit, whom the Father will send in my name, will teach you all things and will remind you of everything I have said to you"* (NIV). Have you ever faced a tough situation, and then all of a sudden a verse comes to mind that brings you hope? That's the Holy Spirit reminding you of what you've read before.

This same principle is true in every area of your life, not just spiritual matters. He cares about every detail concerning you. He is always teaching, leading and reminding. Listen.

godly sorrow vs. worldly sorrow

2 Corinthians 7:10 – *Godly sorrow brings repentance that leads to salvation and leaves no regret, but worldly sorrow brings death* (NIV).

Our oldest son Noah loves socks, and if we'd let him, he would wear them year round. The top drawer of the dresser in his bedroom is dedicated to underwear and socks. To him it's like a treasure chest! For whatever reason, he gets a kick out of digging around in there.

When he was younger, he would change his socks six or seven times a day. As he repeatedly destroyed the sock drawer and dirtied up all his socks, Heidi and I finally had to ban him from his "treasure chest." If he needed socks, or *thought* he needed socks, he would have to come ask us for them.

Unfortunately, many times he would still sneak into his room and wear all of his socks. He wasn't very good at covering his tracks, so we would always bust him. He would cry and tell us how sorry he was, but a couple of days later we'd find the sock drawer in shambles again. We'd confront him, he'd cry, say he was sorry and then the scene would play out again a few days later.

So why did he continue to do wrong? Simple...he wasn't really sorry for what he had done. If he were truly sorry, he would not have continued being disobedient. He would have changed his behavior. The only reason he said he was sorry because he got caught. This story illustrates the difference between godly sorrow and worldly sorrow.

When we sin, godly sorrow causes us to repent and make a lifestyle change. We will make it our aim to change our behavior because we know we've hurt the heart of God. On the other hand, worldly sorrow will cause you to get upset when you get busted, but you will make no effort to change. True repentance brings liberty, but worldly sorrow brings death. Choose wisely.

Matthew 3:8 – *"Prove by the way you live that you have repented of your sins and turned to God"* (NLT).

the emotion Healer

Luke 7:12 – *As he approached the town gate, a dead person was being carried out—the only son of his mother, and she was a widow. And a large crowd from the town was with her* (NIV).

In Luke 7, Jesus and the disciples went to a town called Nain. As they neared the town gate, they encountered the funeral procession of a certain widow's only son. I want to focus on the condition of this poor woman. There are many people today who likely find themselves in a similar position. If you're one of them, I pray you are encouraged by this story.

This woman was obviously in great need. She had already lost her husband, and now her only son was dead. The Bible says a large crowd of people surrounded her, but I imagine she had never felt so alone. Her physical needs were great, but notice how Jesus approached her. **Luke 7:13** – *When the Lord saw her, his heart went out to her and he said, "Don't cry"* (NIV).

The widow must have been in agony. She was probably inconsolable, and who could blame her? Jesus' heart went out to her, and I can picture Him walking up and embracing her. He recognized that her heart was broken, and He immediately ministered to the emotional need first.

Early in our ministry, Heidi and I encountered a young lady who had been sexually molested by a family member. She was eventually removed from the situation and was living in a safe place when we met her. We recognized early on that she was emotionally unstable, and when she finally shared her story with us, we understood why. Her physical need was met when she moved into a safer home, but she was still carrying around the emotional trauma from the abuse.

The point I want to make is that a person cannot be completely healed unless his or her emotional needs are met. That's why Jesus ministered to the widow's emotions first. If you find yourself on an emotional rollercoaster today, Jesus is crossing paths with you right now. He is more than able to meet your emotional needs. Allow Him to embrace you.

stop the funeral

Luke 7:14 – *Then he went up and touched the coffin, and those carrying it stood still. He said, "Young man, I say to you, get up!"* (NIV).

Yesterday we saw how Jesus ministered to the emotional needs of a widow who had lost her only son. Today I want to bring to your attention how Jesus went about healing her physical need as well. He is concerned about every area of your life, and His desire is for you to be made completely whole. Hallelujah!

By earthly standards, when Jesus arrived in Nain, He was too late. The widow's son was dead, and family and friends were on their way to bury him. The funeral procession was already taking place. Notice Jesus was undeterred. He walked up to the young man's emotionally distraught mother and embraced her.

I can only imagine what went through her mind as Jesus hugged her, "You're a little late there, Jesus. My only son is in that coffin. Thanks for the hug, but he is still dead!" Jesus met her emotional need, but that did not erase the fact she had experienced a great loss. In her mind she probably thought it was over. She was going to bury her son just like she had buried her husband.

Sadly, there are many people today holding funeral processions for various situations in life that they consider to be dead. Maybe you're one of them. Perhaps you have lost hope of ever receiving a certain physical healing. Do you have an unsaved family member that you've given up on? Maybe you are currently making arrangements for the funeral of your marriage. The truth is you could have any number of dead circumstances in your life, but God has the power to breathe life back into all of them!

The key is to stop the procession, and give Him an opportunity. Those who were carrying the widow's son stopped when Jesus touched the coffin. They could have brushed by Him, but they didn't. Don't tie Jesus' hands with your unbelief.

Luke 7:15 – *The dead man set up and began to talk, and Jesus gave him back to his mother* (NIV).

don't be alarmed

Acts 20:9 – *Seated in a window was a young man named Eutychus, who was sinking into a deep sleep as Paul talked on and on. When he was sound asleep, he fell to the ground from the third story and was picked up dead* (NIV).

Paul was in Troas speaking to a group of people in a room located on the third story of a building. Scripture indicates that there were lamps lit in the room, and Paul taught until midnight. A dimly lit room, and a man talking on and on into the wee hours of the morning, sounds like a perfect recipe for sleep to me.

As it would turn out, a teenage boy named Eutychus was there sitting on the sill of an open window. He drifted off to sleep and fell out of the building to his death. I'm sure this was not the kind of publicity Paul was looking to get for his ministry: "Teaching so boring, it kills." I used to think this story sounded more like a bad cartoon than something I could apply to my life. Then God showed me something I want to share with you today.

Eutychus' dead body represents whatever the crisis is in your life right now as you read this. You may have multiple crises, and that's okay. The same principle applies. Look at what happened next in the story. **Acts 20:10** – *Paul went down, threw himself on the young man and put his arms around him. "Don't be alarmed," he said. "He's alive!"* (NIV)

Your response to crisis is crucial in determining the final outcome of your situation. You can respond to your circumstance in one of two ways. Notice the first thing Paul said was, "Don't be alarmed." Can you imagine the chaos that ensued after a room full of people watched someone die? Most people respond irrationally to difficulty, but I want to encourage you to react as Paul did.

He calmly and confidently walked down the steps, and God used him to breathe life back into the boy. God asked Paul to do something very unusual to bring Eutychus back, but he would not have known what to do if he had responded like everyone else did. God can use you in much the same way concerning your crisis. Don't flip out. Trust Him, and listen to His voice.

fruit...what fruit?

Listed above are the nine fruits of the Spirit. Read them again and honestly ask yourself, "Which of these areas am I lacking in?" The fact is we could all do better in each area, but I'd venture to say that most people's lives are completely absent of multiple fruits of the Spirit. And the tragic thing about it is they are not willing to do anything differently. Some people don't know how to have a fruitful life, and others just don't care.

Before we go any further, let me give you a couple truths concerning these fruits. First, it's God's intention for *every* believer to have *all* of the fruits of the Spirit in increasing measure. Please don't confuse the fruits with the gifts of the Spirit. The Spirit gives the gifts to each person as He chooses, but *we* choose whether His fruit will be produced in our lives.

Secondly, you cannot pick fruit from someone else's tree. If you are an impatient person, a person who is extremely patient cannot give you a portion of his patience. There are certain things that can be imparted from one person to another, but the fruits of the Spirit cannot. The fruits of the Spirit flow out of our relationship with Him.

Galatians 5:24-26 lists three steps we must take in order to produce the fruits of the Spirit in our lives. Number one, we have to crucify the passions and desires of our sinful nature (5:24). Next, we have to live in step with the Spirit (5:25). We cannot follow someone we don't know. Cultivating a relationship with the Holy Spirit takes self-discipline. Lastly, as you grow in the Lord, do not become conceited (5:26). The fruit you do have will rot when you begin to think you are better than others. People will know you by your fruit.

loathing God's blessing

Numbers 21:5 – *And the people spoke against God and against Moses, "Why have you brought us out of Egypt to die in the wilderness? For there is not bread, neither is there any water, and we loathe this light (contemptible, unsubstantial) manna"* (AMP).

If you go back and read the story of Israel's deliverance from Egyptian bondage, you will find that they were a very ungrateful bunch. On multiple occasions they grumbled against God and the leadership He had established over them. Though God had set them free and promised them a glorious inheritance, they remained thankless.

God performed numerous miracles during the exodus. He always made provision for everything the Israelites needed. When they were about to be captured, He provided a way out. When they were thirsty, God gave them something to drink. There were many times Israel complained about being hungry, and He sent manna from heaven to satisfy them.

Now we read in the above verse that Israel was whining again. They were disgruntled about the lack of water and food, but this time look at what they said about the manna, "We loathe this light manna." The NIV reads, *"And we detest this miserable food."* In other words, they actually hated the blessing from God.

Manna was God's answer to their prayers, yet they loathed the very thing they should have been thankful for. I wonder how many times I've treated God's blessings the same way. Many times we hold His blessings in contempt because they do not come to us in the package we think they should.

Many people get angry when they feel God is withholding certain things from them that they want, but such instances are often times a blessing in disguise. I encourage you today to be thankful for the needs that God has met, and continues to meet, in your life. Even if He doesn't do so in the way you expect Him to.

Philippians 4:19 – *And my God will meet all your needs according to his glorious riches in Christ Jesus* (NIV).

I quit complaining

Philippians 2:14 – *Do everything without complaining or arguing* (NIV).

Complaining is easy, but it is not beneficial at all. Nothing good can come from complaining, yet many people do so without even realizing it. There are some people who complain about everything, and then there are others who only complain about certain things. Complaining is never justified no matter how awful your life may seem. In fact, the Bible instructs us to do *everything* without complaining.

If you find yourself grumbling often, I want to encourage you today to stop. Complaints are an outward reaction to an inward condition. So if you are going to stop whining about things, you are going to have to change your mindset. Negative thoughts are what eventually cause you to complain.

If you sit around and think about how awful your job is and how unfairly your boss treats you, eventually those thoughts will drop down into your heart. Then they will come out in your words and actions. You will drag your feet and hang your head when it is time to get ready for work. And while on the job, you will mope around and poison your coworkers with negative criticism.

Negativity is often contagious. People who are surrounded by chronic complainers many times find themselves whining about things they were once content with. Don't be a complainer, and don't make it a habit to hang out with one. Sometimes negativity cannot be avoided, but do not allow yourself to entertain unpleasant thoughts for too long. Scripture says to take such thoughts captive and make them obedient to Christ.

Perhaps today you are displeased with people or circumstances in your life. Rather than complain, think about the blessings you have. Be thankful. Learn from Israel's example. Complaining will lead you down a path to destruction.

1 Corinthians 10:10 – *And don't grumble as some of them did, and then were destroyed by the angel of death* (NLT).

I quit arguing

Philippians 2:14 – *Do everything without complaining or arguing* (NIV).

Arguments birth out of disagreement. There are at least two sides to every argument, and both are in it to prove that their point of view is right and that the other is wrong. Disagreement is inevitable and unavoidable, yet we are instructed not to argue.

This is a hard truth to swallow, especially if you are the one who is "right" about a certain discrepancy between you and someone else. Few things are as frustrating as trying to prove the truth to a person who refuses to listen. Even if your viewpoint is correct, arguing typically does not lead to an agreement with someone who thinks he is just as right as you think you are.

Countless relationships are destroyed because many people are in a relentless pursuit to be right about everything. Listen to me carefully: Nobody is right about everything all of the time, including *you.*

Some people will even argue when they are obviously wrong. I believe they do so because they are more concerned about *being* right than *doing* right. They would rather defend themselves because doing what's right is often pride-swallowing. Admitting fault makes our human nature very uncomfortable, but arguing makes the flesh happy.

I'll admit I have a really hard time with this "no arguing" command because my flesh flares up every time someone attacks me with untruth. I want to get in the face of the person, and spit the truth at him or her. It's in times like these that I'm so grateful for the fruit of self-control in my life.

I've realized that I can be right without having to prove it. Besides, arguing my case does not make me more right. In fact, I've learned that as long as I'm at peace within myself, I can live at peace with even those who oppose me. So can you.

Romans 12:18 – *If possible, so far as it depends on you, be at peace with all men* (NASB).

285

equip yourself

Many Christians feel inadequate. Perhaps you're one of them. Maybe you feel incompetent and unworthy to fulfill the call of God on your life. The truth is God will equip you with everything you need to do His will (**Hebrews 13:21**), but you have to make yourself available and do your part.

My oldest son Noah decided this past year that he wanted to start playing baseball. We had absolutely nothing he needed— no glove, no bat, no cleats, no baseballs, nothing. If he had shown up to the first practice without any gear, he would have felt embarrassed and very inadequate.

So we went to Academy. They had all the equipment Noah needed in order to play baseball. We walked around for over an hour looking at everything from gloves to bats to uniform pants, but we didn't just look at all of it. We bought it, and took it home. Then when it came time for practices and games to start, he was ready. He put on his uniform and cleats, got his glove and bat, and he confidently went out to play.

In much the same way, God's word provides you with all the equipment you need to successfully carry out His plan for your life. Scripture teaches, rebukes, corrects and trains you in righteousness, but reading over the Word is not enough. Just like Noah has to put on his baseball gear before he goes out to play, you must apply the principles found in God's word to your life. Otherwise, you will always feel unqualified.

I encourage you today to thoroughly study the word of God. Equip yourself with its principles, and inadequacy will go.

Ephesians 2:10 – *For we are God's workmanship, created in Christ Jesus to do good works, which God prepared in advance for us to do* (NIV).

watch your step

Psalm 1:1 – *Blessed is the man that walketh not in the counsel of the ungodly, nor standeth in the way of sinners, nor sitteth in the seat of the scornful* (KJV).

I have never met a person who does not want to be blessed. People can joke around, put up a front and pretend like they don't need or want anything. But if they are truly honest with themselves, everyone will admit they want to live a blessed life.

Christians want to be blessed by God, but He withholds His favor from many of them. God cannot bless a person who is disobedient. The keys to receiving His blessings are found in the word of God. If you are lacking God's favor today, I encourage you to pay careful attention. I believe God is going to unlock His blessings in your life. Hallelujah!

There are three things listed in **Psalm 1:1** that God does not want us to do. If He is going to be able to bless you, you have to stop doing these things. First of all, do not walk in the counsel of the ungodly.

Please understand that ungodly counsel is unavoidable and readily available. We cannot get away from it no matter how hard we try. People, media and society in general will try to get us to speak and act in an ungodly manner. Bad advice is readily available, but you must not walk in it.

Sometimes we will even be given ungodly counsel by people we trust. Perhaps you've already walked down this road before. We must be able to discern what is *good* advice and what is *godly* advice. Just because something sounds right, and appeals to our emotions, does not mean it is from God.

I want to encourage you today. If you have listened to ungodly counsel and made some ill-advised decisions, repent and ask God to redirect you. He will help you get back on track. Consult His word and pray. Walk in the counsel of the godly.

Psalm 33:11 – *The counsel of the Lord stands forever, the thoughts of His heart through all generations* (AMP).

dead-end road

Psalm 1:1 – *Blessed is the man that walketh not in the counsel of the ungodly, nor standeth in the way of sinners, nor sitteth in the seat of the scornful* (KJV).

If you want to be blessed, do not stand in the way of sinners. This has nothing to do with keeping sinners from coming to know God. While I would not advise you to prevent people from knowing Christ, this is not what the psalmist is referring to.

Another version says that a man is blessed if he does not stand submissive or inactive in the path where sinners walk (AMP). The Message Bible says not to slink along Dead-End Road. In other words, God will not bless a person who idly stands on the path with sinners.

In fact, many well-meaning believers adopt "ways" that do not please God because they have casually stood in the way of sinners. Because they condone the sinful habits of others, they eventually take on some of the same shameful characteristics. This is usually a gradual process that can slip in undetected.

Christians who were once gentle and loving become angry and impatient. Encouragers start tearing others down. Optimists begin complaining. Households that were once peaceful give into turmoil and chaos. Holiness is traded for self-righteousness, and excuses replace repentance. When confronted, those who stand in the way of sinners often respond, "That's just the *way* I am." God does not bless this kind of behavior.

I want you to be honest with yourself today. Are you standing in the way of sinners? Have you adopted some ways that are not pleasing to God? Are you increasingly impatient? Does anger have a hold of you? Does your tongue need to be tamed? Do you lack self-discipline? Are you sabotaging your relationships? If so, allow God to change the way you do things. God cannot bless you if you are slinking down Dead-End Road.

Psalm 1:6 – *For the Lord watches over the path of the godly, but the path of the wicked leads to destruction* (NLT).

misery loves company

Psalm 1:1 – *Blessed is the man that walketh not in the counsel of the ungodly, nor standeth in the way of sinners, nor sitteth in the seat of the scornful* (KJV).

The scornful are mockers, and they are full of contempt. They are miserable, and their mission is to make everyone else around them miserable. If we are going to be blessed by God, we cannot relax and share fellowship with scornful people.

In order to avoid sitting in the seat of mockers, we have to be able to recognize them. Today we are going to identify three characteristics of the scornful. Evaluate yourself and your relationships. Sitting on a seat of contempt will rob you of God's blessings, so listen carefully.

Mockers resent correction, and they refuse wise counsel (**Proverbs 15:12**). Scornful people have a hard time admitting fault, and they have an even harder time asking for help. They would rather fall flat on their faces than seek sound advice.

Mockers are also full of pride and act in arrogance (**Proverbs 21:24**). They are self-seeking and have their own best interest at heart. This kind of attitude is not godly. You can choose to hang around with scornful people, but they really don't care about you. They want you to be miserable like they are.

Mockers thrive in strife. They feel at home where confusion and chaos reside, but **Proverbs 22:10** says that quarrels and insults come to an end when mockers are driven out. If your relationships are a source of strife in your life, evaluate your company. Associate with peacemakers.

My prayer is that you will live the blessed life God has purposed for you to have, but you must put yourself in position to be blessed. Avoid scornful people because they will rub off on you. If you already struggle in the areas listed above, receive forgiveness and purpose to live differently. God is merciful.

Proverbs 13:1 – *A wise son heeds his father's instruction, but a mocker does not listen to rebuke* (NIV).

3-D vision

God blesses the person who delights in His word. Delight has to do with desire. I have a great desire to get to know my wife better, so I am delighted to spend time with her. I find pleasure in every chance I get to be around her because being around her meets my desire to know her more intimately. Spending time with her is never a drag.

If you want God's blessings, you have to desire to know Him better. That desire will cause you to be delighted every time there's an opportunity for you to spend quality time with Him. You will find His presence to be very gratifying.

One of the ways we come to know Him better is by spending time in the Word. God blesses those who meditate on His word day and night. This means that pondering and studying the word of God should become a habit in your life. A person who desires to be blessed by God cannot have a casual relationship with His word. God does not bless His acquaintances; He blesses His children.

Habits can be very frustrating. I have often found that starting good habits can be difficult, but it takes very little effort to stop them. On the other hand, starting bad habits is fairly simple, but stopping them can be quite a challenge. I believe this is true because maintaining good habits takes self-discipline, which many people lack. Bad habits just come naturally.

If you haven't already, begin spending quality time in God's word today. Remember these three d-words: desire, delight and discipline. If you desire to know Him more intimately, you will delight in His word, and you must discipline yourself to make studying His word a habit. Be encouraged. God's blessings are released through His word. Hallelujah!

make like a tree

So far we have learned that God blesses a person who does not walk in the counsel of the ungodly, stand in the way of sinners or sit in the seat of the scornful. He also blesses those who delight in His word and meditate on it habitually. The above verse likens such a person to a tree. Being called a tree may not sound too much like a blessing, but allow me to share with you three characteristics the psalmist uses to describe this tree.

First of all, this tree will be planted by rivers of water. Water is a life-giving source, but you will not be planted by just one river. You will be like a tree planted by multiple rivers that will bring you life. What an awesome blessing!

This tree will also produce fruit in due season. God blesses you to be a blessing. While it is very gratifying to bring forth godly fruit in your life, the fruit you produce is meant to benefit the people you come in contact with. Your relationships will be positively affected when you align yourself with God's word. Life, healing, love, reconciliation and a host of other benefits will flow out of you onto others. What an indescribable feeling.

Lastly, the leaves of this tree will not wither. This is a powerful promise. Those who are planted by the rivers of water will not be overwhelmed or blown down by the storms of life. They will not shrivel up or become ineffective. Old age and adversity will not prevail because God's strength is made perfect in weakness (**2 Corinthians 12:9**). Praise the Lord!

Stay close to God today. His desire is for you to prosper and to be a blessing to others all the days of your life. Glory!

Ezekiel 47:9 – *There will be swarms of living things wherever the water of this river flows. Fish will abound in the Dead Sea, for its waters will become fresh. Life will flourish wherever this water flows* (NLT).

the parable of the oldest son

> **Psalm 1:3** – *And he shall be like a tree planted by the rivers of water, that bringeth forth his fruit in his season; his leaf also shall not wither; and whatsoever he doeth shall prosper* (KJV).

I'm going to explain the latter part of this verse to you by using a parable of sorts. Keep in mind that this is a fictional story, but I believe it will help you to better understand God's blessings.

My oldest son Noah is very artistic. He loves to draw, build and create. He has a brilliant imagination, and he thinks outside of the box. One of the activities he enjoys most is drawing. He can take a handful of blank paper and turn it into an elaborate picture book. Normally, when he finishes such a project, he brings it to my wife or me for our approval. He wants us to be proud.

One day I gave Noah a handful of paper. He returned to me about thirty minutes later and handed me his work. As I looked over the pages, he longingly looked up at me and asked, "What do you think, Daddy? Isn't it great?"

He stood there waiting to receive my blessing, but I did not know what to say. The pages were still blank. He had not drawn anything. There was nothing for me to approve of. I handed the paper back to him and said, "Why don't you go and finish, and then come back to me when you're done." He wanted me to bless something he did not do.

If you align yourself with **Psalm 1:1-2**, the third verse says that whatever you *do* will prosper. God cannot bless what you do not do. Many people want the blessings of God, but they don't do anything to deserve them. He does not owe us anything, nor does He prosper us because we have a sense of entitlement.

God's blessings are for everyone, but they're also conditional. He can only prosper what you do, but He does not approve of just anything. As my wife says, "Stop asking God to bless what you're doing, and begin doing what it is He is blessing."

> **Deuteronomy 15:5** – *You will receive this blessing if you are careful to obey all the commands of the Lord your God* (NLT).

thirty sterling principles

Proverbs 22:19-20 – ₁₉ *To make sure your foundation is trust in God, I'm laying it all out right now just for you.* ₂₀ *I'm giving you thirty sterling principles—tested guidelines to live by* (MSG).

Most scholars agree that Solomon compiled the vast majority of the book of Proverbs. He is widely heralded as the wisest man who ever lived. In **1 Kings 4:32** it is said that Solomon uttered three thousand proverbs (I've had a hard enough time uttering three thousand coherent sentences). Needless to say, he is definitely someone you and I can learn from.

Solomon said in **Proverbs 22:17**, *"Pay attention and listen to the sayings of the wise; apply your heart to what I teach"* (NIV). Then over the next couple of chapters he goes on to teach thirty principles that, if applied to your life, will ensure your foundation is trust in the Lord. These principles are tested, and they work.

Solomon had a wealth of wisdom, but like so many of us, sometimes he lacked sound judgment and made mistakes. I believe Proverbs reflects the knowledge he acquired from both his successes and blunders. God's desire is for us to learn from Solomon's experience and the experiences of others.

If something works for someone else, why change it? Many people frustrate themselves trying to reinvent an idea or principle that is proven to work. Changing something that works is not being unique or cutting edge. Often times it is foolish. Some things in life are fine the way they are.

On the other hand, it is also foolish to repeat our mistakes and those made by others. We can gain a lot of wisdom from learning what not to do. I want to encourage you today to take advantage of every learning opportunity you get. Be teachable, and do not pretend to have everything figured out. Purpose to learn from the examples of others. As we look at these thirty principles in Proverbs 22-24, I pray you will never be the same.

Proverbs 22:21 – *Believe me—these are truths that work, and will keep you accountable to those who sent you* (MSG).

don't walk on the poor

Proverbs 22:22-23 – 22 *Don't walk on the poor just because they're poor, and don't use your position to crush the weak,* 23 *because God will come to their defense; the life you took, he'll take from you and give back to them* (MSG).

The first principle you need to apply to your life is don't walk on the poor, and don't use your position to crush them. Why? The Bible says that He will come to the defense of the needy if someone tries to take advantage of them. I don't know about you, but I do not want to get caught walking all over a person whose back is guarded by almighty God.

It is God's desire for His people to look after those who are less fortunate. Even if you feel you don't have a lot to offer, you can still be a blessing to others. Simply begin asking God to show you how to have a positive impact on those around you.

Many people are ruthless when it comes to those who are in need. They tend to judge people instead of showing compassion. If we will be obedient to bless those who are less fortunate than we are, we will develop a sincere desire to help others. We will also learn to appreciate more the things God has blessed us with.

I once received an e-mail from a certain young man. His family had fallen on really hard times. His mom was not around, and his dad became very ill and was hospitalized. He was made to live with his grandmother, and he contacted me out of desperation. It was near the end of the summer, and with school rapidly approaching, he did not have proper school clothes.

The Holy Spirit quickly prompted Heidi and me to take him shopping. What a joy it was to see his face after our trip to the store! He was very thankful, and his eyes had new life behind them. But he wasn't the only one with newfound joy. Heidi and I were blessed, and there's no doubt that God was too. Glory!

1 John 3:17 – *If anyone has material possessions and sees his brother in need but has no pity on him, how can the love of God be in him?* (NIV)

don't hang with hotheads

Proverbs 22:24-25 – 24 *Don't hang out with angry people; don't keep company with hotheads.* 25 *Bad temper is contagious—don't get infected* (MSG).

Another version reads: 24 *Don't befriend angry people or associate with hot-tempered people,* 25 *or you will learn to be like them and endanger your soul* (NLT). Everyone gets angry, even Jesus did. You can read the account of Him turning over the tables and chairs of the money changers in Matthew 21. What we need to understand, though, is there is a distinct difference between getting angry and being an angry person.

The second principle you need to live by is don't hang out with angry people (hotheads). God does not expect us to avoid people who get angry. If He did, then we would have to go into isolation. We could not associate with anyone because, as I mentioned before, everyone gets angry.

The word *angry* is an adjective. Adjectives characterize people and things. When an adjective is attached to the name of a person or thing, that person or thing is then defined by the qualities of that adjective. In other words, an angry person will produce fruit characterized by anger. You need to be able to recognize such fruit in others and in yourself. Allow me to help.

Angry people lack self-control in their actions and words. They are typically very harsh and unforgiving toward others. They have routine outbursts and vent their frustrations inappropriately (**Proverbs 29:11**). Their foolishness is habitual, and they generally make decisions they later regret (**Ecclesiastes 7:9**).

I do not believe that God's desire is for you to completely cancel the relationships you have with angry people. The truth is they need to be influenced by the love of God in your life, but be careful. Your inner circle of friends should not include hotheads. The Bible teaches that anger can be learned. Avoid that lesson.

Proverbs 14:29 – *He who is slow to anger has great understanding, but he who is quick-tempered exalts folly* (NASB).

295

sober management

The third principle you need to apply to your life is do not gamble with your security. In other words, don't risk losing what God has blessed you with by taking chances. A lot of people have problems with the "do nots" found in Scripture, so I'm going to share with you the right thing *to do.*

When most people hear the word *gamble,* they immediately think of casinos and neon lights, slot machines and the craps table. While this is a prominent form of gambling, I do not believe that the majority of Christians struggle with this addiction.

So as I was watering the flowers at our church one afternoon, I asked God to give me revelation concerning this passage. The Holy Spirit quickly spoke this to me, "Every time you are a poor steward of what I have blessed you with, you are gambling with your security." This was eye opening for me.

The Bible teaches in **James 1:17** that every good and perfect gift comes from our heavenly Father. This means that no matter how much (or how little) we think we have, everything that is beneficial to our lives comes from Him. This includes our family, relationships, time, finances, food, clothing, vehicle, home, etc. Anytime we misuse these things, or make ill-advised decisions concerning them, we are gambling with our security.

You cannot afford to be a poor steward of God's blessings. When you are unfaithful with what He's given you, what you have will eventually be taken from you. I encourage you to prayerfully consider every decision you make regarding your security. Do not act hastily or lazily. Be a sober manager of your relationships and assets.

stealth stakeouts

Proverbs 22:28 – *Don't stealthily move back the boundary lines staked out long ago by your ancestors* (MSG).

In ancient Israel, land had a special meaning because it was owned by God (**Leviticus 25:23**). So when the original boundary lines were set, it was more than just an agreement between neighbors. The ancient boundaries of Israel were an agreement between the people and God. To compromise those lines was to reject God's law.

In **Deuteronomy 19:14**, the people were told not to move the boundary stones. This command was no doubt given because there were some who would attempt to secretly move the boundaries (perhaps to add to the size of their own property). I call these missions "stealth stakeouts."

I imagine such missions were widely successful because the boundaries could be moved subtly without detection. There were likely many who were able to enlarge their properties without the knowledge of their neighbors.

Not much has changed today. Boundaries are used to mark limits, and God's people continue to push those limits. Boundaries are often viewed negatively. Many people feel as if they limit potential or fun, but boundaries are a necessary part of life. They provide protection, stability and focus.

Parents set boundaries to help protect their children. Employers have boundaries in place to optimize the performance of their employees. God has set boundaries in His word to guide His children to holiness. Pushing the limits in secrecy is rebellion. Some boundaries may eventually need to be moved, but God says not to do so stealthily. Otherwise, we will be judged accordingly.

I encourage you today not to push the limits. Don't ignore boundaries just because you can get away with it. Be a person of integrity, and you will remain protected, stable and focused.

1 Samuel 15:23 – *For rebellion is like the sin of divination, and arrogance like the evil of idolatry* (NIV).

297

backseat workers

Proverbs 22:29 – *Observe people who are good at their work— skilled workers are always in demand and admired; they don't take a back seat to anyone* (MSG).

There are not too many things more annoying than a backseat driver. I have been driving now for about half of my life and have experienced my fair share of backseat drivers, and every experience has been equally unpleasant. No one wants to be told how to drive while he is driving. It's really very irritating.

Keeping this in mind, I want you to read the above verse again. There is an important principle to be learned here. Those who are diligent and skillful at their work will be held in high regard, and they will not take a back seat to anyone. Another version says such workers will stand before kings (AMP).

You could also say that people who have a *poor* work ethic will not be valued or in demand. They will take a back seat to those who do things with excellence. I call them "backseat workers." Many times these backseat workers will fault find and pick apart the people who work hard. This is not the will of God.

I want to encourage you today not to be a backseat worker. People who have a poor work ethic are a strain to those who really do work hard. I am a hard worker, and it is very frustrating to have to pull someone else's wait while he or she is critiquing what I do from the back seat. I challenge you to be honest with yourself. When there is a job that needs to be done, are you someone who is sought after or avoided?

God's desire is for backseat workers to get out of the back seat. Observe those who are good at what they do, and learn from them. Study people who have a solid work ethic and who do things with excellence. Do not be content with taking a back seat to those who work. God promotes diligence. Don't expect to be promoted if you are comfortable riding around in the back seat.

Proverbs 12:24 – *The hand of the diligent will rule, but the slothful will be put to forced labor* (AMP).

bridle your appetite

Proverbs 23:1-3 – 1 *When you go out to dinner with an influential person, mind your manners: 2 Don't gobble your food, don't talk with your mouth full. 3 And don't stuff yourself; bridle your appetite* (MSG).

I believe the message of this passage is two-fold. There is a principle here that God desires us to apply to both our physical and spiritual health. Today I want to address the physical application, and tomorrow we will look at the spiritual. What you will find, though, is the two go hand-in-hand.

God sent Jesus so that we may believe and have life to the full (**John 10:10**). After Jesus went to be with the Father, the Holy Spirit was then sent to lead us into that abundant life. The Spirit dwells on the inside of believers. In fact, the Bible says that our bodies are His temple, and we should glorify Him with our bodies (**1 Corinthians 6:19-20**). With that said, the message I want to convey to you today is not a popular one.

If you are going to live the abundant life God desires you to have on this earth, you are going to have to take care of your body. Many people argue that much of the Bible is figurative and that there is deep, hidden meaning behind certain passages. While this is true sometimes, there are also scriptures that are meant to be taken literally and applied practically. This is one of them.

Scripture says that when we sit down to eat, we need to consider what is in front of us. **Proverbs 23:2** then says to put a knife to your throat if you are given to gluttony (NIV). This does not mean to end your life if you have an unhealthy relationship with food. It means to practice restraint. The Message Bible says not to stuff yourself, to bridle your appetite.

If you are controlled by what you eat, you lack self-control and the abundant life God desires you to have. Overeating zaps your strength and ruins your self-image. I want to encourage you to practice healthy eating habits. It is also important that you exercise regularly. Being healthy means living a balanced life with proper nutrition, exercise and an appropriate amount of rest.

don't desire dainties

Proverbs 23:1-3 – 1 *When you sit down to eat with a ruler, consider who and what are before you; 2 for you will put a knife to your throat if you are a man given to desire. 3 Be not desirous of his dainties, for it is deceitful food [offered with questionable motives]* (AMP).

As I mentioned yesterday, I believe the message behind this passage is two-fold. The practical application is for you to live a healthy life. But this passage not only challenges us not to overeat, but also to avoid giving into temptation, period. There are some valuable lessons you need to learn concerning temptation.

Avoiding sin is only possible if you make a proper judgment call at the moment you are tempted. The devil disguises temptation by making it look attractive to you. If he initially showed you the ugly effects sin has on your life, you likely would not have a problem saying no. Often times the decision is tough because the line between right and wrong has been blurred.

As it is, sin is made to look fun and beneficial, so giving into temptation has become commonplace both in the world and in the church. Most people do not feel remorse until they have to face the consequences of their actions. Much guilt and shame could be avoided if we would simply heed the advice offered in **Proverbs 23:1-3**.

When you are faced with a decision, and you don't have clear direction as to what to do, the Bible says to consider who and what is before you. Do not act impulsively. Ask God to reveal to you what is right. If you are someone who is prone to jumping at opportunities that look good but really are not, restrain yourself. Satan tempts us with things that are desirous, but his motives are evil. You must discern which potential blessings are godly and which are wicked. Then you can make the correct decision.

Matthew 26:41 – *"Keep watch and pray, so that you will not give in to temptation. For the spirit is willing, but the body is weak!"* (NLT)

wealth sprouts wings

The next principle you need to apply to your life is do not wear yourself out trying to get rich. Please understand that there is nothing wrong with being rich. There is a common misconception that Christians should be lowly and poverty stricken. God does not want you to pursue riches at the expense of your well-being, but He also does not want you to purposefully become a charity case.

Proverbs 15:6 teaches that great wealth is in the house of the righteous, but trouble is in the income of the wicked (NASB). When we live the righteous, balanced lives that God has planned for us to have, He will supply all of our needs according to His riches and glory. On the other hand, when gaining riches becomes an idol to you, there will be trouble in your house.

Finances are one of the main causes of strife is marriages today. More times than not, financial discord between husband and wife results from poor stewardship or a lack of funds. In either case, often times the belief is that there would be no issue if there were more money. So many people then allow money and materialism to govern their lives. Riches become their god, and they embark on a relentless pursuit to get more.

This type of behavior doesn't only affect married couples. Countless individuals have developed a love for money. **1 Timothy 6:10** – *For the love of money is a root of all kinds of evil. Some people, eager for money, have wandered from the faith and pierced themselves with many griefs* (NIV). When a person loves money, his or her faith is no longer in God. It's in stuff.

I challenge you today to keep perspective when it comes to your finances. Increasing your wealth should not be your life's ambition because one day it will sprout wings and be gone.

the meal's a sham

Another version says not to eat the bread of a person with a hard, grudging and envious eye (AMP). Have you ever had an experience with someone who seemed pleasant on the surface, but they really had some sort of personal vendetta against you?

Like the tightwad described in the above passage of Scripture, this type of person tells you what he thinks you want to hear in order to take advantage of you. "Eat and drink!" he says, but he doesn't mean it. His desire is to gain your trust and get you to open up. Then he uses what is said to manipulate you or others.

These kinds of people are unavoidable. In fact, your current relationships likely consist of multiple tightwads. There have been numerous people in my life that I could only get *so close* to because I knew they did not really care about me or my family. Their motives were self-seeking, but many times I did not realize what their true intentions were until I was burned by them.

There are also others who are nice to you so you will be nice to them. Their generosity has nothing to do with a desire to meet your needs; they're just "fishing for compliments." They want you to shower them with praise, but they resent the fact that they're being nice to you.

My goal today is not for you to become a cynic, but rather for you to use discernment. The majority of people are not out to get you, but some really are. Do not allow yourself to be enticed by them. **Proverbs 23:8** teaches that being taken advantage of will make you sick. While I've found this to be true, relationships are a gift from God. Invest yourself in them wisely.

talking sense to fools

Proverbs 23:9 – *Don't bother talking sense to fools; they'll only poke fun at your words* (MSG).

I once heard someone define *stupidity* as doing the same thing over and over expecting to get different results. Another word for *stupidity* is *foolishness*.

Before I go any further, I want to make sure you understand the difference between a fool, and a person who makes mistakes. Everyone makes mistakes. Humans are all flawed creatures, and you've probably found that you make multiple mistakes daily. Fools are people who do not learn from their mistakes. They have a habit of making wrong choices. Then they murmur and complain about the unfavorable results, but they still make no changes.

I used to think that fools were waiting on me to correct their stupidity. I figured they would be delighted for me to tell them how to change their behavior and get the results they desired, but I was wrong. Fools are not interested in gaining wisdom. They're more interested in proving conventional wisdom wrong. **Proverbs 18:2** – *A fool does not delight in understanding, but only in revealing his own mind* (NASB). If you don't support what they're doing, fools would rather you just leave them alone. They are going to do things their way no matter what the outcome might be. That's why it's called foolishness. If you try to "talk sense" into such people, they will either blow you off or ridicule you. Either way you are wasting your breath.

Fools generally have to learn lessons the hard way, and for someone like me, this is a hard truth to swallow. It goes against my nature to have to sit back and watch someone fall flat, but I have to admit that following this principle has saved me from a lot of frustration. It's aggravating to give someone sound advice, and then watch as that person makes a poor choice anyway. Do yourself a favor today: Don't debate with a fool.

Proverbs 28:26 – *He who trusts in himself is a fool, but he who walks in wisdom is kept safe* (NIV).

don't cheat orphans

> **Proverbs 23:10-11** – 10 *Don't stealthily move back the boundary lines or cheat orphans out of their property,* 11 *for they have a powerful Advocate who will go to bat for them* (MSG).

James defined religion that is pure and acceptable to God as to look after orphans and widows (**James 1:27**). The conventional definition of an orphan is a child that does not have parents. Children become orphans for one of two reasons. They either lose both parents through death, or they are abandoned by their parents.

There are also countless children who are neglected by one or both of their parents. Mom, Dad or both may be present in the child's life, but they do not care for the child properly. There are still others whose parents are unable to meet their needs. The parents do their best to get by, but their efforts often fall short. While these children are not labeled as orphans in our current society, I believe the church should look after them as such.

My definition of an orphan is a child whose physical, emotional and spiritual needs are not being met by his or her parents for whatever reason. Children whose needs are not being met are never at fault, and no child deserves to be neglected no matter the circumstances.

The Bible says not to cheat orphans. Most Christians know they should not be running around taking advantage of orphans, but I do believe many miss out on opportunities to bless them. How many children do you know whose needs are not being met for whatever reason? I believe we cheat them when we *can* help but don't.

I want to encourage you today to become more aware of the needs around you. Maybe there is an orphanage near you that you can volunteer at or support financially. Perhaps you can bless a family that's barely getting by. Even if you are only able to do a little, it will mean a lot. Share God's love through your generosity.

> **Isaiah 1:17** – *Learn to do good; seek justice, reprove the ruthless, defend the orphan, plead for the widow* (NASB).

open your ears

Proverbs 23:12 – *Give yourselves to disciplined instruction; open your ears to tested knowledge* (MSG).

As I studied this particular principle, I discovered that its message is three-fold. Applying this verse to your life will help prevent you from making unnecessary mistakes and poor decisions. I pray that you are blessed.

First, nobody knows everything, and this includes you. We must be teachable. Be open to learn from anyone in any situation. If we were able to know everything, then we would be on an even playing field with God. I hate to break it to you, but that is never going to happen.

Secondly, you must apply your heart and mind to discipline. Because you do not know everything, you are going to make mistakes. Discipline is meant to get you back on track when you mess up, and it also serves as a reminder not to repeat your mistakes.

The Bible says to give, or apply, yourself to disciplined instruction. I used to get in trouble when I was in school because I did not apply myself. I knew what to do and how to do it, but I just didn't do it. God places people in your life to help guide you. Learn to apply the sound instruction you receive to your life.

Lastly, open your ears to tested knowledge. The key word here is *tested*. Many people inadvertently lend their ears to foolishness. Your life is too valuable to allow yourself to be governed by other people's opinions. There is a lot of knowledge to be gained from the experiences of others, but you must be able to discern what is beneficial to you and what is not.

I encourage you today to take advantage of the opportunities you will have to learn. Though discipline is often uncomfortable, allow it to bring correction and structure to your life. Godly knowledge is readily available to you. Listen for it.

Proverbs 15:32 – *He who ignores discipline despises himself, but whoever heeds correction gains understanding* (NIV).

discipline doesn't kill

> **Proverbs 23:13-14** – 13 *Don't be afraid to correct your young ones; a spanking won't kill them.* 14 *A good spanking, in fact, might save them from something worse than death* (MSG).

Some of the greatest compliments my wife and I have ever received have come as a result of the good behavior of our children. It is not uncommon for teachers, friends or family to say things to us such as, "Your boys are so well-behaved." "They are very polite," or "I can't believe they can sit still in church so long." Heidi and I are always very grateful for the positive feedback.

Many times people will follow their compliment by saying something like, "I wish I could get my children to behave like that, but they are out of control. How do you guys do it?" Heidi and I are very proud of ourselves and our children, but Noah and Jack were not born compliant, and being good parents is a constant learning process for us.

Because no child or parent is perfect, both have to be disciplined. Children must be disciplined by their parents, and parents must discipline themselves in order to effectively raise their kids. This is a very tough, but necessary, balance to maintain. It also helps that we serve a very gracious and merciful God.

As a parent, if you do not discipline your children, you are living in disobedience. What you need to do is ask God to help you be consistent in every area of parenting, including discipline. Consistency is key, and it is vital for you and your spouse to be on the same page. Otherwise, your children will play you guys against each other. You also need to be willing to admit fault.

I am not going to tell you whether or not to spank your kids, but I will say that doing so is not unbiblical. You ultimately decide what methods to use and whether they work or not. Do not be afraid to ask for help or to try something new. Raising children is the most important job a parent has. Do it well.

> **Ephesians 6:4** – *Do not provoke your children to anger, but bring them up in the discipline and instruction of the Lord* (NASB).

become wise

My wife and I once bought a brand new, full-size truck. It was our dream vehicle! We owned it for about a year and a half, and we paid down our loan considerably during that time. One day we were driving along, and I asked Heidi if she thought it would be a good idea to trade in the truck. She had actually been thinking the same thing for some time, but she did not mention it because she knew I loved the truck so much.

We began to weigh the pros and cons. The decision wound up being a no-brainer. We were tired of not driving anywhere but still having to fill it up with gas. While we had no problem paying the monthly note on the truck, we figured our monthly payments would be less if we traded for a four-door car. Also, our car insurance premium would likely decrease.

We went ahead and made the trade for a newer car with fewer miles and a longer warranty. It gets double the gas mileage of the truck, and it more than meets all of our family's needs. All in all, we ended up giving ourselves more than a $300/month raise! Trading in our dream truck proved to be a very wise decision.

I remember telling my dad that we had made the trade. He was very excited. He told me that he did not understand why we wanted a truck to begin with. Owning the truck was not detrimental, nor was it practical. He was very pleased with our decision. It made him happy because he wants what is best for us.

Our heavenly Father responds in much the same way when we make wise choices. He always knows what is best, but He allows us to make our own decisions. When you make wise choices, His heart rejoices. I encourage you to include God in your decision-making. You will be the one who benefits from doing so.

307

an armload of nothing

The careless rebels referred to in this passage are sinners. We are instructed not to allow our hearts to envy them. So ask yourself, "How often do I covet the possessions or lifestyles of sinful people?" Probably more times than you would like to admit.

I will be very honest. There have been numerous times that I have looked at a magazine and wondered why *that* person gets to be on the cover. I am also aware of the lavish lifestyles that some openly sinful people have. They drive luxury vehicles, wear designer clothes, and they seem to be above the law. It sometimes seems as if sinners prosper while those who try to live righteously suffer. It can be quite frustrating.

If you are not careful, it is very easy to find yourself coveting the devil's blessings. Satan blesses his children, but the blessings of a sinful life are fleeting (see **Hebrews 11:25**). They have no eternal value. Satan knows this, but he is able to make a sinful lifestyle look attractive. He lures well-meaning people in and then ultimately leaves them with an armload of nothing.

On the other hand, fearing the Lord brings hope and blessing. The fear of God promises both temporal and eternal benefits. If Satan blesses his people, then how much more does God want to bless His children! God's blessings are far superior. **Proverbs 22:4** – *The reward of humility and the fear of the LORD are riches, honor and life* (NASB). He also gives confidence to those who fear Him (**Proverbs 14:26**). Fearing God also brings life, wisdom and knowledge. If you take the time to study the fear of the Lord, you will realize that serving God and obeying His commands has so much more to offer than a lifestyle of sin does. Don't get caught up in the hype. Fear Him today.

to drink, or not to drink?

> **Proverbs 23:19-21** – 19 *Oh listen, dear child—become wise; point your life in the right direction.* 20 *Don't drink too much wine and get drunk; don't eat too much food and get fat.* 21 *Drunks and gluttons will end up on skid row, in a stupor and dressed in rags* (MSG).

Alcohol and gluttony are two things that can derail our lives very quickly, and there is probably not enough sound teaching on either subject coming from the pulpit. There are other substances, besides alcohol and food, that are plaguing the church, but I want to focus on this particular passage today. I have already addressed overeating, so I want to look specifically at alcohol.

I recently read a conversation between multiple young ministers on the message board of a particular social network. There were probably twenty to thirty men and women participating in the dialogue. I read as each of them voiced their opinions on whether pastors and other church leadership should consume alcohol or not.

Many of them shared about their personal experiences and struggles. They also gave biblical principles and scientific facts to support their positions. They all shared one of two views. Ministers should either abstain from alcohol altogether, or they should drink in moderation under certain conditions. All of them agreed that drunkenness was sinful. Thank God!

I will honestly tell you that my heart was grieved as I read the conflicted conversation between the church leadership of this generation. If the leaders cannot agree, how confused those underneath them must be! How do you teach people to drink in moderation? It is not possible. The definition of moderation will differ from person to person and pastor to pastor.

The Bible does teach not to be drunk, but it does not say to avoid alcohol altogether either. However, we are to abstain from all appearance of evil (**1 Thessalonians 5:22**). Ask yourself, "Does alcohol have the appearance of evil or godliness?" Scripture links alcohol to ruin, not holiness. Use sober judgment.

buy, buy, buy, buy

Proverbs 23:22-25 – 22 *Listen with respect to the father who raised you, and when your mother grows old, don't neglect her.* 23 *Buy truth—don't sell it for love or money; buy wisdom, buy education, buy insight.* 24 *Parents rejoice when their children turn out well; wise children become proud parents.* 25 *So make your father happy! Make your mother proud!* (MSG)

I have a great love and appreciation for my father. I respect my dad more than any other man on the planet. I am thankful for the example he has set for me as a godly father and husband. He is a patient and hardworking man (even in retirement).

My mother is a peacemaker. She will bend over backwards to make sure everyone in her life is happy. My mom is a giver and a good friend. I am grateful for the support she has given me in every area of my life. She was always the mom hollering in the stands at my sports games.

I have always appreciated my parents, but I have learned to value them more as I have grown older. Good parents are priceless, and I want nothing more than to make them proud. I want to encourage you to do the same. Even if your parents have not met your expectations, show them love and respect. If one or both of your parents has gone on to eternity, continue to honor their memory by living a godly lifestyle.

One of the ways you can make your parents proud is by being truthful. The Bible says to buy truth and not to sell it for anything. Be a person of integrity, and back up your words with action. Pursue wisdom and value education. Never stop learning. With wisdom and education comes insight and understanding. Making these things a priority will set you up for success.

I want to be a person worthy of receiving my parents' respect, and I'm sure you do too. Live your life in a way that will cause them to rejoice over you. Make your parents proud!

Proverbs 6:20 – *My son, keep thy father's commandment, and forsake not the law of thy mother* (KJV).

worse than thieves

Proverbs 23:26-28 – 26 *Dear child, I want your full attention; please do what I show you.* 27 *A whore is a bottomless pit; a loose woman can get you in deep trouble fast.* 28 *She'll take you for all you've got; she's worse than a pack of thieves* (MSG).

Getting a child to focus is no easy task. Our boys are no different. There are plenty of little "teaching moments" that come along when you're a parent, and I have found they are often disciplinary in nature. Usually, Heidi or I will get down on eye level with the culprit and ask him to look at us in the eyes. It's amazing how difficult it is to get their full attention. They will look from side to side, over our heads and down at the ground, all while rocking back and forth playing with their hands.

I imagine God must feel the same way about His children sometimes, especially when the teaching moment is sexual by nature. I want to encourage you to give God your full attention today (no matter how awkward it might be). Sexual sin is plaguing the body of Christ, and I don't want you to be its next victim. I pray that if you struggle in this area, you will be set free today to the glory of God!

This particular passage is obviously directed at men, but it can also be applied to women. Sexual immorality is not gender sensitive, though I do believe men and women often enter into it for different reasons. Men are typically (but not always) tempted to sin in this particular area because of the physical appeal. Whether you are married or not, men, you need to learn and practice self-control. Don't make excuses for the urges you have.

Women often times (but not always) are tempted by sexual sin because of an emotional need. Ladies, if you find yourself entertaining the idea of sinning in this area, seek the face of God today before it's too late. Do not give yourself to someone who is not your spouse. Doing so will only compound the emotional torment you may feel. Allow God to heal you today.

Sexual immorality is worse than a pack of thieves. Thieves take what you don't want to give. Don't fall victim to them.

be like John

Proverbs 23:29-35 – 29 *Who are the people who are always crying the blues? Who do you know who reeks of self-pity? Who keeps getting beat up for no reason at all? Whose eyes are bleary and bloodshot?* 30 *It's those who spend the night with a bottle, for whom drinking is serious business.* 31 *Don't judge wine by its label, or its bouquet, or its full-bodied flavor.* 32 *Judge it rather by the hangover it leaves you with—the splitting headache, the queasy stomach.* 33 *Do you really prefer seeing double, with you speech all slurred,* 34 *reeling and seasick, drunk as a sailor?* 35 *"They hit me," you'll say, "but it didn't hurt; they beat on me, but I didn't feel a thing. When I'm sober enough to manage it, bring me another drink!"* (MSG)

Once again Scripture warns us of the consequences of drunkenness. Many will argue that alcohol is not outlawed in God's word, but I would like to reiterate something I said on a previous day. The Bible links alcohol to ruin, not holiness.

When so much is written in the Word about the destruction that alcohol brings, why would a Christian even want to take a sip? God expects believers to live a life of holiness because He is holy (**Leviticus 19:2**). You could also say that we are to be holy *as* He is holy. There are not different kinds of holiness.

If you have a drink every once in a while, I do not want to make you angry or call you a sinner. What I do want to do, however, is give you a New Testament example of a man who never drank alcohol. John the Baptist was commissioned to prepare the way for the first coming of Christ. He was set apart from birth to live a life of holiness unto God. One of the requirements he had was not to consume any alcohol (Luke 1).

God has commissioned us as believers to prepare the way for Christ's second coming. Countless lives were changed through John's ministry because he was unique and did not blend in with the people he was trying to reach. He was uncompromising. I believe that Jesus is looking for some "John the Baptists" to rise up in this generation. Will you be one of them?

don't envy anyone

Proverbs 24:1-2 – 1 *Don't envy bad people; don't even want to be around them.* 2 *All they think about is causing a disturbance; all they talk about is making trouble* (MSG).

I had a friend in school that was very outgoing and well liked. He was athletic, smart and loved by the ladies. He had a lot of charisma, and he excelled in many areas that I struggled in. I was very insecure as a teenager, and I honestly envied him. My parents did not care for him, and for the longest time I could not understand why. I thought he was great!

As I grew older, though, I began to realize that my friend always seemed to be in trouble. He was rebellious and disrespectful to authority. He was always involved in some kind of mischief. I noticed that many of his conversations consisted of trouble he had just been in or trouble that he was about to start. I started to understand why teenagers loved him and why adults were suspicious of him. The Holy Spirit convicted me of my desire to be like him. We remained friends, but I stopped spending as much time with him.

I now understand why my parents had such a difficult time with the friendship I had with him. They did not want me to be influenced in a negative way. What I didn't realize was that I had developed some rebellious characteristics. My friend was definitely *not* to blame, though. It was by my own choice that I began to act differently, but his influence did not help matters.

Envy is never beneficial. We should not envy sinners, nor should we envy those we view as "spiritual." Wherever there is envy, there is confusion and every evil work (**James 3:16**).

I want to encourage you today to get rid of every kind of envy. Envy births from discontentment and will only add to any disappointment you may be feeling. My prayer is that you will find your identity in Christ. Allow Him to shape your character.

Proverbs 14:30 – *A heart at peace gives life to the body, but envy rots the bones* (NIV).

the Holy Spirit's blueprints

> **Proverbs 24:3-4** – 3 *It takes wisdom to build a house, and understanding to set it on a firm foundation;* 4 *it takes knowledge to furnish its rooms with fine furniture and beautiful draperies* (MSG).

I have very limited knowledge when it comes to the ins and outs of building a house. If I decided to start construction on one today, it would not end well. I have a general idea of what a finished home should look like, but I have no idea how to get from a vacant lot to an inhabitable home. I might be able to create something that resembles a house, but it would not be a place anyone would want to live in.

Even if I followed a blueprint and had the steps outlined in front of me, I would still lack the skills necessary to finish the project. The wise thing for me to do would be to hire someone to build the house for me. I would need to seek out a competent builder, and then trust that he will do the job right.

I believe this same concept can be applied to building your relationship with God. You cannot live a godly life without help and the wisdom that comes from the Holy Spirit. Everyone has access to the word of God (the blueprint). But unless you receive a revelation of the Word by the Spirit of God, your relationship with Him will be as unstable as any house I try to build by myself.

Jesus is the only sure foundation for you to build your life on. After you establish Him as your foundation, the Holy Spirit will instruct you as to how to build your life. He will give you the knowledge you need in order to fill your house with fine furniture and beautiful draperies (qualities that are pleasing to God).

> **1 Corinthians 3:9-11** – 9 *For we are God's fellow workers; you are God's field, God's building.* 10 *By the grace God has given me, I laid a foundation as an expert builder, and someone else is building on it. But each one should be careful how he builds.* 11 *For no one can lay any foundation other than the one already laid, which is Jesus Christ* (NIV).

knowledge increases strength

> **Proverbs 24:5-6** – 5 *It's better to be wise than strong; intelligence outranks muscle any day.* 6 *Strategic planning is the key to warfare; to win, you need a lot of good counsel* (MSG).

The King James Version says that a wise man is strong, and a man of knowledge increases strength. The adverse of this verse is also true: A foolish man is weak, and a man without knowledge loses what strength he has. We are engaged in a battle with the powers of darkness. Our adversary is a worthy opponent, and he will take advantage of ignorance.

We must seek wisdom and add to our knowledge of the Word on a daily basis, and it's imperative that we do so with an attitude of humility. The enemy will destroy an arrogant opponent just as quickly as he would an ignorant one. Many knowledgeable people fall because of arrogance.

Knowledge can puff a person up (**1 Corinthians 8:1**), but it is also necessary for victory. Once a person begins to increase his or her knowledge of the word of God, the devil goes to work. God uses knowledge to propel believers to victory, but Satan uses it to birth religion. Developing a religious spirit will cause you to let your guard down. Then you are susceptible to attack.

This is where accountability comes into play. The Bible says that strategic planning is the key to warfare. One of God's goals is for His children to work together. Unfortunately, many believers are battling each other over petty differences. Friendly fire is often the product of religion.

I want to encourage you to unite with fellow believers. Pray and study the Word together. Encourage one another, and develop a strategy to reach the lost of your community. Ask God to give you wisdom, and pursue knowledge. But do so in humility, motivated by love. With knowledge comes great responsibility.

> **Ecclesiastes 7:12** – *Wisdom is a shelter as money is a shelter, but the advantage of knowledge is this: that wisdom preserves the life of its possessor* (NIV).

I don't get it

Proverbs 24:7 – *Wise conversation is way over the head of fools; in a serious discussion they haven't a clue* (MSG).

I was recently at a meeting with seven or eight other men. We meet together on a monthly basis at our church for a time of food, discussion and prayer. The night typically starts with food and fellowship. After about an hour or so, the meeting then shifts to a time of Bible study. We discuss Scripture and apply it to everyday life. Then the evening closes with prayer and clean up.

On this particular night, we were sitting around eating and catching up when the topic of discussion turned to cars. If they would have started talking about the Disney/Pixar animated films, I would have been the life of the conversation. But as it turned out, they began discussing the inner workings of automobiles and how to fix a certain problem one of the guys was having with his vehicle. Needless to say, I was lost.

I sat there and listened trying to learn something new, but the same four-word phrase kept bouncing around in my mind. "I don't get it," I said to myself over and over. I occasionally nodded my head in agreement and made grunts and noises that made it sound like I knew what was going on, but I was clueless. I am a fool when it comes to cars, and any conversation that goes above how to clean or put gas in one loses me very quickly.

It was extremely awkward being in the middle of a conversation about something I know very little about, but I don't have to remain a car fool forever. If I want to become wiser in that area, I need to study and learn from others who are knowledgeable.

The same is true in your relationship with the Lord. God does not expect you to know everything, but He does expect you to pursue wisdom. Don't remain a fool. Admit that you don't know everything, and take advantage of every learning opportunity.

Titus 3:14 – *Our people must learn to devote themselves to doing what is good, in order that they may provide for daily necessities and not live unproductive lives* (NIV).

prince of rogues

Proverbs 24:8-9 – 8 *The person who's always cooking up some evil soon gets a reputation as prince of rogues.* 9 *Fools incubate sin; cynics desecrate beauty* (MSG).

How would you describe your reputation? What would your spouse, children, pastor, coworkers and others say about your character? Are you a person of your word, or do you lack integrity? I want to challenge you today to take a good, hard look at yourself. Everything you do and say shapes who you are and forms the perception that people make of you.

Everyone can be lumped into one of two categories. Your reputation will either portray you as godly or ungodly. The qualities that make up who you are will either point others to God or away from Him.

The above passage of Scripture describes the reputation of an ungodly individual. Such a person is a troublemaker, and the Bible calls him the prince of rogues (I guess such a woman would be the princess of rogues). These people incubate sin. In other words, they nurture, develop and protect sinful habits. Do you make excuses for your sinful behavior? Be honest with yourself.

Now I want to share with you the reputation of a godly individual. Paul describes the character of Epaphroditus in **Philippians 2:25-30**. Paul calls him his brother and a fellow worker and soldier. Epaphroditus served Paul and took care of his needs. He was submitted to authority. Paul goes on to say that such men should be honored and received with gladness (vs. 29). Epaphroditus risked his life for the work of Christ.

If you are unsure today as to how others view you, ask them. Tell them to be honest with you. Ask for both positive and negative feedback. You also need to ask the Holy Spirit to shine His light on your character. You may not like all that you see, but God will give you the grace to change what needs to be changed.

Proverbs 22:21 – *Choose a good reputation over great riches; being held in high esteem is better than silver or gold* (NLT).

strength in crisis

After reading this verse and exploring other versions of it, I began to think about the times in my life that I have folded under pressure. I also thought about the countless others who have allowed crisis to get the best of them. It is not uncommon for someone to approach me in a panic because something has gone terribly wrong. Crisis is an unavoidable part of life, but we do not have to be overcome by it.

The message of **Proverbs 24:10** is very clear. A person falls to pieces in a crisis because he or she lacks strength. One version says that if we are slack in the day of distress, it's because our strength is limited (NASB). The King James states that people faint during adversity because their strength is small. My desire today is for you to be strengthened by the word of God. You *will* be able to stand up under pressure. Hallelujah!

The Lord is your strength and shield. Let your heart rejoice because He is your help! He saves His anointed (**Psalm 28:7-8**). God is your strength in times of trouble, and He is your ever-present help in time of need (**Psalm 37:39, 46:1**). Are you getting this yet?!

Crisis is not a time for you to crumble; it's a time for God's strength to be made perfect in you! He is your defense (**Psalm 59:17**), and He strengthens those whose ways are upright (**Proverbs 10:29**). God is your salvation, and there is no need to be afraid (**Psalm 27:1; Isaiah 12:2**).

I want to encourage you today. If you are facing a crisis, do not fall to pieces. Find your strength in Him! Open His word, and begin to study it. God is strength, and if you are in relationship with Him, He will be yours. Be at peace. Jesus has already overcome the world (**John 16:33**).

caution or fear?

Proverbs 24:11-12 – 11 *Rescue the perishing; don't hesitate to step in and help.* 12 *If you say, "Hey, that's none of my business," will that get you off the hook? Someone is watching you closely, you know—Someone not impressed with weak excuses* (MSG).

A person hesitates due to uncertainty of mind or fear. Hesitancy implies delayed action. Many people have a tendency to be hesitant when faced with a new, uncomfortable or potentially dangerous circumstance.

While being hesitant can protect a person from harm, it can also cause a person to become bound by timidity. If you are going to enjoy your life, you must find the balance between using caution and being afraid. Fear can cause us to miss out on new and exciting things.

My boys are perfect examples of this. My oldest son Noah is hesitant. He is very aware of his surroundings, and he rarely puts himself in danger. He looks both ways before he crosses the street, and he avoids strangers. My wife and I don't have to worry about Noah getting into trouble because he is so careful to avoid it.

Unfortunately, his tendency to hesitate often causes him to stress over things that are meant for his enjoyment. For instance, Heidi and I decided to teach him how to swim one summer. Even though we made the lessons as safe as is humanly possible, it was like pulling teeth to get him to cooperate. He was in tears more than he was in the water. We want him to be cautious, not fearful.

Our son Jack, on the other hand, is rarely hesitant. When he was three, he dove off the back of my parents' ski boat into the lake without knowing how to swim. He will try anything at least once, and he does not think about potential dangers.

Everyday life requires a balanced approach to hesitancy, but sharing the love of Jesus with others does not. The Bible says not to hesitate when it comes to helping those who are perishing. Do not be overcome by the fear of rejection. Use wisdom, but don't talk yourself out of possibly doing something great for God. He is watching to see if you will be obedient to His word.

your future is secured

Proverbs 24:13-14 – 13 *Eat honey, dear child—it's good for you—and delicacies that melt in your mouth.* 14 *Likewise knowledge, and wisdom for your soul—Get that and your future's secured, your hope is on solid rock* (MSG).

The main uses of honey are in cooking and baking. It can also be used as an addition to certain beverages, such as tea and coffee. Honey mustard is a popular sauce flavor. Honey is very versatile, and it serves a variety of purposes. Not everyone may like honey, but everyone would agree that it is sweet to the taste.

Honey may not be the featured ingredient in very many dishes, but it enhances the flavor of everything it touches. In much the same way, knowledge and wisdom enhance every area of your life. Most people do not make obtaining knowledge and wisdom a focal point of their lives. If you happen to be one of them, my prayer is that you will become a student of God's word.

Be knowledgeable in every area of your life. Familiarize yourself with the information you need in order to make everyday decisions. Many people sacrifice their futures for one of two reasons. They either make decisions because they lack knowledge in a certain area, or they have the knowledge but don't use wisdom in their decision-making.

Be led by the Spirit of God. He will make you look like a genius. **Galatians 5:25** – *If we live by the [Holy] Spirit, let us also walk by the Spirit. [If by the Holy Spirit we have our life in God, let us go forward walking in line, our conduct controlled by the Spirit]* (AMP). If the Holy Spirit controls your conduct, your future will be secure.

I want to encourage you to begin thinking about your legacy. Do not be narrow-minded in the way you run your life. The decisions you make today affect the future of the generations to come. Don't allow your expectation to be cut off.

Ephesians 1:8 – *He has showered his kindness on us, along with all wisdom and understanding* (NLT).

Christians vs. Christians

> **Proverbs 24:15-16** – 15 *Don't interfere with good people's lives; don't try to get the best of them.* 16 *No matter how many times you trip them up, God-loyal people don't stay down long. Soon they're up on their feet, while the wicked end up flat on their faces* (MSG).

There are two lessons to be learned from this passage. First of all, those who try to meddle in the lives of godly people will fall flat. And secondly, those who are loyal to God will stumble, but they won't stay down long.

There are many people who wait anxiously for God's people to fall. They are ruthless individuals who find pleasure in the failures of the righteous. You would expect ungodly people to act this way, but there are many Christians rooting for other Christians to fail. This is a heartbreaking reality, and I pray you are not one of them.

We must make up our minds not to be judgmental and conniving. **Romans 14:13** – *Therefore let us stop passing judgment on one another. Instead, make up your mind not to put any stumbling block or obstacle in your brother's way* (NIV).

Causing someone to fall, or rejoicing when they do, is wicked behavior. It's unacceptable in the eyes of God, and such a person will not prosper in any way. I encourage you to examine yourself right now. Are you cheering for someone to fail? Jealousy is often the root of such conduct. It causes well-meaning people to applaud the failures of others. Cheering for others to fail sets us up for a fall.

Everyone is loyal to something or someone; be loyal to God. There will be times that you trip, but God will never allow the righteous to fall (**Psalm 55:22**). If you struggle with jealousy, ask the Holy Spirit to help you rejoice in the success of others. Be an encourager. Otherwise, your heart may become hardened.

> **Hebrews 3:13** – *But exhort one another daily, while it is called today; lest any of you be hardened through the deceitfulness of sin* (KJV).

no crowing

Proverbs 24:17-18 – 17 *Don't laugh when your enemy falls; don't crow over his collapse.* 18 *God might see, and become very provoked, and then take pity on his plight* (MSG).

Enemies are anyone who you believe opposes your ideals, beliefs, goals, family, etc. If someone is not in agreement with you in a certain area, then he or she opposes you in that particular area. They become your enemy, and it's only natural to rejoice when such a person falls.

In competitive sports, it's engrained into the athletes by their coaches to do everything possible to take opposing teams down. When victory is achieved, it is not uncommon to see the winning team jumping around embracing one another. While this type of demonstration can escalate and get out of hand from time to time, there is nothing wrong with celebrating victories if it is done tastefully and respectfully.

Unfortunately, many people are bad sports, and bad sports are not always on losing teams. Many "winners" have poor character and bad attitudes. Whether in sports, the corporate world, or life in general, gloating over the fall of an enemy is never appropriate. Hurling insults and bragging are not actions that please God. He wants us to be victorious, but it does not bring Him joy when anyone falls, enemy or not.

When someone who opposes you fails, recall a time when you were down. How did you feel? What did you need? Did someone rub it in your face? If you begin to think this way, you will not laugh or crow over the collapse of your enemies.

It is important for you to keep in mind that everyone has the potential to recover from a fall, and God may want to use you to aid in that process. You also need to understand that not everyone who opposes you is your enemy. I challenge you today to be a good sport. Win honorably and lose graciously.

James 4:16 – *But as it is, you boast in your arrogance; all such boasting is evil* (NASB).

snuffed out

Proverbs 24:19-20 – 19 *Don't bother your head with braggarts or wish you could succeed like the wicked.* 20 *Those people have no future at all; they're headed down a dead-end street* (MSG).

Many people mortgage their futures to indulge in sinful habits. There is no stability for a person who lives an ungodly lifestyle. He or she forfeits temporal and eternal security for short-lived pleasure. Do not envy such people! They lack discipline, and they have no hope for the future.

In fact, the Bible says that the wicked are headed down a dead-end street. The NIV teaches in three different places that the lamp of the wicked will be snuffed out (**Proverbs 13:9, 20:20, 24:20**). Once the lights go out, the conscience is seared, and hope is lost.

There are many ungodly people who appear to be thriving by worldly standards. They have money, sex, fame, good looks and the latest gadgets, but their lives are hopeless and empty. In his book, Power, Money & Sex, Deion Sanders writes: "I tried everything. Parties, women, buying expensive jewelry and gadgets, and nothing helped. There was no peace. I was playing great, and every time I turned on the TV I could see myself on three or four commercials, but there was no peace, no joy, just emptiness inside."

This quote describes Sanders' feelings at the pinnacle of his career. He was a successful two-sport athlete with a magnetic personality. Endorsement deals were knocking down his door. He had a record-setting contract, and his persona was larger than life. Even so, he is quoted above as twice saying, "There was no peace." What a sobering reality.

The pleasures of sin are nothing to be envied. This world cannot offer anything more valuable than peace. Purpose to live obedient to God's word, and your light will not be snuffed out.

Matthew 6:33 – *"But seek first his kingdom and his righteousness, and all these things will be given to you as well"* (NIV).

323

ifs and buts

We do not have to be openly defiant to disrespect God or the leadership He has established. Before I further explore this truth, allow me to clarify something. When we dishonor any earthly authority—parents, bosses, government leaders, coaches, pastors, etc.—we dishonor God. It does not matter whether the person in that particular position is godly or not.

It is very possible that you currently lack respect for a certain leader who is in your life. You may not demonstrate your contempt for all to see, but your conduct behind closed doors is just as important as how you act publicly.

You do not have to stand in a picket line or lead a revolt to directly oppose someone in leadership. Rebellion originates in your thoughts. The enemy tries to plant "ifs" and "buts" in your mind. If you do not take unruly thoughts captive, the birthing of insubordination begins.

You will start thinking things such as, "*If* my pastor would just visit me more often, then I'd respect what he teaches," or "*If* politicians were not so crooked, then our country would not be going down the toilet." Many people reason, "I know I should be submitted, *but* I don't agree with how he or she does things." These mindsets dishonor God, and they will dominate your life.

Once rebellion is established in your mind, your words and actions will follow suit. Even if your feelings are founded on truth, dishonoring authority is sinful. If you have a difficult time submitting to a particular leader in your life, I encourage you to develop a greater fear of God. You cannot properly honor anyone else if you are not submitted totally to Him.

are you a blasphemer?

Are *you* a blasphemer? Most Christians would be offended if I asked them this question. Blaspheming is typically reduced to slandering or cursing the name of Jesus or the Holy Spirit, and no one is going to admit to doing that. Jesus said that a person who blasphemes the Holy Spirit will not be forgiven (**Mark 3:29**), so believers are careful to avoid doing so.

But I'm not asking if you publicly defame God. In the above verse, Paul addresses social authorities. These individuals include employers, bosses, teachers, coaches and so on. Given this information, we could rewrite this verse to say: Let as many as are *employees* under the yoke count their own *employers* worthy of all honor, or let as many as are *students* under the yoke count their own *teachers* worthy of all honor.

God expects us to give all honor to social leaders. If we don't, we personally blaspheme the name of God and His word, and we pollute the view that others have of Him as well.

I once worked in shipping and receiving for a well-known, snack food manufacturer. My supervisor was not a Christian. He had a foul mouth and a bad attitude. He was aware of my faith, which caused him to be skeptical of me from the beginning. I didn't understand why he was unsure about me until I was about to leave the company some time later.

He approached me one day and said he had been watching me carefully. It turned out that he had previously employed a Christian man who was lazy and disrespectful. He expected nothing less from me because I shared similar beliefs, but instead he thanked me for my hard work. His perspective of God changed.

Are you a blasphemer? I want to encourage you to read **Ephesians 6:5-8** today. This passage demonstrates how to honor authority. Respect your leaders, and serve them as you would Christ. Work well privately and publicly with all of your heart.

blame shifting

Genesis 3:12-13 – 12 *The man said, "The woman you put here with me—she gave me some fruit from the tree, and I ate it." 13 Then the Lord God said to the woman, "What is this you have done?" The woman said, "The serpent deceived me, and I ate"* (NIV).

The above exchange occurred because Adam and Eve ate fruit from the only tree God had forbidden them to eat from. God confronted their sin, and Adam and Eve were quick to point the finger at someone else. This scene is not uncommon today.

Blame shifting is a human reflex used to avoid facing the truth about one's self. People only point the finger at someone or something else when they have done something wrong. You don't blame another person for your right actions. That would be ludicrous. In fact, most people are quick to accept all the credit they can get when they do something well.

The reason most people blame shift is because it can be emotionally painful to face the truth about themselves and their behavior. When we do something that displeases God, Satan begins to work hard on our minds to prevent us from owning up to our fault. He fills our minds with excuses as to why we did what we did so that we will evade personal responsibility. It's always easier to face the truth about someone else.

The devil wants us to justify our wrong behavior instead of cutting it off at the root. Joyce Meyer teaches that you may have a legit reason for why you act poorly, but don't use it as an excuse to stay that way. Adam and Eve were deceived into eating the forbidden fruit, but instead of owning up to their sin, they committed another blunder by trying to hide from God. Then they started blame shifting. Not facing the truth about themselves caused a chain reaction of poor behavior.

Ask God to show you the truth about yourself. Perhaps you have been hurt, and your actions and attitude are a direct reflection of the pain you feel. Take responsibility for your behavior. Don't blame circumstances or other people. Then your healing will come, and your behavior will change.

faith to forgive

Luke 17:3-5 – 3 *"So watch yourselves. If your brother sins, rebuke him, and if he repents, forgive him.* 4 *If he sins against you seven times in a day, and seven times comes back to you and says, 'I repent,' forgive him."* 5 *The apostles said to the Lord, "Increase our faith!"* (NIV)

Jesus was teaching His disciples about forgiveness, and as His message reached the midway point, the disciples cried out in unison, "Increase our faith!" There was a sense of urgency in their voices. They realized it was going to take more faith than they already had in order to forgive certain offenders.

Jesus mentioned two different scenarios in **Luke 17:3-4**, the first of which I want to talk about today. He began by saying that if a brother sins against you *one* time and repents, you are to forgive him. Most people have said something like, "I don't know if I'll ever be able to forgive that person for what he or she did." And the truth is there are certain sins that we may not be able to forgive in our own strength.

All offenses hurt, but there are some that *deeply* hurt (such offenses vary from person to person). They wound us and leave scars that serve as a constant reminder of what was done to us. All it takes is *one* such offense to ruin a person's life.

Many people rehearse a sin that was committed against them years ago. They go over and over it in their minds and are unable to let it go. It's really sad, but some people have allowed one unfair moment in time to completely destroy their lives. Lord, give us the faith to forgive even the deepest of offenses!

Maybe today you are struggling with unforgiveness. Someone hurt you deeply, and you are unable to forgive him or her in your own strength. My prayer is that your faith will be increased. Let go of what was done to you. By faith, you *can* forgive because His love has been shed abroad in your heart!

Romans 5:5 – *The love of God is shed abroad in our hearts by the Holy Ghost which is given unto us* (KJV).

more faith to forgive

Luke 17:3-5 – 3 *"So watch yourselves. If your brother sins, rebuke him, and if he repents, forgive him.* 4 *If he sins against you seven times in a day, and seven times comes back to you and says, 'I repent,' forgive him."* 5 *The apostles said to the Lord, "Increase our faith!"* (NIV)

We often need an increased measure of faith in order to forgive someone who has deeply offended us just *once*. Even more faith is required in order to forgive someone who offends us multiple times. Jesus said that if a brother sins against us seven times in a day and repents, we are to forgive him each time. Let me remind you what the disciples said after Jesus revealed this truth to them. They cried out together, "Increase our faith!"

Keep in mind that this teaching is directed toward believers. Why is it that those who have been forgiven often have such a hard time forgiving? I believe Jesus explains why in **Luke 17:6** – *"If you have faith as small as a mustard seed, you can say to this mulberry tree, 'Be uprooted and planted in the sea,' and it will obey you"* (NIV).

At a glance, it might be a little difficult to understand what mustard seeds and mulberry trees have to do with forgiveness. Allow me to explain. I believe a "mulberry tree" is planted the moment someone offends us. If we forgive the offense promptly and properly, the tree will not take root and will be thrown out. It's much more beneficial to deal with offenses as they come.

But if the initial offense is not forgiven, roots will begin to grow. Then with the next offense, a root of bitterness may shoot down. Perhaps a root of anger or distrust will begin to grow after the next offense. Cynicism may take root after that, and the list goes on. When a person fails to forgive multiple offenses, his or her life will eventually become entangled in a deeply rooted mess.

Jesus said that the faith of a mustard seed is needed in order to uproot, or to forgive, multiple offenses. In fact, the same measure of faith is needed to move mountains (see **Matthew 17:20**). My prayer today is that you will have the faith to forgive.

our duty to forgive

Luke 17:7-10 – 7 *"Suppose one of you had a servant plowing or looking after the sheep. Would he say to the servant when he comes in from the field, 'Come along now and sit down to eat'?* 8 *Would he not rather say, 'Prepare my supper, get yourself ready and wait on me while I eat and drink; after that you may eat and drink'?* 9 *Would he thank the servant because he did what he was told to do?* 10 *So you also, when you have done everything you were told to do, should say, 'We are unworthy servants; we have only done our duty'"* (NIV).

Jesus revealed a valuable truth in this passage as He concluded His teaching on forgiveness. He told the story of a servant that had just finished working all day in the field, and how it would have been inappropriate for his master to give him preferential treatment for doing what was expected.

The servant was supposed to work in the field, wait for his master to eat and then eat and drink himself. The master was not obligated to thank the servant for simply doing his job. It would have been wrong for the servant to expect his master to reward him for doing what he was told to do.

Jesus used this parable to show us that it is our duty to forgive, and we should not expect a pat on the back for doing something that God requires of us. It is our duty to forgive whatever grievances we have against one another and to forgive others as the Lord forgave us (**Colossians 3:13**).

Forgiveness is unconditional, and it should not only be given to those who we think have earned it. T. D. Jakes once said, "When we refuse to forgive, we basically insist on setting our standards higher than God's." When we choose to forgive, we are upholding the standards that God has set. And we should not expect to have a party thrown in our honor for doing what is required of us.

Romans 4:7 – *"Blessed are those whose lawless deeds are forgiven, and whose sins are covered"* (NKJV).

here we go 'round the mulberry bush

> **Luke 17:6** – *He replied, "If you have faith as small as a mustard seed, you can say to this mulberry tree, 'Be uprooted and planted in the sea,' and it will obey you"* (NIV).

Today I want to take a closer look at the mulberry tree Jesus mentioned in the above verse. The roots of a mulberry tree can become a nuisance because they have a tendency to travel along the surface of the ground. When this occurs, the roots can be a trip hazard to unsuspecting feet.

In order to prevent such a problem, many people plant their mulberry trees with a root guard around the root ball of the tree. This guard helps encourage the roots to grow down deep before they spread wide and create a surface root issue. When we apply this information to the life of a believer, it's easy to see why Jesus used the mulberry tree to illustrate offense.

When someone is offended, a mulberry tree is planted in his or her life. If the person is able to forgive, the tree will not take root and is easily removed. Unfortunately, many people harbor offenses because they empower the emotions that come with them. Every negative emotion gives root to the mulberry tree, or offense.

Like mulberry trees, the roots of offense often grow on the surface of a person's life and can be hazardous to others. Many people live their lives governed by their feelings, and if those feelings are the product of offense, everyone pays. A life controlled by emotion is volatile at best, and when the roots of offense run close to the surface, someone is going to get hurt.

Other people put a root guard around the emotional hurt they incur from offense. This causes the roots of offense to shoot down and go deep. These people mask their pain and try not to bring attention to themselves. They appear okay, but they are dying inside because of their unhealthy emotional state.

Perhaps you need to forgive today. Is someone walking on eggshells around you? Forgiveness is not a feeling; it is a decision. Most people choose not to forgive because they don't feel like it. Don't be led by your emotions. With forgiveness comes freedom!

330

emotions and millstones

Luke 17:1-2 – 1 *Jesus said to his disciples: "Things that cause people to sin are bound to come, but woe to that person through whom they come.* 2 *It would be better for him to be thrown into the sea with a millstone tied around his neck than for him to cause one of these little ones to sin"* (NIV).

I want to begin today's devotion the same way I ended yesterday's: Forgiveness is not a feeling; it is a decision. Most people choose not to forgive because they don't feel like it. Then there are those who make the decision to forgive, but they don't *feel* like they have forgiven. It's for this reason that faith is needed in order to forgive.

Many people battle within themselves after they've chosen to forgive. Their minds constantly nag them, and their emotions tell them they are still angry with the person for what he or she did. This is why it's not uncommon for a person to feel animosity toward someone they've already let off the hook. Your flesh wants to breathe life back into the offense, while your spirit tries to remind you that you've already let it go. You have to make the decision to forgive by faith because you may never *feel* like it.

Unforgiveness is fueled by emotion. Emotions are the roots of offense. They attach you to the offense and give it life. Jesus said that it would be better for a person to be thrown into the sea with a millstone tied around his neck than for him to cause another person to sin because of offense.

Offended people tie themselves to the millstone and jump into the sea when they choose not to forgive. Offense will either cause a person to grow or sink. So many people justify unforgiveness because their feelings have been hurt. I pray that you are not one of them. If you are, make today the day you stop letting your emotions get the best of you. Choose to forgive.

Luke 6:37 – *"Do not judge, and you will not be judged. Do not condemn, and you will not be condemned. Forgive, and you will be forgiven"* (NIV).

unmerited forgiveness

> **Luke 23:34** – *Jesus said, "Father, forgive them, for they do not know what they are doing." And they divided up his clothes by casting lots* (NIV).

Before we further explore this verse, let's rewind a few chapters to Luke 17. If you'll recall, Jesus was teaching the disciples about forgiveness. He told them that if someone was to sin against them and come back later to repent, that they were to forgive him each time (**17:4**). But what if someone sins against us, and doesn't ask for forgiveness? What if they are unaware that they've even offended us? What is our responsibility to those people as believers?

Jesus answered these questions in the above verse. As He suffered the most horrible death ever devised by sinful man, He looked at those crucifying Him and prayed for their forgiveness. The Jewish leaders, Roman politicians, soldiers and bystanders really believed they were killing a worthy criminal. They were not playing a sick joke or trying to get away with something they knew was wrong. They truly believed in their cause. Jesus even said so Himself, "For they know *not* what they do."

Even though they were unaware of what they were doing, Jesus chose to forgive them. They didn't ask for mercy, and they didn't tell Him they were sorry. They didn't try to make restitution. They murdered Him, but before Jesus took His last breath, He understood the importance of letting go of offense.

I believe if He had not forgiven them from the cross, He would have nullified the purpose of His death. How could Jesus have made restitution for the sins of mankind if He had taken unforgiveness to the grave with Him?

Maybe today there are people who have offended you unknowingly. Some people refuse to forgive because they're waiting on an apology. What if *your* apology never comes? Will you still forgive? I encourage you to do so because if you don't, you're only hurting yourself. We must choose to forgive whether our offenders ask for it or not.

pardon the interruption

Psalm 51:17 – *The sacrifices of God are a broken spirit; a broken and contrite heart, O God, you will not despise* (NIV).

There's a verse from an old song that says, "Brokenness, brokenness is what I long for. Brokenness is what I need. Brokenness, brokenness is what You want from me." What an amazing truth! Brokenness is vital if God is going to be able to do anything in you and through you.

As I studied the word *broken*, I came across many definitions and synonyms, but one really grabbed my attention. Another word for *broken* is *interrupted*. God wants us to be willing to allow Him to interrupt our lives.

Most people get aggravated when they are interrupted for anything. Just tonight, before I sat down to write this, I was watching the World Series (my hometown team was playing). Like most men, I don't necessarily care to be distracted while I am watching my favorite teams play, especially if they are playing in the championship series!

My youngest son Jack came into the room and stood right in the path between me and the television (and it was not on commercial). Jack is one of those children that keeps saying what he wants over and over and over until you acknowledge him with a response. He started asking me repeatedly for a drink of water. I tried to ignore him and look around him, but he kept maneuvering himself between me and the TV, all the while firing off his drink request machinegun style.

Needless to say, I was aggravated. I did not want to get him a drink of water. He didn't need one, and I was trying to watch the game! Then he pooched out his bottom lip and started to tear up. I immediately felt six inches tall. I got him some water.

One of the most miserable feelings in the world is rejection. Nobody wants to be rejected. Yet every time you don't allow God to interrupt you, you reject Him. I wonder how many times I have grieved the heart of my Maker because I have been unwilling to bend my schedule for Him. I pray for you to be broken today.

why can't we be friends? (pt.1)

> **Proverbs 12:26** – *The righteous choose their friends carefully, but the way of the wicked leads them astray* (NIV).

Choose your friends wisely. It's not inappropriate to require something from those you are in relationship with. Setting standards, and expecting people to meet them, is a sign of health in any relationship. There are some people that you cannot afford to have close to you. If you have no way of determining who those people are, you will be led astray by them.

My purpose today is for you to evaluate your circle of influence. Take a long, hard look at those who are closest to you. I'm going to give you some biblical qualities that make a good friend. Set these qualities as the standard for both your current and future relationships. If someone does not meet these criteria, the relationship may need to be cut off or left at surface level.

First of all, you need to beware of repeat offenders. *He who covers over an offense promotes love, but whoever repeats the matter separates close friends* (**Proverbs 17:9**). You will offend and be offended at some point in every relationship. When you wrong someone, you no doubt want him to forgive and love you anyway. You should expect no different. If someone constantly offends you without remorse, that person does not deserve your friendship. You are more valuable than that.

Secondly, your friends should be in it for the long haul. Have you ever noticed that certain people seem to disappear when your life falls on hard times? **Proverbs 17:17** – *A friend loves at all times, and a brother is born for adversity* (NASB). A true friend will stick by you when the going gets tough. If someone abandons you every time you face a crisis, he has nothing invested in the relationship. He can cut ties with you at anytime because it costs him nothing to get out.

I pray that your friends possess these two qualities. If not, you need to prayerfully consider on what level (if any) you should continue having a relationship with them. Tomorrow we are going to look at some more characteristics your friends should have.

why can't we be friends? (pt.2)

Proverbs 19:4 – *Wealth attracts many friends, but even the closest friend of the poor person deserts them* (NIV).

Don't surround yourself with "takers." There will be certain people who come into your life for the sole purpose of getting something from you. They will invest nothing but want to benefit from everything. Takers will be around only as long as your resources are plentiful, but as soon as you appear to have nothing more to offer them, they will desert you.

These "friends" will not only take of your finances. They will often take advantage of your relationships, job position, knowledge and anything else that seems valuable. The sad reality is that you cannot give to takers enough to change them. Giving to them, or allowing them to take from you, just feeds their disease.

They also have a way of making you feel bad about yourself if you don't give to them. Many takers are master manipulators. Keep in mind **Proverbs 19:6** – *Many curry favor with a ruler, and everyone is the friend of one who gives gifts* (NIV). As soon as you run out of gifts, takers will bail. I pray God brings you friends who give more than they take.

You also need friends who will hold you accountable. **Proverbs 27:6** – *Faithful are the wounds of a friend; but the kisses of an enemy are deceitful* (KJV). Sometimes it's necessary for someone to tell you hard truths about yourself. If your character gets out of line, you need people in your life who don't mince words. Hearing the truth may hurt your feelings initially, but all wounds heal if they are treated properly.

If you surround yourself with people who are constantly kissing up to you, you will have a warped view of yourself. The kisses of an enemy are deceitful. Some people we perceive to be friends are really enemies.

Don't get me wrong. I'm not telling you to avoid encouragers, but there is a difference between being encouraged and having your ego stroked. Every relationship needs balance. I encourage you to set these standards and stand by them.

esteem others highly

Philippians 2:3 – *Let nothing be done through selfish ambition or conceit, but in lowliness of mind let each esteem others better than himself* (NKJV).

Maybe you read this verse and immediately thought, "I can't do this. There are some people I just don't think very highly of." I want to encourage you today. You can do what God says you can do because He freely gives you the grace to do it.

He has made an unlimited amount of grace available to you. **Hebrews 4:16** – *Let us then approach the throne of grace with confidence, so that we may receive mercy and find grace to help us in our time of need* (NIV). Receive an extra dose of His grace today, and He will enable you to esteem others better than yourself. Hallelujah!

Jesus said, *"A new command I give you: Love one another. As I have loved you, so you must love one another"* (**John 13:34**, NIV). In order for you to love others as Christ loved you, you must first understand the love Jesus has for you. He esteems you so highly, that He willingly gave Himself up for you. He separated Himself from the Father and became poor so that you might live eternally. I am floored by His love for us!

God has given every believer the *potential* to love others in this same way. **Romans 5:5** says, *"For God's love has been poured out in our hearts through the Holy Spirit Who has been given to us"* (AMP). We have to cooperate with the Holy Spirit in order to love others as Christ does. Valuing others higher than you do yourself is made possible by the unconditional love shed abroad in your heart by the Holy Spirit.

My prayer is that you will honor those you are in relationship with. Do not use people for personal gain or self-promotion. Humbly respect others, and show them the love of God through your words and actions.

Romans 12:10 – *Be devoted to one another in brotherly love. Honor one another above yourselves* (NIV).

you are highly esteemed

Philippians 2:3 – *Let nothing be done through selfish ambition or conceit, but in lowliness of mind let each esteem others better than himself* (NKJV).

I briefly mentioned yesterday that Jesus esteems you so highly that He willingly gave up His life for yours (see **1 Peter 2:24**). I want to take this truth one step further. Maybe today you don't think very highly of yourself. I believe this message will bring you great encouragement and restore your self-esteem.

Did you know that Jesus actually esteems you better than He does Himself? This revelation was difficult for me to understand because He is God. How could the Creator esteem the creation better than He does Himself? You may be asking yourself this same question, so I'm going to prove it by the word of God.

Philippians 2:3 tells us that we are to esteem others better than we do ourselves. Here's my point: The Lord does not ask His people to do anything that He does not already do Himself. God is not hypocritical. He does not set standards for His children and then live by a different set of rules. He honors you as His child by living by example.

Many homes are in disarray today because parents require things of their children that they don't do themselves. Many parents punish their kids for fighting, and then they argue right in front of them. When parents do what they tell their children not to do, or they don't do what they tell their children to do, they dishonor their children.

God does not treat His kids this way. He values you too much to be a hypocritical parent. Are you getting this today? This kind of good news has the power to change your life forever! I pray that you receive this message by faith. You are special to God. Ask Him to help you see yourself the way He does. If you can grasp this truth, your life will never be the same again!

1 John 3:1 – *How great is the love the Father has lavished on us, that we should be called children of God!* (NIV)

cut me off

> **Romans 9:1-3** – 1 *With Christ as my witness, I speak with utter truthfulness. My conscience and the Holy Spirit confirm it.* 2 *My heart is filled with bitter sorrow and unending grief* 3 *for my people, my Jewish brothers and sisters. I would be willing to be forever cursed—cut off from Christ!—if that would save them* (NLT).

When I was in high school, I was not a part of the *in* crowd. In fact, I was far from it. I had some friends, but they were mostly from my home church. There was a faction of unchurched kids at school who ridiculed and made fun of me from time to time, but I was content with myself for the most part. I wasn't going to let their stupidity shape my identity.

Unfortunately, I used their ignorance as an excuse to build up contempt toward them. I resented them, and I told myself they would eventually get what they deserved. I allowed my heart to become calloused, and I missed out on hundreds of opportunities to bless them with the love of God. How foolish I was!

This same kind of bitterness toward the ungodly is not uncommon in the church today. Many Christians stereotype, slander and are even offended with those who do not know Christ. This is especially true of someone who has been wounded by an unbeliever. This is not the heart of God.

Reread the above passage in **Romans 9:1-3**. Read it three or four times if you have to. This could be one of the most radical statements a minister of God's word has ever made. Paul's heart was overflowing with bitterness and grief, but not because he was persecuted by his countrymen. He was broken over their unbelief.

He was so overcome by love for the lost that he proclaimed he would forfeit his own salvation for theirs. Wow! Pray this prayer with me today: "Lord, make my heart like Paul's. I repent for the ill feelings I've had toward those who don't know You, and I receive Your forgiveness now. I purpose today to do whatever it takes to see people come into the kingdom of God. I activate my potential to love the unlovable. Thank You, Lord. Amen."

rolling away the reproach

Joshua 5:9 – *Then the Lord said to Joshua, "Today I have rolled away the reproach of Egypt from you"* (NIV).

After living in Egyptian captivity for hundreds of years, the Israelites crossed over the Jordan and were on the brink of the Promised Land. God had already brought them through so much, but He had one more requirement before they could inherit what was promised: consecration.

As a sign of leaving the lifestyle they had grown accustomed to in Egypt, He had Joshua circumcise all the males. After Joshua did this, the Lord declared, "Today I have rolled away the reproach of Egypt from you." They then went and conquered Jericho and entered into the Promised Land. This was one of the most significant moments in Israel's history.

It's important for you to understand that the reproach had to be rolled away from the Israelites before they could inherit the promise. The word *reproach* means blame, disgrace and shame. Though almost everyone who had originally been rescued from Egypt had died because of disobedience, the disgrace of their past was apparent in the next generation. God's people were unfit to receive the promise, so He wiped away the shame of their past.

Maybe today you are burdened by your past. Many people believe that they don't deserve the blessings of God. They feel unworthy because of past failures. God's desire is to roll away your blame, disgrace and shame, but you must first receive His forgiveness by faith. You also need to learn to forgive yourself.

Consecrate yourself to Him today. Repent and circumcise your past. Today is a new day! Jesus Christ forgave you once and for all. Your reproach has been rolled away. Hallelujah!

Ephesians 1:4 – *Even as [in His love] He chose us [actually picked us out for Himself as His own] in Christ before the foundation of the world, that we should be holy (consecrated and set apart for Him) and blameless in His sight, even above reproach, before Him in love* (AMP).

be part of the solution

Daniel 5:12 – *This man Daniel, whom the king named Belteshazzar, has exceptional ability and is filled with divine knowledge and understanding. He can interpret dreams, explain riddles, and solve difficult problems. Call for Daniel, and he will tell you what the writing means* (NLT).

Dr. David Remedios says that a proposed problem without a potential solution is just a complaint. A lot of people have a knack for pointing out faults, but they fail to offer any help in finding solutions. If you have ever been in any kind of leadership position, you have no doubt come across someone who acts in this manner. They tell you what needs to be fixed and how to do it, but they do not participate when it's time for work to be done.

In Daniel 5, we can read the account of King Belshazzar and the writing on the wall. He was an unruly king. One day he asked for the gold and silver cups that had been taken from the house of God in Jerusalem. They were brought to him, and he and his nobles, wives and concubines drank from them. They praised their many idols, and then a hand appeared and wrote something on the wall of the palace.

The king did not understand the writing, but he knew he had a problem. Scripture says that his face turned pale, his knees knocked together and then he collapsed. He was in trouble, and he needed help. He sent for the enchanters, astrologers and fortune-tellers, but none of them could interpret the writing. After all of the wise men came in, and no one came up with a solution, everyone quaked with fear. They needed a problem solver.

None of those men could tell the king anything other than the obvious: he had a problem on his hands. Enter Daniel. He was known as having the exceptional ability to solve difficult problems, and he explained the writing on the wall to the king.

Isn't that how *you* want to be known? I want to challenge you today. Don't just recognize problems; be a part of their solutions. God will give you divine knowledge and understanding, just like He did Daniel. Be someone who is sought after for help.

weighty consequences

Romans 5:19 – *For as by one man's disobedience many were made sinners, so by the obedience of one shall many be made righteous* (KJV).

Disobedience and obedience both carry weighty consequences. Because of Adam's disobedience, sin entered the world. The downfall of many came through the inappropriate actions of one man. This is amazing to me. What's even more amazing is that Jesus made righteousness available to *everyone* by His obedience. Now those are some weighty consequences!

It gets even heavier than that, though. It was not a series of disobedient acts on Adam's part that many were made sinners. It only took one! The same is true concerning righteousness. Through one act of obedience, death on a cross, Jesus restored hope to mankind. Hallelujah!

I tell you this because the decisions you make carry great weight, not only in your life, but also in the lives of those connected to you. If people would take this truth into consideration before they act, much collateral damage could be avoided. It may seem unfair, but life is unfair and sometimes the truth is as well.

Do you make decisions with your spouse, or your family, in mind? As a husband or father, if you decide to make a major decision that produces negative results, without talking it over with your wife first, you are not the only one who has to deal with the negative consequences. Your wife and children have to deal with them also. In fact, your lives may be affected for years to come.

Many people sabotage future relationships by making poor judgments calls in their present ones. The choices you make are important, and they have the potential to impact people positively or negatively both now and for years to come. Be obedient to God's word. Make a positive impact on the people around you.

Proverbs 5:23 – *Death is the reward of an undisciplined life; your foolish decisions trap you in a dead end* (MSG).

give and receive

2 Corinthians 6:11-13 – 11 *Our mouth has spoken freely to you, O Corinthians, our heart is opened wide.* 12 *You are not restrained by us, but you are restrained in your own affections.* 13 *Now in a like exchange—I speak as to children—open wide to us also* (NASB).

I want to share with you today a new revelation I received concerning relationships. I believe it has the potential to bring healing to you and to those you are connected to.

I grew up thinking that healthy relationships were ones that have a balance of giving and taking. I never questioned this concept because it seemed to make sense. Perhaps you are someone who was taught something similar. The giving part is right on the money. We need to invest into those we are in relationship with, and we should expect the same in return. Givers make great friends.

The problem lies with the taking part. God gave me fresh insight as I was studying relationships for a message I recently preached. I was actually writing into my sermon that healthy relationships have a balance of giving and taking, when suddenly I heard the voice of the Holy Spirit.

He said, "You take something from somebody who does not want to give it to you. Do you really think such behavior makes for a healthy relationship?" "No," I replied (I had just finished writing about setting boundaries for takers). I felt rather sheepish as He continued. "A healthy relationship is one that has a balance of giving and *receiving*."

In the above passage of Scripture, Paul writes about how he had freely given to the Corinthians and that his heart was open to receive from them. But the Corinthians were restrained. Their relationship was out of balance.

I want to encourage you today to be a giver, but also learn to receive from others. Many people who are truly givers have a difficult time receiving from anyone. This is not healthy behavior. Give *and* receive, and your relationships will go to a new level.

342

unclean to clean

Isaiah 6:5 – *"Woe to me!" I cried. "I am ruined! For I am a man of unclean lips, and I live among a people of unclean lips, and my eyes have seen the King, the LORD Almighty"* (NIV).

I am always amazed by the relevance of God's word. I love how He can repeatedly show me something new from a passage that I've read and studied time and time again. My prayer is that you will develop a deeper appreciation for His word. Be open to fresh insight, and God will show Himself to you.

At the time of this encounter with the Lord, Isaiah was the prophet appointed to be the spiritual leader of Israel. He obviously had an intimate relationship with God and knew the voice of the Lord. Even so, Isaiah was undone after catching a glimpse of Him seated on the throne. After beholding the Almighty, Isaiah was immediately made aware of his unclean condition.

A friend of mine once said, "We don't truly see ourselves until we have seen the Lord." This is so true. I encourage you today to seek the face of God. Many people appear to have it together, when in fact, God is trying to make them aware of some changes that need to be made. I believe a lot of Christians avoid making eye contact with God because they don't want to face the truth about themselves.

Maybe there are some areas in your life that you are ashamed of. Perhaps you know full well what the things are that you struggle with. Isaiah confessed he was a man of unclean lips; then look what happened. **Isaiah 6:6-7** – 6 *Then one of the seraphs flew to me with a live coal in his hand…*7 *With it he touched my mouth and said, "See, this has touched your lips; your guilt is taken away and your sin atoned for"* (NIV). Hallelujah!

God is ready to take what is unclean in your life and make it clean. But before He can do a work on the inside of you, you have to be aware of your condition and confess your shortcomings to Him. Hold your life up to the word of God and seek His face today. You may not like what you see, but He will gladly clean you up a little. Thank You, Jesus!

to and for

Galatians 6:2, 5 – 2 *Carry each other's burdens, and in this way you will fulfill the law of Christ...*5 *for each one should carry his own load* (NIV).

The truth I want to share with you today has the power to set you free and bring balance to your life. Many people do not have a clear understanding of what they are responsible for. They take on things they shouldn't, and they delegate to others what they should take care of themselves. This is a very unhealthy way to live, but this kind of behavior is the norm for a lot of people.

This problem usually results from insufficient boundaries, or the absence of boundaries altogether. Boundaries define where you end and someone else begins. Some people have a hard time setting boundaries because they are under the misconception that boundaries are confining. This couldn't be further from the truth. Having appropriate boundaries in place can actually be quite liberating.

The Bible teaches that we are responsible *to* others and *for* ourselves. Paul says in **Galatians 6:2** that we are to carry each other's burdens. The Greek word for *burdens* in this verse means excess burdens. As believers, we have a God-given responsibility to help those who cannot help themselves. When a burden becomes too big for any one person to handle, believers should come alongside that person to help.

Galatians 6:5 teaches that each person should carry his own load. The word *load* in this verse comes from the Greek word meaning cargo; burden of daily toil. Every individual is responsible for his or her own load. We are to work and be productive. There are certain tasks and duties that we are responsible for. No one else is supposed to do them for us.

If you are carrying someone else's load today, I want to encourage you to stop. You are not responsible for pulling another person's weight. Also, do not delegate your personal responsibility to others. If you have already blurred the lines, ask God to help you redefine what your job *is* and *isn't*.

working it out

Philippians 2:12-13 – 12 *Therefore, my dear friends, as you have always obeyed—not only in my presence, but now much more in my absence—continue to work out your salvation with fear and trembling, 13 for it is God who works in you to will and to act according to his good purpose* (NIV).

A lot of people act as if they are allergic to work. There are many definitions and interpretations of the word *work*, but I want to offer you my personal definition. To work means to put forth the appropriate amount of effort needed in order to be productive.

Many believers offer minimal effort and expect to produce optimum results. Others give nothing of themselves and assume everything will work itself out. This is a delusional mindset. Most things worth having require work, or maximum effort, in order to achieve them. This includes working out our salvation.

What does it mean to work out your salvation? I'm glad you asked. Salvation does not begin and end with a "sinner's prayer." When you prayed and received Christ as your Lord and Savior, a form of conception took place. With that prayer, you made a commitment to go to work.

All believers have the responsibility to put forth the appropriate effort needed to produce godly fruit in their lives. To work out your salvation means to strive daily to become more like Him and to live in obedience to His word. Paul instructs us to do so with fear and trembling.

Most people fail to work out their salvation because they do not have a holy fear of God. They don't reverence Him or hold Him in high esteem. Those who honor God appropriately work to be godly, and they do what He says. Their great love for Him compels them to do whatever is necessary to be like Him. Maybe you're laying down on the job today. If so, get back to work!

1 Corinthians 3:13 – *But on judgment day, fire will reveal what kind of work each builder has done. The fire will show if a person's work has any value* (NLT).

345

God works

While it is absolutely necessary for you to work out your salvation, it is impossible for you to become more like God in your own strength. We all need His help!

This truth should come as a relief to you. Many believers are frustrated today because they are trying to live a godly life without God's involvement. They put forth an honest effort to please Him, but they constantly fall short. A lifetime of righteous deeds does not necessarily make you more like God. In fact, Isaiah likens our attempts to be righteous to filthy rags (**Isaiah 64:6**).

You cannot produce spiritual fruit in your life by using fleshly means. Galatians 5 lists nine fruits of the Spirit. Working out your salvation includes the production of these nine fruits in your life. I have genuinely tried to generate these fruits in myself by myself. It never works. The end result is usually a set of empty promises. If the fruits of the Spirit could be produced solely by our fleshly efforts, they would be called the fruits of the flesh.

Think about it. Unconditional love is a fruit of the Spirit. But you know as well as I do that there are certain people we just can't seem to love in our own strength. Only God gives us the ability to love the unlovable. Peace is also one of these fruits. Unlike worldly peace, the peace God gives is not circumstantial. No matter how hard we try, we will not be able to manufacture a peace that transcends all understanding on our own.

I pray this message has been a liberating one. God works in you to will and to act according to His purpose. He does not expect you to work out your salvation alone. Allow Him to help.

just say no

Contrary to popular belief, everyone has a conscience. Your conscience gives you an inner sense of what is right and wrong. It judges conduct and motives, and it impels you toward right action. When a person's conscience becomes weak, he or she has a distorted view of right and wrong.

Many people have developed a tainted idea of what is right and what is wrong because they were mistreated. Emotional, physical, sexual or verbal abuse can all hinder a person's ability to judge between good and evil.

Others have been taught that poor behavior is acceptable. Countless children are shown the *wrong* things to do by their parents, and they learn to accept them as normal. If they are never shown the *right* things to do, they grow up to be adults who believe that wrong is right.

Unfortunately, this is the predicament many well-meaning people find themselves in today. Their consciences have been made weak by no fault of their own. As a result, they live their lives without proper boundaries. They get taken advantage of, and they do not stand up to mistreatment. A weak conscience will often cause a person to say "yes" to the bad.

Perhaps you are someone who has a hard time saying "no" when you know you should. Maybe you've been taught that only difficult or unreasonable people say no. I want to encourage you today. Standing up for yourself when you are mistreated does not make you a difficult person. Saying no to someone who tries to get you to take on tasks that you are not responsible for does not make you unreasonable or lazy.

Allow the Holy Spirit to partner with your conscience. When that still, small voice says "no," listen to it, and don't feel bad about it. Don't allow guilt or fear to back you into a corner. You do not have to tolerate mistreatment. Wrong will never be right, and it will never be right for you to do wrong.

homecoming

Mark 6:1-2 – 1 *Jesus left there and went to his hometown, accompanied by his disciples.* 2 *When the Sabbath came, he began to teach in the synagogue, and many who heard him were amazed. "Where did this man get these things?" they asked. "What's this wisdom that has been given him, that he even does miracles!"* (NIV)

I want you to think about an instance in your life when you left home for an extended period of time. Perhaps you went off to college or summer camp for two or three months. Maybe you served in the armed forces and spent some time overseas. It's possible that you got married, started a family and currently live somewhere away from your hometown.

Now I want you to think about how you felt to return home after being away. A homecoming should be a glorious occasion (though I realize it's not for everyone). Most people would want their return home to be an exciting time, a joyous reunion with family, friends and neighbors.

I'm sure Jesus felt the same way as He arrived in Nazareth. His visit began favorably. As Jesus taught in the synagogue, Mark recorded that the people were amazed. They marveled at His great wisdom and the miracles He had done. Jesus was probably felt pretty good about Himself, but everything quickly changed. Their amazement turned to offense (**Mark 6:3**).

Jesus must have been devastated. I can only imagine the feelings of rejection He must have felt. Maybe today you don't have to imagine how Jesus felt; you know exactly what He went through because you have faced similar opposition. Perhaps those closest to you have withdrawn their love and support. I want to encourage you today. If you have done something to cause that rejection, make it right. If you are an innocent victim (as Jesus was), stand firm knowing who you are in Christ.

Proverbs 18:24 – *A man of many companions may come to ruin, but there is a friend who sticks closer than a brother* (NIV).

could not vs. would not

Mark 6:5 – *He could not do any miracles there, except lay his hands on a few sick people and heal them* (NIV).

I believe this is one of the most tragic verses in all of Scripture. Jesus left his hometown to go into full-time ministry. The fruit of His efforts was quite impressive. Multiple people were healed of diseases, the demonized were set free and paralytics walked. Jesus cured the woman with the issue of blood, and He even raised Jairus' daughter from the dead (see **Mark 5:21-43**).

Jesus no doubt arrived in Nazareth intending to do similar exploits, but He was rejected. In fact, the Bible says that He could not do any miracles there, except to heal a few of the sick. Mark was very specific in his writing. Jesus *could not* do what He desired to do in His hometown. It does not say he *would not*.

In other words, the lack of miracles Jesus did in Nazareth was not a matter of His will. He was restrained. I believe there is a parallel here that is often overlooked. Many individuals, families and churches have a shortage of the supernatural. Countless believers live their lives absent of God's favor and miracle-working power. Maybe you're one of them. If so, it's not because God is unwilling to work on your behalf. He's being restrained.

The question that needs to be answered is, "Why?" Jesus could not do as He intended in Nazareth because the people were offended at Him. People become offended at God for different reasons, but believers particularly have a problem receiving a blessing that comes in a package they don't expect, like or understand. The Nazarenes did not receive their blessing because they did not approve of Jesus, the package God had sent.

Jesus was also unable to perform many miracles there because they did not show Him honor. The same is true in many households and churches today. Begin to evaluate the condition of your heart concerning these matters. Over the next couple days, we are going to further explore offense and honor and the role each plays in receiving or restraining the miraculous in your life. My prayer is that you will begin to experience the supernatural!

right blessing, wrong package

Mark 6:3 – *"Isn't this the carpenter? Isn't this Mary's son and the brother of James, Joseph, Judas and Simon? Aren't his sisters here with us?" And they took offense at him* (NIV).

Many believers become offended at God when His blessing comes in a package they don't expect, like or understand. In fact, people often miss out on the blessing entirely because they discard the package before they ever open it. Sometimes God requires us to endure a tough process in order to receive His greatest blessing.

When I was a small child, I wanted a Nintendo for Christmas. I'm not talking about the Wii or the 3DS or whatever the latest system is today. I wanted the original game system with 8-bit graphics, the one with Super Mario Brothers and Duck Hunt. I had been good all year and the years prior, so I deserved it. I made my request known to my parents, and I anticipated receiving one come Christmas day.

When Christmas finally came, I was full of expectation. I ripped through my presents, and with each one my excitement began to wear off. I started to get upset...no Nintendo. I looked at the final, wrapped box, and I quickly decided it was too big to be a Nintendo. To say I was discouraged would be an understatement. I was offended at my parents. How could they do this to me?!

I slowly began to open it. I removed the wrapping paper to discover a giant, cardboard box. I pried it open to find dozens of socks. Have you ever received a gift you didn't like, but you tried to play it off so you wouldn't hurt the feelings of the person who gave it? That's what I did.

I picked up some of the socks, and I moved others around. As I tried to look interested, I suddenly felt another box! I dug a little deeper. A Nintendo! I was beside myself.

Can you imagine how foolish it would have been for me to stop digging and remain offended? This may sound a little extreme, but the same scenario is played out in the lives of countless believers. Don't miss God's blessing because you're offended with its packaging. Be willing to endure the process.

without honor

Mark 6:4 – *Jesus said to them, "Only in his hometown, among his relatives and in his own house is a prophet without honor"* (NIV).

Offense causes a breach between you and the person you are offended at. You are unable to give anything of value to that person, and you are unable to receive anything of value either. In fact, if the person were to make a kind gesture, offense would cause you to question his or her motives. And when you are offended with someone, you certainly cannot show that person honor. This is what Jesus was up against at His homecoming.

The word *honor* originates from the Greek word translated time. Honor is assigned to a thing or person considered to be precious or valuable. Such items or people are given preferential treatment, but familiarity is often the cause of *dishonor*.

I bought my first laptop about seven years ago. I was so excited! I had always wanted one, and I was determined to take care of it. I honored that laptop. It was extremely valuable to me. I bought a nice case for it and stored it in a secure place. I only took it out to use it, and I would always put it back when finished.

Over time, though, I became more and more familiar with the laptop. I started to be a little rougher with it. I wasn't as concerned about keeping it clean and safe as I was before. I even began to leave it out from time to time after using it.

One day I left it open out on a table in our house, and I left the room for a few minutes. When I came back, I found our youngest son Jack holding a handful of keys. He had pulled some of the letters off of the keyboard. Familiarity caused me to treat something valuable as common, and I got burned.

Jesus could not work the miracles He desired to in Nazareth because they treated Him as common. They were familiar with Him because He had grown up among them. They hung out with His family; they sat at tables He had made. They viewed Jesus as the carpenter He had once been, and they missed out. I challenge you not to become too familiar with Jesus. Give Him a place of honor in your life. Value Him. He longs to bless you.

something worth mentioning

2 Corinthians 8:1-3 – 1 *And now, brothers, we want you to know about the grace that God has given the Macedonian churches.* 2 *Out of the most severe trial, their overflowing joy and their extreme poverty welled up in rich generosity.* 3 *For I testify that they gave as much as they were able, and even beyond their ability* (NIV).

Are you walking through a severe trial today? Have circumstances robbed you of your joy? Perhaps your finances have taken a hit. You may be in great need today, but I want you to be encouraged by the above testimony. God's grace gives you the ability to do what you cannot do in your own strength.

Extreme difficulty often causes people to become selfish, but I believe that it is God's desire for us to be a blessing to others during the times we feel we need to be blessed. This may seem like an impossibility, but please listen to me.

Paul testified that the Macedonian churches had fallen on hard times. In fact, he records that they faced the *most* severe trial and that their finances had bottomed out. They had every reason to feel sorry for themselves, but they did not. Rather than sulk and beg for help, the Macedonians gave as much as they were able.

How were they able to do this? The Bible says that they had overflowing joy. One of the first things to go at the sign of trouble is joy. If your joy is depleted, so is your strength. When your strength is gone, it's easy to become selfish. Selfish people hoard their time, money and resources. I exhort you today: Do not forfeit your joy no matter how dreadful your life may seem!

Watch this. Not only did they give what they were able to, but they even gave beyond their ability. How? God's grace. It's only by His grace that you can give of yourself when you have nothing left to give. Receive more grace today. I encourage you to be a blessing, even if you are in desperate need of one yourself.

John 1:16 – *From the fullness of his grace we have all received one blessing after another* (NIV).

keeping zeal and fervor

Romans 12:11 – *Never be lacking in zeal, but keep your spiritual fervor, serving the Lord* (NIV).

The above verse gives believers two instructions: never lack zeal and keep spiritual fervor. Zeal and fervor speak of a person's passion or enthusiasm. In this case, Paul is encouraging us to maintain our passion for the things of God.

Unfortunately, many believers have lost their zeal and spiritual fervor. The fire that once burned brightly and out of control has been snuffed out. You may be someone whose spiritual tank is close to empty. If you are, Paul gives the key to restoring or preserving your passion for God. Serve Him.

Perhaps you've heard of The Pareto Principle or the 80-20 Rule. It's a theory that states, for many events, roughly 80% of the effects come from 20% of the causes. While this principle is only theory, there are various studies that confirm Pareto's beliefs.

In fact, many Christian researchers, pastors and authors have applied the 80-20 Rule to the church. They imply that 20% of a church's congregation does 80% of the work of the ministry. Drawing from my personal experience, I can understand how they came to such a conclusion, but I realize not every church is dysfunctional to this degree. Tragically, though, many believers are idle in their faith.

I want to encourage you today. Maybe you lack the passion you once had for God. Perhaps you've allowed circumstances to steal your joy. There could be many reasons as to why you have lost spiritual effectiveness, but God wants to restore your zeal and fervor.

Keep in mind, though, that He cannot restore the passion of someone who is content with doing nothing. Get involved in the work of your local church. Ask the leadership what *they* need you to do. Purpose to meet a need instead of being needy.

Romans 12:6-7 – 6 *We have different gifts, according to the grace given us…*7 *If it is serving, let him serve* (NIV).

sea of forgetfulness?

Micah 7:19 – *You will again have compassion on us; you will tread our sins underfoot and hurl all our iniquities into the depths of the sea* (NIV).

God has the supernatural ability to literally forget about all of the times people have wronged Him. This is mindboggling but true. **Hebrews 8:12** – *"For I will forgive their wickedness and will remember their sins no more"* (NIV). Wow! I am so thankful that God does not hold all the wrong I've done over my head. He is so good! Take a moment right now, and thank Him in your own way. Lord, You are awesome!

Don't you wish you had the same ability to forget about all of the wrongs you've incurred over the years? Unfortunately, there are certain wrongs you and I may never forget. God has a sea of forgetfulness, but we don't. This fact makes it vitally important for us to handle our painful memories appropriately.

There is a difference between *remembering* what people did to us and *holding* what they did to us against them. *How* do you remember the wrongs you've had to endure? That's the question I want you to ask yourself right now.

You may think, "Well, I will just try to avoid people who could possibly hurt me." Jesus said in **Luke 17:1** that it is impossible that no offenses should come. In other words, offenses are inevitable. You are going to be wronged, period.

Pain always accompanies offense. When someone wrongs you, it's going to hurt on some level no matter how strong of a person you are. It's in that "hurt stage" that you have a very important decision to make: Are you going to seek healing, or are you going to become offended. Dr. David Remedios says, "Hurt people look to be healed, and offended people look to hurt."

Since forgetting about the times people have wronged you is unrealistic, you have two options when it comes to dealing with your hurt. You can either choose justice or forgiveness. One of them will cause you to be offended, and the other will set you free. We will look at justice tomorrow and forgiveness the next day.

354

justice

Justice seeks to pay back or to make the person pay for his or her wrongdoing. Most hurt people become offended and choose justice. Such a person sets himself up as judge and the person who wronged him as a felon. Offended people want to be compensated.

I believe there are two types of offended people, and both want restitution for the wrongs that have been committed toward them. The first group of offended people is passionate. They are out for revenge. It's obvious they are offended, and they are determined to pay back their offender or make their offender pay. They do things solely to hurt the people who have hurt them.

Those who are passionate in their offense purpose to be a stumbling block. They may gossip about their offender or try to ruin that person's reputation. They will poison work environments if their offender is a coworker. They even make attending church awkward. Many people commit the same offenses that were committed against them in an attempt to give their offender what they think he or she deserves.

There are also offended people who are passive. These people don't look offended on the surface. They may never voice their displeasure, but their offense is very real and deeply rooted. They keep a record of wrongs and harbor unforgiveness. They allow themselves to be offended for the "right" reasons. Their feelings are justified because they are not openly seeking revenge. They don't gossip, but many silently hope, and may even pray, for their offenders to get what they deserve.

Are you offended? Have you chosen the way of justice? Stop hoping for those who have wronged you to get what you think they deserve. Remember: God sacrificed Jesus so you would not get what *you* deserve. I encourage you to imitate His love.

the way of love

1 **Peter 4:18** – *Above all, love each other deeply, because love covers over a multitude of sins* (NIV).

Forgiveness is the way of love. Forgiveness is not a feeling; it's a commitment. It is the road less traveled. Many hurt people choose not to forgive for reasons mentioned yesterday, but the person who truly loves God will express that love by forgiving his or her offenders.

We have to consciously make the decision to pardon those who have hurt us. Forgiveness does not happen by chance; it happens by choice. Choosing to forgive is rarely easy. 1 **Corinthians 13:6** says that love always perseveres. This truth is important to understand, especially when someone hurts you repeatedly.

Peter and Jesus had an enlightening conversation concerning this truth in **Matthew 18:21-22**: 21 *Then Peter came to Jesus and asked, "Lord, how many times shall I forgive my brother when he sins against me? Up to seven times?" 22 Jesus answered, "I tell you, not seven times, but seventy-seven times"* (NIV).

I'm sure Peter thought seven times was a very generous offer. When someone consistently hurts us, it's not uncommon to think, "When is enough, enough?" Have you ever been there before? Are you there right now? Jesus basically told Peter that he was to forgive his brother every time he was wronged by him. God requires the same of us today.

Forgiving is difficult because forgetting offenses is not always possible. Gary Chapman once wrote, "We cannot erase the past, but we can accept it as history." Forgiveness is a choice to show mercy and live today free from the failures of yesterday. Forgiveness does not make the wrongs you've suffered right, nor does it wipe away the hurt, but it is the first step toward recovery.

Colossians 3:13 – *Bear with each other and forgive whatever grievances you may have against one another. Forgive as the Lord forgave you* (NIV).

thoughts and faith

Mark 5:27-28 – 27 *When she heard about Jesus, she came up behind him in the crowd and touched his cloak,* 28 *because she thought, "If I just touch his clothes, I will be healed"* (NIV).

Thoughts are very powerful. Your attitude, words and actions are a direct reflection of your thought life. Thoughts are what separate creative people from those who are unproductive. They are the difference between persevering and giving up. Thoughts cause one person to plan ahead and another to fly by the seat of his pants. Thoughts give confidence and cause depression.

Today I want to talk to you about thoughts as they relate to your faith. Thoughts can either partner with your faith or quench it. In Mark 5, you can read the account of a woman who suffered from an undisclosed blood disease. She had been subject to bleeding for twelve years. She was a social outcast, doctors could not help her, her finances were depleted and she was dying.

Then she heard about Jesus, and her faith level increased. She believed in His ministry so much so that she fought through a large crowd to get to Him. I can't even begin to imagine the struggle she faced physically and emotionally to get there. She had every reason in the world to feel sorry for herself and focus on her issues, but she did not think that way. Mark records that she thought, "If I just touch his clothes, I will be healed (**5:28**). She grabbed Jesus' cloak, and immediately her bleeding stopped!

Her thoughts lined up with her faith, and she received her miracle! Notice that not one word was spoken between the woman and Jesus. Tell me your thoughts are not powerful! Many people miss out on God's best for their lives because their thoughts crush their faith and abort their miracle.

Romans 10:17 – *So then faith comes by hearing, and hearing by the word of God* (NKJV). If you can get the word of God on the inside of you and make your thoughts line up with that Word, your faith will skyrocket! I encourage you today to fill up on God's word. Then when a crisis comes, your thoughts will turn to His word, and you can face adversity with confidence.

thoughts and fear

1 Kings 19:3-5 – 3 *Elijah was afraid and ran for his life. When he came to Beersheba in Judah, he left his servant there,* 4 *while he himself went a day's journey into the desert. He came to a broom tree, sat down under it and prayed that he might die. "I have had enough, LORD," he said. "Take my life; I am no better than my ancestors."* 5 *Then he lay down under the tree and fell asleep* (NIV).

Thoughts can either partner with our faith or propagate fear. Nobody demonstrates this truth better than Elijah. He was a prophet who had great faith. In 1 Kings 17-18, you can read about some of the miracles God worked on his behalf.

Elijah was used by God to raise a widow's son from the dead and to defeat the prophets of Baal on Mount Carmel. His prayers also ended a three-year drought. Elijah knew that God answered prayer so it's safe to believe that when he fell asleep under the broom tree, he did not expect to wake up. After all, he prayed that he might die! But how did it come to that? How could a man with such great faith pray for God to kill him?!

He received a death threat. Jezebel heard about Elijah's victory on Mount Carmel and vowed to kill him. Elijah was afraid and ran away. The thought of someone wanting to kill him overwhelmed his faith. He became depressed and decided his life was over.

Please listen to me. Fear originates in your mind. Countless people live in fear because doubt, worry and unbelief clutter their thought life. They allow what they see to control their faith instead of allowing their faith to control how they respond to what they see. **2 Corinthians 4:18** encourages us not to fix our eyes on the seen (or temporary) but the unseen (or eternal).

There is something fundamentally wrong with your faith if a Christian lives in fear. It is vitally important for you to meditate on God's word daily (**Joshua 1:8**) and discipline yourself to pray (**1 Peter 4:7**). Then your thoughts will likely line up with your faith, not promote fear. Think about it, and have a great day!

thoughts and the fundamentals

> **Proverbs 14:8** – *The wisdom of the prudent is to give thought to their ways, but the folly of fools is deception* (NIV).

A prudent person is not necessarily a prude. Prudes are those who are excessively proper or snobbish. The prudent are wise and practical. They are sober and are careful to provide for the future. The prudent person does not shoot from the hip, nor does he wait for a crisis to act. He takes the steps necessary to help prevent crisis from happening.

You've probably heard it said of certain people that they don't think before they speak or act. If you are like me, you have likely had someone (or multiple people) say something like this about *you*! The truth is everyone thinks before they speak or act. Some just don't think enough, and others think too much.

Many people make poor decisions regarding their family, careers and the future because their thoughts are out of whack. Bad habits all start because of a lack of self-discipline, but healthy habits are the product of a disciplined thought life.

God has given each of us the ability to think soberly and plan appropriately. It's His desire for us to be prudent. He did not create us to be bound by bad habits, nor does He want us to be blindsided by life's curve balls. We are victorious!

Perhaps today you are struggling with a certain habit that you know does not please God. You may be someone who has difficulty planning for the future. Maybe you've even made some ill-advised decisions, and you are now reaping the consequences. Don't lose heart! You are not alone, and you *can* change.

Many people refuse to change because they believe they are bound by their personalities. This is a myth. The *real* reason people refuse to change is they are bound to a certain way of thinking. People with various personality types change everyday, and so can you. You just have to make up your mind to do so.

> **Proverbs 14:15** – *A simple man believes anything, but a prudent man gives thought to his steps* (NIV).

faithful to the faithless

> **Romans 3:3-4** – 3 *What if some did not have faith? Will their lack of faith nullify God's faithfulness?* 4 *Not at all! Let God be true, and every man a liar* (NIV).

This is one of the greatest truths in all of Scripture. The faithfulness of God is not contingent on the faithfulness of any human being. Another version says that even if everyone else is a liar, God is true (NLT). Isn't it comforting to know that God is who He is no matter what we do? Hallelujah!

Every Christian's faith gets tested, and many fail the test miserably. I know there have been times in my life when I have questioned God's faithfulness because my faith was exhausted. I have been angry with Him, and I was the one who had changed.

God does not compromise. He is constant. He has always been the same, and He will always remain the same. God's character does not go through developmental stages as He gets older. **Deuteronomy 32:4** – *He is the Rock, his works are perfect, and all his ways are just. A faithful God who does no wrong, upright and just is he* (NIV). God is, always has been and always will be, perfect and just. Let this truth sink in today.

Many believers have the tendency to beat themselves up when they feel as if their faith has failed. You may be one of them. Please listen. God does not punish us when our faith is tested, so stop punishing yourself. Guilt is unhealthy for you and everyone else connected to you.

But remember: Just because God doesn't beat you up because of a lack of faith does not mean you should be content when your faith level is low. It's His desire for you to lean on Him when your faith is struggling. If you are being tested today, allow Him to strengthen you. He is faithful even when you're not.

> **2 Corinthians 12:9** – *But he said to me, "My grace is sufficient for you, for my power is made perfect in weakness." Therefore I will boast all the more gladly about my weaknesses, so that Christ's power may rest on me* (NIV).

think legacy

> **Titus 2:2-3** – 2 *Teach the older men to be temperate, worthy of respect, self-controlled, and sound in faith, in love and in endurance.* 3 *Likewise, teach the older women to be reverent in the way they live, not to be slanderers or addicted to much wine, but to teach what is good* (NIV).

No matter how old or young you think you are, there is someone in your life that is younger than you. It's because of this fact that you need to purpose to develop the above characteristics. Developing character is as beneficial to others as it is to you. If believers would understand this concept and apply it to their lives, it would have a positive affect on the next generation.

The world we live in does not promote the characteristics mentioned in the **Titus 2:2-3**. In fact, many people adopt unhealthy counterfeits. Rather than practice self-control, those who are out of balance in a certain area of their lives get a prescription. Instead of living a life worthy of respect, many live however they want and demand to be respected.

Many Christians lack respect for people who do not share their same ideals or beliefs. This kind of behavior contradicts the love of God. They often defame others and have shameful addictions. God's desire is for believers to set the standard rather than conform to the poor one that currently exists. Who is going to lead the next generation? Every person must answer this question.

Paul said to teach the young men and women what is good and to show integrity and seriousness. Do your children see God in the way you conduct your life? Do you model respect and hard work for your younger coworkers? Are you a person of integrity? Begin thinking about your legacy and what kind of impact you are making on those who are younger than you are. If you are not modeling godliness, you are promoting godlessness.

> **Titus 2:7-8** – 7 *In everything set them an example by doing what is good. In your teaching show integrity, seriousness* 8 *and soundness of speech that cannot be condemned* (NIV).

play no favorites

James 2:1 – *My brothers, as believers in our glorious Lord Jesus Christ, don't show favoritism* (NIV).

People tend to favor what is familiar and shun what they don't understand. I've learned that a lot of what is unfamiliar to me makes me feel uncomfortable. I imagine this is probably true for most people. Some people show favoritism because they are uncomfortable, and others do so because they are mean-spirited. In either case, believers are instructed not to play favorites.

Those who show favoritism discriminate and become judges with evil thoughts (**James 2:4**). As I looked at this verse more closely, the part about *evil thoughts* kept jumping off of the page at me. Showing favoritism originates in a person's thought life. What kinds of thoughts promote favoritism? That's the question I want to answer.

People often play favorites because they think they're better than others. They accept those who they believe to be of equal or higher status, and they look down on those who appear to be beneath their level. They draw these conclusions based on looks, wealth, occupation, influence, ethnicity, etc. These people often show favoritism based on stereotypes (see **James 2:2-3**).

Others play favorites because they think they will benefit personally by doing so. Many people favor those who might be able to help escalate their careers, or they may try to butter up certain individuals for financial gain. They think that being seen with the "right" people will bring promotion and that being seen with the "wrong" people somehow brings demotion.

Bottom line: When favoritism is shown, somebody gets hurt, and it's usually the one who gets slighted. I want to encourage you today not to show partiality. Maybe you tend to think you are better than certain people, or perhaps you have favored people who somehow benefit you personally. If so, receive forgiveness today, and purpose to live free from favoritism.

James 2:13 – *Mercy triumphs over judgment!* (NIV)

have faith in God

Jesus was walking with His disciples one day when He decided to teach them about faith. He began with a four-word statement, "Have faith in God." He could have stopped right there and made an altar call. What a powerful statement! If you are reading this today, I believe Jesus wants to give you the same four-word message: Have faith in God!

Did you notice that the disciples were the audience Jesus chose to share this message with? There is a valuable lesson to be learned here. It doesn't matter how close we walk to Jesus, we all need a reminder to keep our faith in Him.

It's so easy to put our faith in other things and other people, especially when everything in our lives seems to be going as we think it should. Many people put their faith in their relationships, finances, health, knowledge, experiences, etc. But even the most intimate relationships will fail us, our finances will fluctuate, our health will go up and down, our knowledge is limited and we will eventually run out of experiences.

Maybe you have the tendency to slack off in your relationship with God when your life appears to be in order. This is a dangerous place to be. Adversity is inevitable, and if you're in cruise control when it hits, your life will be thrown into chaos. You will go into panic mode. When you have not made building your faith in God a priority, fear will overwhelm you at the sight of trouble. Perhaps you understand where I'm coming from today.

God is the only constant. He has not changed, and He will never change. He is reliable, and He loves you. The circumstances surrounding your life will vary from day to day, but you can trust God no matter what. If you have put your faith in something or someone else today, have faith in God!

you're a whoever

Another version says, "Truly I say to you" (NASB). The NIV puts it this way, "I tell you the truth." For Jesus to begin this teaching on faith by saying, "I tell you the truth," it leads me to believe that there was some faith-related *untruth* being taught and adhered to. Perhaps there was some confusion among the disciples. The same could be said of today.

There are many believers who have adopted an unbalanced view of faith. Some have fashioned a faith that is conducive to their personal ideals. Others have been told what to believe, but they don't know why they believe it. Countless others have no clue what it is they believe at all.

It's because of the church's currently confused faith that Jesus has the same message today as He did to His disciples then: "Listen to me. I am the voice of reason. Don't pay any attention to teaching contrary to what I'm about to tell you. What I speak is truth." If you don't have a clear understanding of what it means to have faith in God, I encourage you to listen to His words.

Jesus defined faith in **Mark 11:23**. The first thing you need to understand is that *you* can have great faith. Jesus said, "*Whoever* says to this mountain." Other versions say if *anyone* says to this mountain. I personally like the NLT. It reads, "*You* can say to this mountain." Are you a *whoever*? Of course you are!

Great faith is not reserved for a select few, well-known preachers and evangelists. There is no elite faith club, and if there were, you wouldn't want to join it. God has unlimited power, and when you partner with Him, there is no limit as to what He can do through you. Hallelujah! Be encouraged; you have great faith!

the voice of faith

> **Mark 11:23** – *"For assuredly, I say to you, whoever says to this mountain, 'Be removed and be cast into the sea,' and does not doubt in his heart, but believes that those things he says will be done, he will have whatever he says"* (NKJV).

Mountains are impossibilities. They are circumstances we cannot overcome in our own strength. Mountains have a way of exposing a person's faith, or the lack thereof. Perhaps you are staring at Pike's Peak right now, or maybe you are facing an entire mountain range. If so, this message is for you!

My wife Heidi recently said in a sermon on a Wednesday night, "You have to give your faith a voice." The truth is we give our *fear* a voice all the time. Your mountain has been taunting and belittling you.

The enemy of our souls wants to frame your world with fear, doubt, confusion and anxiety. His desire is to overwhelm you with situations that he knows you cannot overcome on your own. He bombards your thoughts with hopelessness and worry in hopes that you will speak negatively about your life. The devil also knows that the power of life and death is in the tongue.

Impossibilities will either cause a person to turn to God or away from Him. Many people have a hard time understanding why bad things happen to good people. I have often wondered this myself. I pray that you are able to grasp the truth I'm about to share with you: God allows things that are contrary to His will to happen to us, but we may never fully understand why.

He allows certain mountains to arise in our lives for multiple reasons, but I believe His main reasoning is to test our faith. He wants to hear what your faith has to say. Jesus told us to *speak* to our mountains. Your mountain cannot read your mind.

Open your mouth, and declare God's word over your situation. If your faith doesn't have anything to say, you need to spend more time with Jesus on a daily basis. Monitor your thought life as well. If your thoughts are out of order, your faith will remain in disorder, and the voice of faith will be muzzled.

knockout roses

1 Corinthians 5:6-7 – 6 *Don't you realize that this sin is like a little yeast that spreads through the whole batch of dough?* 7 *Get rid of the old "yeast"* (NLT).

My wife recently shared the following illustration with me. Our house is tastefully landscaped with a variety of nandina, hydrangea and ferns. There is also a row of six or seven knockout roses right off of our front porch. They are a very beautiful and hardy. Most people are impressed by them.

Last year some sort of disease infected our roses. They all developed white spots on their leaves. It was frustrating because we took pretty good care of them. One day Heidi decided to treat them. It took four or five months, but the spots eventually cleared up on all but one of the rosebushes.

Heidi figured it would be a good idea to dig up the one that remained diseased, but she opted to leave it alone. The other roses were clear for about eight months, and then she began to notice the white spots coming back. The disease spread from the one infected bush to all the others. Just the other day she had to treat all of them again. The relapse probably could have been avoided if the infected bush had been dug up to begin with.

Many people follow this same pattern when it comes to treating the sin in their lives. They allow certain areas to remain infected because they are okay for the most part, but a lot of people do not take into account that sin spreads. If you condone even a small amount of sin, it will eventually spill over into all areas of your life. Pretty soon even your strengths will become infected.

You can also apply this concept to your relationships. All it takes is one person to poison an entire group. Have you been giving a free pass to someone who probably should not be influencing your life? Take an honest look at yourself today. You may need to dig up some rosebushes.

1 Corinthians 5:7 – *Get rid of the old yeast that you may be a new batch without yeast—as you really are* (NIV).

believe in God's ability

As Shadrach, Meshach and Abednego faced King Nebuchadnezzar and the fiery furnace, they respectfully spoke the words you just read above. What a declaration of a faith! "The God we serve *is able* to save us," they said. Their words define faith for us. Faith is believing in God's ability.

They believed God was able to save them, even if He chose not to. These three men were determined to trust God even unto death. They refused to bow to the foreign gods. Shadrach, Meshach and Abednego were willing to sacrifice their lives so that their faith might live on.

Maybe today you are believing God for something that has not happened yet. You've remained steadfast, but the days, months or years that have passed have started to take a toll on our faith. Don't stop trusting Him. Believe God is able because He is! Your faith will struggle at times, but He remains faithful always.

Become familiar with Hebrews 11. This chapter is dedicated to men and women who possessed great faith. While God was faithful to each of them, they all took their faith to the grave. They did not receive everything God had promised, but they saw His promises and welcomed them from a distance (**Hebrews 11:13**).

The Bible says they *saw* His promises. Can you still see His promises? Perhaps you've lost sight of them today. Remember this: Faith is being fully persuaded that God has the power (or ability) to do what He has promised (**Romans 4:21**), even if what you see doesn't line up with what He's said.

mustard seed-sized faith

Matthew 13:31-32 – 31 *He told them another parable: "The kingdom of heaven is like a mustard seed, which a man took and planted in his field.* 32 *Though it is the smallest of all your seeds, yet when it grows, it is the largest of garden plants and becomes a tree, so that the birds of the air come and perch in its branches"* (NIV).

Mustard seeds are typically one to two millimeters in diameter. They are one of the smallest seeds in the world. I find this interesting because Jesus taught that faith as small as a mustard seed is necessary to forgive offenses and to move mountains (see **Luke 17:6** and **Matthew 17:20**). Mustard seed-sized faith doesn't sound like enough faith to cure a toothache, let alone to forgive or to move a mountain.

So what is so significant about a mustard seed? Why did Jesus use something so small to describe sin-forgiving and mountain-moving faith? I'm glad you asked.

Jesus said in the above passage that though the mustard seed is the smallest of seeds, it grows into the largest of garden plants and becomes a tree. Mustard seeds may be small, but they are alive and growing. They don't look like much in the beginning, but they produce big results in the end.

All it takes is a very small amount of genuine faith to produce big results in our lives. Your faith may be very small today, but as long as it is alive and growing, God can do great things in and through you. Our faith should never reach a place where it stops growing. Mature faith grows continuously.

I want to encourage you today. Don't allow unanswered prayers to stunt the growth of your faith. Mustard seed-sized faith may not be great in measure, but it's amazing how God can take what little we have, multiply it and produce supernatural results.

2 Corinthians 13:5 – *Examine yourselves to see if your faith is genuine. Test yourselves. Surely you know that Jesus Christ is among you; if not, you have failed the test of genuine faith* (NLT).

what you *were*

> **1 Corinthians 6:9-11** – 9 *Do you not know that the wicked will not inherit the kingdom of God? Do not be deceived: Neither the sexually immoral nor idolaters nor adulterers nor male prostitutes, nor homosexual offenders* 10 *nor thieves nor the greedy nor drunkards nor slanderers nor swindlers will inherit the kingdom of God.* 11 *And that is what some of you were. But you were washed, you were sanctified, you were justified in the name of the Lord Jesus Christ and by the Spirit of our God* (NIV).

Paul wrote that if anyone is in Christ, he is a new creation (**2 Corinthians 5:17**). Everyone has things in their past that they're not proud of, but the moment a person receives forgiveness, he becomes a new person in Christ.

Paul listed a few types of sinners in the above passage. You may be able to relate to one or more of them. There is no room in heaven for any kind of sin, but look at what he wrote in verse 11: And that is what some of you *were*. When we are in Christ, our identity changes. We are no longer identified by our old sinful nature. When He looks at you, He doesn't see the liar or the thief that you *were*. He sees the new creation that you *are*. The one that He washed, sanctified and justified.

He washed us from our sins in His own blood (**Revelation 1:5**). We are also sanctified in Christ (**1 Corinthians 1:2**). He set us apart and called us to submit to His will, resist sin and seek holiness. **1 Thessalonians 4:7** – *For God has not called us for the purpose of impurity, but in sanctification* (NASB). We have also been justified. Sanctification is a process, but justification is a declaration of innocence. Hallelujah!

I pray that this message has encouraged you today. If you are in Christ, you *are* a new creation. Your identity has changed, so stop identifying yourself with what you used to do and who you used to be. He justified you—so it's just as if you never sinned!

> **Romans 5:1** – *Therefore, having been justified by faith, we have peace with God through our Lord Jesus Christ* (NASB).

Made in the USA
Lexington, KY
14 June 2012